Emancipation, the Media, and Mo

Emancipation, the Media, and Modernity

Arguments About the Media and Social Theory

Nicholas Garnham

OXFORD
UNIVERSITY PRESS

OXFORD

UNIVERSITY PRESS

Great Clarendon Street, Oxford OX2 6DP

Oxford University Press is a department of the University of Oxford.
It furthers the University's objective of excellence in research, scholarship,
and education by publishing worldwide in

Oxford New York
Athens Auckland Bangkok Bogotá Buenos Aires Calcutta
Cape Town Chennai Dar es Salaam Delhi Florence Hong Kong Istanbul
Karachi Kuala Lumpur Madrid Melbourne Mexico City Mumbai
Nairobi Paris São Paulo Singapore Taipei Tokyo Toronto Warsaw

and associated companies in Berlin Ibadan

Oxford is a registered trade mark of Oxford University Press
in the UK and certain other countries

Published in the United States
by Oxford University Press Inc., New York

© Nicholas Garnham 2000

British Library Cataloguing in Publication Data

Data available

Library of Congress Cataloging in Publication Data
Data available
ISBN-0-19-874225-8
ISBN-0-19-874224-X (Pbk.)

1 3 5 7 9 10 8 6 4 2

Typeset by Best-set Typesetter Ltd., Hong Kong
Printed in Great Britain
on acid-free paper by
T. J. International Ltd,
Padstow, Cornwall

To Linda and Sophie

Contents

1 | Introduction: The Media, Emancipation, and Modernity

All human beings are granted a limited time on this earth and limited stocks of energy and aptitudes. I, the author of this book, and you, its readers, are no exception. Since we cannot do everything, to lead a life is, unavoidably, to make choices. And this is no less true of how we choose to deploy our intellectual energies and the social resources necessary to that deployment. Thus the choice of a field or object of study, and within that field the questions posed and the methodologies used, have to be justified against some hierarchy of priorities—some things are more important and more interesting than others.

There are many reasons for and ways of studying the media. But the position taken in this book is that the media are worth studying because they raise some very old but central questions in social theory. That lying behind the major questions about the media and how to study them that are debated today lie some very old problems. That both to avoid reinventing the wheel, but also to clarify what is really at stake in these debates, it is necessary to unpack the intellectual tradition and the historical development within which those problems have been posed and solutions attempted. In short this book is consciously placed within a long tradition of social theory and within an ongoing historically rooted argument.

Modernism, Post-modernism, and Social Theory

In seventeenth-century France there was a celebrated dispute in the field of literary and artistic criticism between the Ancients and the Moderns. The Ancients argued that the standards of beauty established in the classical age and revived in the Renaissance were timeless and universal and should continue to be applied to the creation and judgement of contemporary works of art. The Moderns on the other hand argued that, while classical standards of beauty were appropriate to the age that produced them, the new modern age was so different from that which had preceded it that works of art appropriate to it should be judged by standards of beauty which were new and different. Tradition was no longer an adequate guide. New rational enlightened standards of judgement were required.

We are now participants in a new battle between the Ancients and the Moderns and this book is a contribution to that debate. The old Moderns have become the Ancients and the new Moderns are the post-modernists. In this new battle we find in one camp those who wish, whatever their internal differences, broadly to uphold those Enlightenment standards of truth, justice, and beauty originally developed in response to modernity; those who believe that, however flawed in its execution, the Enlightenment project remains unfinished business so long as human social life continues to be stunted by coercive inequality and avoidable ignorance. Indeed for this camp the human sciences themselves, to which this book is a modest contribution, derive their purpose from the contribution they can make to this more general emancipatory project. In the other camp, often in strange alliance, stand both those who derive their position from the Ancients and from that strand of counter-Enlightenment thought stemming from Hamman, Herder, and Nietzsche who never accepted the Enlightenment project as either possible or desirable, seeing the attempt to break with tradition and bring human life under rational control as dangerous hubris, and also those who argue that the Enlightenment was a false dawn and that the Dialectic of Enlightenment has betrayed the original emancipatory thrust by erecting Reason, particularly in its economic and bureaucratic forms, as the new source of domination. This post-modernist school of thought argues, just as the old Moderns did, that we are entering or have entered a new age which requires us to throw off the chains of enlightenment thought and emancipate ourselves from its universalistic rationalist pretensions in the name of difference and desire.

The aim of this book will be to trace these often complex and difficult arguments across the terrain of media studies. In so doing I define the object of study of media studies as the structure and processes of social communication.

The human species is, in evolutionary terms, distinguished from other species, and owes its survival and development as a species to its exceptionally large brain. This brain has enabled it to develop culture. By culture I mean patterns of behaviour which are not merely instinctual, but are endowed with meanings which can be transmitted through space and time beyond the immediate stimulus/response site of action, and a learning process the lessons of which are cumulative and open to criticism and modification in the light of experience. Culture in this sense is crucially dependent upon systems of symbolic communication.

At the same time, and in part because of their large brain and its organic requirements, humans are social animals. They depend for their survival and reproduction on relatively complex systems of inter-personal and inter-group co-ordination. These systems of co-ordination depend upon the development and deployment of symbolic communication. Human evolution has been characterized by the development of ever more complex and extensive systems of social co-ordination that we call societies or social formations. In part at least this evolutionary development is what historians of technology now call 'path-dependent'. This has two aspects: (a) one stage of development is built on the foundations of the previous one—'Humans make their own history but not in conditions of their own making'; (b) the process cannot be reversed because, whatever the costs involved, the level of population supportable by the new stage would be unsupportable by the previous stage. Thus a social group dependent upon agriculture will not willingly return to hunter-gathering, nor an industrial to an agrarian society.

This process of general historical social evolution should not be confused with either progress or historical teleology. Progress implies the notion that each successive evolutionary stage is better, in some sense to be defined, than the previous one—that evolution is a process of improvement. While in my view a case, over some historical periods and for some societies, can be made for progress in this sense, it is no part of the argument I am making here. Historical teleology implies a notion of predetermined development paths towards a goal—for instance the path from feudalism to capitalism to socialism—through which all societies will pass, as was argued in some versions of Hegelian Marxism, or the fulfilment of human destiny, as in the neo-Hegelian version of the triumph of capitalism.

One strand in the general process of human social evolution (or development) has been the development of the systems of inter-personal communication necessary for social co-ordination, beyond the context of unmediated face-to-face communication dependent on the natural endowments of speech and gesture, and beyond the systems for the inter-generational communication of culture and learning dependent on human memory, into systems of communication extended through space and time. These systems for the production, distribution, and appropriation of symbolic forms have been based on the development and deployment of technologies of communication. First, and still most important, forms of writing; subsequently technologies for the reproduction, distribution, and reception of symbolic forms of all types.

This process required the deployment of scarce material and cultural resources (all humans, unless brain-damaged, are equally endowed with the resources required for face-to-face communication within the codes of their specific culture), and thus their deployment both reflected and reinforced other structures of social power and legitimacy. In particular the development of these systems of social communication accompanied and made possible a growing social specialization or division of social labour. The skills of symbolic communication were then, within this general process of development, unevenly distributed through the population and were associated with a class of specialists—priests or intellectuals.

Looked at in this way we can see that the structures and processes of social communication are deeply embedded within the wider structures and processes of a given social formation. Who can say what, in what form, to whom, for what purposes, and with what effect will be in part determined by and in part determine the structure of economic, political, and cultural power in a society. Thus one cannot be studied without the other.

Looking at the media in this way has important consequences. First it enables us to avoid too narrow a focus on what has generally been seen as the major focus of media studies, the mass media of print publishing, radio, and television consumed domestically in leisure time. This leaves out two crucial elements of media as I am here defining them. First it totally neglects the role played by the media within the modes of production and coercion *per se*, and thus largely loses sight of the driving forces within the sphere of production rather than consumption, behind the creation and continued operation of media systems, particularly modern telecommunication systems from the telephone to Internet. Secondly, if we define media as systems for the production, circulation, and appropriation of meanings carried by symbolic forms, then in modern societies the education system must by any reckoning—in terms of money invested, people employed, time spent—rank as a, if not the, major medium. To see things in this way enables us to place media influence and patterns of cultural consumption within the context of societies based upon exogenous training and accreditation as the major mode of socialization and social stratification, as for instance Bourdieu does. While I do not have space in this book for a substantive treatment of the education system either in its own right or in relation to other media, the issue of the pedagogic versus the entertainment role of media, not just as one internal to the mass media themselves, but also as an aspect of a struggle between systems of formal education and other public media for dominance as agents of socialization and legitimation, is central to the treatment of the producers in Chapter 5, the audience in Chapter 6, the content in Chapter 7, and politics in Chapter 8. Indeed it can be argued that the central question underlying all debates about the media and how we study them concerns the way in which and the extent to which humans learn and thus how through time identities are formed and actions motivated.

Once we see the media in this way it becomes obvious that questions about the media are questions about the kind of society we live in and vice versa. The study of the media is thus a part of, and must be grounded in, the human sciences more generally. We study them because they give us a way in to the general questions of social theory. The questions we ask about the media and the answers we might give to those questions can only be understood within the context of social theory more generally.

Social Theory, the Enlightenment, and Modernity

I will be arguing in this book that what is at stake in current debates over social theory in general and over social communication in particular are debates that go back to the origins of modernity and of the attempt to understand it in the Enlightenment and its intellectual successors. Habermas has usefully reminded us in his introduction to *The Philosophical Discourse of Modernity* that this debate stemmed from an awareness of a new sense of historical time. This involved both a changed sense of the past, the sense that tradition, whether we liked it or not, was dead, as a way of orienting ourselves in this new world. We had to construct new understandings of what was happening. It also involved a sense of the future, of living and acting in a world oriented towards a future for which our world would become the past, and thus an unavoidable sense of our responsibility for the future. This could of course take the form of a complacent, whiggish view of progress, of the world necessarily becoming better. But more importantly it involved a sense of the possibility of constructing a future world that was different and thus the chance that it might be better. That is, modernity and the attempt to understand it involved both a sense of responsibility towards the future and also a sense of hope that made that responsibility possible. If the future was fated we had no responsibility.

Social Theory as Moral Philosophy

In *Enlightenment and Despair* Geoffrey Hawthorn describes social theory as a failed attempt to ground an ethical argument. What does he mean by that? The coming of modernity in Europe posed unavoidably the great question posed by Kant—how to construct a viable community for autonomous rational subjects. The problem was and is one of dealing with what Kant called the 'unsocial sociability' of the human species; how, in the absence of binding traditions, and without relying on a dogmatic theology, it was possible to combine the two grounding conditions of human specificity—humans as individual, autonomous moral agents—moral because endowed with free will—and humans as what Aristotle called *zoon politikon*—animals that not only required developed forms of social intercourse for both physical and psychic survival and health, but whose highest potential as a culture-creating species took social forms. One can see the Enlightenment and the traditions of often conflictual social theory that developed out of it as a continuing attempt to deal with this problem. In confronting this problem we can see a continual danger of abolishing it by collapsing to one side or other—stressing either individual autonomy as the goal over against the social, seen as dominating and repressive, or stressing and placing the highest value on the social and seeing the individual as potentially disruptive, selfish, anti-social, as an animal whose destructive bestial instincts and drives have to be controlled for the higher social and cultural good. In practice actual theoretical stances rarely approach the two limit cases, but work in complex, shifting, and often contradictory ways across the tensions of the divide and the relationship upon which the ethical dilemma is posed.

In confronting this problem it is important to stress, against the image of Enlightenment thought that post-modernism has constructed as its opponent, that the problem is a problem not because the Enlightenment held to a concept of triumphant reason, but precisely because of the pervasiveness of doubt. The project was a project. It was an attempt to test the boundaries of human reason and moral action and the boundaries for the social community within which such reason and action could be grounded. A project the outcome of which was always likely to be partial and fragile, in the face of the death of God and tradition and in cognizance of the limits to human reason and thus the limits to the possible emancipation from necessity. Here the image of the garden is apposite. Recent post-modern thinking has equated the role of the intellectual with that of the gardener (see Bauman 1987), seen as the exploiter of nature in two senses—as the exploiter of external nature and as the dominator of other men and their internal natures as though they were domestic animals to be tamed. But I would rather see the garden as the attempt to carve out a small patch of civilization, of light and of moral action, within the surrounding indifference, darkness, even absurdity, of potentially destructive nature.

The full sense of the nature of the problem and the approach that Kant, among others, set for social theory, and which I am arguing in this book should underline the study of the media, is well captured by Panofsky in his defence of humanism. In his essay 'History of Art as a Humanistic Discipline' (in Panofsky 1966) Panofsky recounts a tale of Kant nine days before his death being visited by his physician:

Old, ill and nearly blind, he rose from his chair and stood trembling with weakness and muttering unintelligible words. Finally his faithful companion realised that he would not sit down again until the visitor had taken a seat. This he did, and Kant then permitted himself to be helped to his chair and, after having regained some of his strength, said 'Das Gefühl für Humanität hat mich noch nicht verlassen'—'The sense of humanity has not yet left me'. The two men were moved almost to tears. For, though the word *Humanität* had come, in the 18th century, to mean little more than politeness and civility, it had, for Kant, a much deeper significance, which the circumstances of the moment served to emphasise: man's proud and tragic consciousness of self-approved and self-imposed principles, contrasting with his utter subjection to illness, decay and all that is implied in the word 'mortality'.

Panofsky goes on to argue that

historically the word humanitas has had two clearly distinguishable meanings, the first arising from a contrast between man and what is less than man; the second, between man and what is more. In the first case humanitas means a value, in the second a limitation. . . . It is from this ambivalent conception of humanitas that humanism was born. It is not so much a movement as an attitude which can be defined as the conviction of the dignity of man, based on both the insistence on human values (rationality and freedom) and the acceptance of human limitations (fallibility and frailty) from this two postulates result—responsibility and tolerance.

Thus in order to understand what is at stake in studying the media from the perspective of social theory we need to make a diversion by way of philosophy in order to understand how and why the debates have been set up in the way they have and what they are in fact about. It is also the case that the debate between modernists and post-modernists takes place largely on the ground of philosophy, as is indicated by the centrality to this debate of the concept of reason and its role in human affairs and by the erection of various Enlightenment thinkers, whether Kant or Rousseau according to taste, as the villains in the story of the Dialectic of Enlightenment, the subjectification of Being or logocentrism.

The problem Enlightenment thought attempts to resolve was handed down by the Greeks. How to lead a good life? In Greek thought such a life was assumed to be a life that fulfilled the full potential of humans as a distinct species. This then had two aspects. On the one hand the study of the relationship, within human nature, between the animal, governed by the laws of nature within the realm of necessity, and human self-consciousness involving a recognition of free will and intentionality which made human actions unavoidably questions of moral choice. This then involved a debate which is ongoing as to whether the good life was the pursuit of pleasure, and moral claims merely the pursuit of self-interest in disguise, or whether on the contrary we had moral obligations of a different or 'higher' sort. On the other hand it was assumed that humans were in their essence social animals—in Aristotle's terms *zoon politikon*—and thus in fulfilling the potential of their sociality ethics was always a social as well as a personal question. Thus this potential could only be fulfilled within a set of social arrangements that were themselves good in a moral sense, or at least which were conducive to leading a good life which was necessarily a social life. The importance within this tradition of thought of the communal is expressed in the common root of *ethos*—a shared set of communal values or customs—and *ethics*. For the Greeks in short the good life combined happiness—the realization of one's full potential as a human being, above all those potentialities that distinguish the human from the animal—with virtue the fulfilment of one's responsibilities as a social being within the polis. The personal and the political were one.

Enlightenment thought, in particular that of Rousseau and Kant, then re-posed these questions under new historical conditions in which the self-conscious moral subject was alone in the world without the prop of either religious dogma or tradition to guide her necessarily moral actions. In particular Kant, following Rousseau, defined the key problem as one of how to deal with the problem of what he called the 'unsocial sociality' of humans, the tension between the autonomous, reflexive moral agents on the one hand and a viable social group within which such agents had to live and act on the other. The Enlightenment project was therefore an enquiry into the possibilities of constructing viable communities for autonomous, reflective moral agents and thus, under the conditions of modernity, combining happiness and virtue.

At this point it is important to stress that central to this project is not the overweening rational subject presented by the post-modernists, but, on the contrary, doubt. The Enlightenment project was founded upon the limits of human reason and was therefore concerned with emancipation as an always partial project, not an achieved and total fact. The question was how, and if so to what extent, could we emancipate ourselves from the limits that our animal natures and our social bonds placed upon us. Here reason is seen as moral intentionality and therefore as a guide to truly human action, not as a conceptual, calculating reflection on the world. Indeed as Onora O'Neil (1989) argues in her fine interpretation of Kant, the truth of conceptual pure reason is, in the Kantian schema, based upon the categorical social imperative that governs the practical reasoning of morality. It is not divorced from it. From this perspective reason is then opposed to desire, action to behaviour, the rational to the instinctual. From this perspective the ethical question was the extent to which we can, in this sense, behave rationally and therefore morally. From the social perspective the question was the extent to which society could be made rational, and this in two senses. To what extent could social structures be built which were acceptable to, and thus necessarily transparent in their workings to, the autonomous moral agents who were the members of the given polity, and which were virtuous, that is to say conducive to enlightenment and thus virtuous behaviour? The problem posed by this relationship between individual moral behaviour and the form of the polis had been clear also to the Greeks. The problem, which Rousseau, in *The Social Contract*, raised acutely, is straightforward: 'The problem is to find a form of association . . . in which each, while uniting himself with all, may still obey himself alone, and remain as free as before. This is the fundamental problem of which the social contract provides the solution.' If people are moulded in their moral behaviour by the social context within which they find themselves how could one ever hope for internal change to an unvirtuous republic, given that presumably that republic would mould unvirtuous citizens whose moral behaviour would be that sanctioned by the ethos of the community? Plato attempted to solve the problem, as is well known, through the device of the guardians and the philosopher king, i.e. an enlightened elite—how they become enlightened is always a mystery—have the duty to impose on the unenlightened a set of political and social arrangements which will lead them to enlightenment, or at least ensure moral behaviour. This raises the problem of virtue as something which is not inherent in the exercise of reflective moral reason for all humans, and thus to the view of enlightenment as a problem of moral education and the passage to enlightenment as one from immaturity to maturity.

The reason Hawthorn calls social theory a *failed* attempt to ground an ethics is because in his view it has never been able to square this circle. As I will attempt to show, however, the key questions which still concern social theory and its approach to the media remain these problems, and the crucial debates circle around them in their various attempts at a solution and in their varying assessment of the possibilities of human reason in the face of both the animality of internal nature and the uncontrollability of what has come to be seen as the second nature of social structure.

Broadly the issues I will be examining are concerned with the following questions: the extent to which, if at all, humans can or should be expected to act rationally in the sense of morally; the extent to which the social can be made transparent and conducive to virtuous moral action, however defined; and the extent to which individual thought and action is moulded by 'society' and what this means for human autonomy and moral action.

The Social Challenge of Modernity

The issue of the viable community raises the question of the nature of the social challenge posed for the ethical project of social theory by modernity. What were the key characteristics of this historical social transformation which challenged the ethical project of combining happiness and virtue—or, to put it another way, the secularization of the project of building the City of God on earth—and how does the development of media fit into this process and thus into the way in which the problem is posed?

To simplify crudely, whatever the arguments about its genesis and its implications, everyone broadly agrees that the transition to modernity involved: (a) increased specialization or division of social labour in all social spheres, not just the economic—although economic specialization may have made the other forms possible; (b) the development of generalized structures of social co-ordination, particularly those called by Habermas, following Parsons, the media of money and power (the one involved the generalization of market relations, the other the development of bureaucratic state forms and systems of law); (c) what is sometimes called secularization but is more accurately described as the rise to dominance of a culture of critical rationalism and its associated 'scientific' world view and the accompanying decline of the doxa of tradition, especially the religious world view.

The media were involved in this development along all three dimensions. The operation of the media became more specialized and autonomous from other social realms; the media were themselves both one of the increasingly generalized and abstract systems for social co-ordination in their ideological role and were also mobilized by and essential to the development of the other 'media' in the Habermasian sense. The media were both effected by and implicated in—by some reckonings a key creator of—the death of tradition and the rise of critical rationality.

The problems these developments raised for the Enlightenment project were the following, and in each case the media are central to the problem. First the question of how to rebuild the ethos necessary for a viable community. For Kant both the truth of rational knowledge of external nature and the validity of moral norms could only be established by the test of a *sensus communis* which in its turn could only be established through public discussion and debate:

> How much and how accurately would we think if we did not think, so to speak, in community with others to whom we communicate our thoughts and who communicate their thoughts to us! We may therefore conclude that the same external constraints which deprive people of the freedom to communicate their thoughts in public also remove their freedom of thought, the one treasure which remains to us amidst all the burdens of civil life, and which alone offers us a means of overcoming all the evils of this condition. (Kant 1970: 247)

For Hegel reason itself was a social construct since it was created out of projection into and interaction with the world external to the subject, both material and social. At the same time, in his view no virtuous state was possible which did not rest upon what he called *Sittlichkeit*—an ethos or set of common cultural norms—since Kant's concept of the categorical moral imperative was, in Hegel's view, too abstract to motivate subjects towards shared social action or to attract their allegiance and commitment to a set of social arrangements which by definition in part require them to subordinate their own personal interests and drives for the greater good. Thus the hunt was on for what became known as either the 'new' religion or the 'new' mythology. It is around this problem that questions of ideology, hegemony, the public sphere, community, culture, identity, and the autonomy of art, all central, as we shall see, to contemporary debates about the media, still revolve.

The second problem was the question of structure and agency and the dialectical relationship between the growth in social specialization and complexity and the necessary accompanying growth in structurally constraining systems of general social co-ordination. It is here we find the problem of what has been called the separation of systems world and life world, or the rise of instrumental reason at the expense of communicative reason. How, from the perspective of emancipation and the attempt to combine happiness and virtue, are we to judge this development? On the one hand such systems, and the social specialization and relative freedom from both material necessity and arbitrary power that they make possible, can be seen as the necessary basis for an increase in autonomy and range of moral choice. At the same time they can be seen as non-transparent and thus not subject to rational control for moral ends. Do they then just have to be accepted as a new nature and as fate—a limit to the realm of reason—or on the contrary can they be brought under rational and communal control? Again the media can be seen as either possible agents of transparency and control—the theory of the media as public sphere—or as themselves examples of the systems world—theories of ideology and problems of ownership and control and the democratic accountability of the media.

The third problem was the relationship between the rational moral subject as individual consciousness and self-identity and the subject as socially formed. Within this broad problematic the media were of central concern for two reasons, or in two forms. First the whole Kantian approach grounded both truth and morality in publicity or a discourse ethics. Kant argued in 'What is Enlightenment?' that, precisely because of the pervasiveness of doubt in the face of the errors attributable to both fantasy and subjectivity, reason could only be disciplined and an approach to a more general truth arrived at through a process of sharing of ideas. True ideas must be subjected to external critique. Secondly, moral judgements always had to be put to the test of the categorical imperative such that they could be distinguished from the mere pursuit of selfish self-interest. Thus such judgements had to be offered in a form that was potentially acceptable to other members of society and had to be disciplined and grounded in a *sensus communis*. Under conditions of modernity, i.e. social specialization and expansion of social scale, such *sensus communis* could only be created within a media-based public sphere.

Plan of the Book

In this book, then, I will trace these often complex and difficult arguments across the terrain of media studies.

In Chapter 2 I will examine the debate about history and our relation to the past that sprang out of the confrontation between Modernity and Enlightenment thought. I will argue that all debates about the media necessarily mobilize historical arguments, and will examine the interrelationship between different perspectives on media history, and the evaluative stances they carry with them, on the one hand and more general histories of modernity on the other.

In Chapter 3 I will examine the media as institutions and processes within the capitalist mode of production and thus as instances of that systems world which it was the purpose of the Enlightenment project to make transparent, and thus bring more fully under human social control. In examining the implications for emancipation, and thus in particular for media policy, of analysing the media from the perspective of the steering system of money and with the tools of political economy I will, in particular, focus on a critique of currently dominant Information Society thinking.

In Chapter 4 I will turn to an analysis of the media as technologies. I will argue that many of the debates about the economic and social impact and future development of the media are part of wider debates, again going back to the Enlightenment, concerning the relationship of human beings, whether for good or ill, to science and technology. In particular I will argue that we need to steer between the two extremes of, on the one hand, a position that sees not only all media development, but now also social development in general in the form of the Information Society, as a technologically determined, even if emancipatory, fate and, on the other, a social constructivism which fails to confront the real limitations placed upon human action by material constraints and thus sees technological development as purely an ideological struggle.

In Chapter 5 I turn to the specialist producers of symbolic forms and examine their social role from the perspective of the debate about intellectuals. I argue that the operation and control by specialists of the systems of social communication, and thus the social distance and distinction between those who produce symbolic forms and those who consume or appropriate them, are an inevitable corollary of the general process of specialization that characterizes modernity. It is for this reason that post-Enlightenment social theory has been continually concerned with the problem of how to think about and evaluate the social role of these 'intellectuals'. Are they the privileged carriers of Enlightenment values pursuing and diffusing truth and criticizing the opaque structures of social power, or, on the contrary, are they technologists of instrumental reason manipulating knowledge in their own interest at the expense of general enlightenment and emancipation?

In Chapter 6 I turn to the audience, or the consumers of symbolic forms. Here I argue that underlying current debates about the audience and the effects of the media are debates, stemming from the Enlightenment, concerning the relationship between learning, identity formation, and action. What is at stake is the relation between individual autonomy, and thus freedom and rational action, on the one hand and the social construction of identity and behaviour on the other. In particular, I argue against the current vogue for ethnographic studies of everyday life and the extreme particularism that results, and for the centrality of statistics and measurements of probability for producing real knowledge of the audience. At the same time I argue that the counterposing of an active audience to a passive audience is not the issue, but rather what, given a general social constructivist approach, are the emancipatory consequences of different instances of audience–media interaction.

In Chapter 7 I turn to the symbolic forms that the media circulate and to the debates over language, culture, and evaluation that these forms raise. In this chapter I mount a critique of the narrow view of language and the now largely incoherent concept of culture that has dominated recent work in the humanities and social sciences and which underpins an extreme social constructivist and relativist approach to cultural evaluation. Apart from the fact that this lets media producers off the hook of any responsibility for what they produce, I argue that evaluation is unavoidable. The question then is whether such evaluation can be based upon anything more than a socially determined taste, whether individual or group. In the search for such possibilities I return to the reasons for the development of aesthetics in Enlightenment thought and, following the argument in Chapter 6, to the argument for art as moral education and as a potential realm of freedom. But in line with the general Kantian position of the book as a whole I then argue that, while common evaluative standards are possible and the search for them cannot simply be dismissed as elitist, the *sensus communis* upon which they must be based can only be created within the discourse ethic of a vibrant critical culture—the public sphere for which the media alone can provide.

Finally in Chapter 8 I examine the role of the media in relation to democratic politics. This chapter focuses on debates over the public sphere and the normative entailments of different uses of the distinction between public and private. I argue that debates about the media and politics are at heart normative debates about the nature of politics. Going back to the central Kantian problem of 'unsocial sociability' and the centrality of the exercise of public reason to Kant's conceptions of truth, justice, and the morally right I argue, following Benhabib and against the communitarians and many advocates of identity politics, for the necessary generalization, under the conditions of modernity and the potential for generalized reflexivity that accompanies it, of a discourse ethic as the necessary normative foundation for democracy. This entails arguing against Habermas's speech–act foundationalism on the one hand and against the communitarians' identity foundationalism on the other. At the same time I argue that we need to hold on to a distinction between the political public sphere, where the issue is the relation between debate and decisions on the necessarily polity-wide actions and their consequences, and a range of other public spheres where people are able to create a *sensus communis* concerning the values they will share and the actions they will take in common. The crucial point is that all these public spheres are dependent in one way or another on media, but the nature of that relationship, the specific media form it takes, and its adequacy from a discourse ethic perspective will differ.

2 | Media Histories, Media Theories, and Modernity

> There are only two reasons for sociologists, anthropologists or even historians to string reports together in a sequence isomorphic to the temporal sequence of what they report: either because the sequence itself is to be explained, described or evaluated, or because it explains, describes or evaluates something in its turn
>
> (Runciman 1983: 102)

This book is written from a historical perspective. All human thought and action is unavoidably historical in the sense that it takes place in time and as a project is oriented towards the future on the basis of the experience of the past. But as Habermas stresses in chapter 1 of the *Philosophical Discourse of Modernity*, entitled 'Modernity's Consciousness of Time and its Need for Self-Reassurance', the concept of modernity and the problems it raised for social theory were born out of the acute sense of a historical break, out of a new and heightened sense both of history as tradition, from the dominating hold of which it was necessary to break free, and of history as a break with the past, the understanding of which might orient action towards the future. When Kant, when asked whether he lived in an enlightened age, replied, 'no . . . an age of enlightenment'; when Hegel wrote in the *Phenomenology of Mind* that 'it is surely not difficult to see that our time is a birth and transition to a new period. The Spirit has broken with what was hitherto the world of its existence and imagination and is about to submerge all this in the past'; when Marx and Engels wrote in *The Communist Manifesto* 'all fixed, fast-frozen relations, with their train of ancient and venerable prejudices and opinions, are swept away. . . . All that is solid melts into air, all that is holy is profaned, and man is at last compelled to face with sober senses his real conditions of life and his relations with his kind'; when Weber posed the 'problem of universal history' as the question why, outside Europe, 'the scientific, the artistic, the political and economic development . . . did not enter that path of rationalisation which is peculiar to the Occident', the question of the nature of modernity and of how it

15

came about was posed as a question of history and of our relationship to the past.

The concept of modernity, and of both the Enlightenment and counter-Enlightenment traditions of thought which developed as a response to the problems it created, grew out of the awareness of historical development that the acceleration of social change foregrounded and out of the associated undermining of tradition, especially religion, which had provided both an explanation of the meaning of history and of the future (which was not in this earthly life) and the norms by which to orientate action in the present. Thus on the one hand an awareness of accelerated change caused a break with a cyclical view of history as human fate, while on the other the descent of the future from heaven to earth placed upon human beings the responsibility of choosing their future. But upon what basis should those choices be made? On what normative basis should the new life of modernity be organized? This question, which is in essence one of the relationship of reason and ethics to tradition, became central and has haunted us ever since. On the one hand you have a current of thought that claimed to break with the past and emancipate itself from tradition on the basis of reason, since a part of human emancipation and autonomy was seen to derive from a reflective critique of tradition. On the other you have those who see the only source of guidance for practical reason as the accumulated wisdom of past generations as it is embedded in tradition. For Herder this wisdom is embedded in natural language as the carrier of the experience and values of a *Volk*. For Burke it is tradition that is the ground upon which he attacks the French revolutionaries and expresses his 'insuperable reluctance in giving my hand to destroy any established institution of government, upon a theory'. Thus it is that in much if not all of the debate in social theory since the Enlightenment readings of history are mobilized, of which post-modernism in its various forms is only the most recent. This indeed is why debates about and in history are so important and unavoidable. For the purposes of this book I want to argue strongly that just as Keynes argued that we neglect economic theory at our peril because the actions of practical men in the present are governed by the ideas of long-dead scribblers, so I would argue that both the questions we pose about the media and the approaches we take to answering them have lying behind them, often unacknowledged and so unreflectively, particular historical explanations.

There is one region in which the reduplication of the world, the supposition of an independently existing substrate, somehow responsible for surface phenomena, is not absurd, presumptuous, circular and unwarranted—an area in which we really are allowed to peep behind the veil of Maia, and habitually do: where the 'other' reality is accessible and really *is* known to exist. That area is the area of human performance. In the human sphere, external experience of reduplication, contact with a second reality behind appearance, occurs in, at any rate, two forms: through the multiplicity of persons and through the passage of time. Let us take time as an example. A strict empiricist, or reduplicationist, positivist attitude to the past, for instance, is to treat it simply as equivalent to the evidence about 'what we call the past' in the present, which alone is now eligible for experience. But we do not really believe that the past is merely the marks of the past in the present (A. J. Ayer attempted at one stage to persuade himself of this and asserted such a view in print, but he now admits that he cannot sustain this heroic piece of positivist puritanism). The past was once present, as *the present*, and it was real. The acts of historical personages that explain certain marks in the present are not merely summaries of those marks. They 'really' existed, and they explain those marks in this philosophically 'realist' way. Their being is not exhausted by their role as premises from which current data follow. They have a true reality of their own, transcending their explanatory instrumentality. And we believe the same, whether or not we can prove it, in connection with the independent existence of ourselves. (Gellner 1985: 134)

Thus this book adopts a historical approach, and it does so in the face of current post-modern scepticism regarding the truth of history for a number of reasons.

First because evidence drawn from history, even if it is from the very recent past, is the only evidence we have against which to test sociological theories. Indeed all study of process, whether in the natural or human world, must of necessity be of the past in the sense that by the time the phenomenon is measured, transcribed, and explicated the process is over. Hence the futile search to capture in reflection the immediacy of experience, a futility that leads some within the Romantic tradition to a refusal of reflection and explanation, indeed to condemnation of reflective intellectual activity as essentially and irrevocably alienated and alienating. To claim for any set of observed phenomena or actions in the social world an existence beyond that of a purely temporary random pattern requires us to demonstrate that they exist through time. For instance, if we wish to claim that there is a tendency to concentration of media ownership or that cultural consumption is related to class membership, we cannot rely on measurements taken at one point in time—the relevant correlation may be a random coincidence. Indeed it is a time series of correlated observations that distinguishes an explanation from a coincidence, and cause-and-effect explanations depend upon the temporal priority of the cause.

Secondly, however much people may argue that we cannot learn anything from history, either because the past doesn't determine the future or because, as some post-modernists claim, any account of the past is a fiction, as human beings we plan our actions on the basis of past experience.

Thus we in fact mobilize the lessons of history inescapably every day of our lives, since it is the only material we have to hand. This is true of us not merely as individuals in the projects of our personal lives. It is also true of us as social decision-makers, whether managing a business or merely running a country. Indeed the historical development of systems of social communication has been in part the extension and efficient mobilization of human memory. This memory, and thus the lessons of history, is not to be found just in history books or in our individual memories. It is solidified into institutions and habitual social practices or routines. Thus we can only emancipate ourselves, in so far as that is possible, from the hold of habit by understanding historically how, why, and with what consequences such institutions and routines were formed. We may wish, we may choose, we may even be able, to change ourselves and the social structures and identities within which perforce we live, but we can only do so on the basis of the structures and identities we inherit from past generations. It is in this sense that we create ourselves, but not in conditions of our own making. We stand on the shoulders of those who have gone before. If we wish to take a critical stance towards the existing structure and performance of the media we need to know why they are the way they are, what historical variations there may have been, if any, between historical periods and between societies or cultures, what historically rooted practices are inscribed in the institutions of social communication we have inherited.

As Craig Calhoun has written regarding critical social theory, 'Breaking with the immediate givenness and immediate facticity of the social world calls not only for historical knowledge as a precondition of theory but for a continual engagement with history and rethinking of historical assumptions' (Calhoun 1995: p. xxii).

Thirdly, precisely because history is the only material we have with which to explain to ourselves who we are, where we are, and where we are going or wish to go, historical evidence, whether fictional or not, is constantly mobilized to explain our social world and to justify social and political projects and policies. I certainly agree with post-modernists that histories can be constructed and mobilized in the service of power. But this is not their only or inevitable use. Nor can we criticize and undermine that particular form of the exercise of power without alternative histories which we can show to be truer than those mobilized for ideological purposes. This indeed is what gives historians their great responsibility for the historical truth, however approximate that may be. Thus in the field of social communication this is particularly true at present where a theory of the Information Society mobilizes a stage theory of historical development in which information and communication technologies are causing a set of interrelated economic, social, political, and cultural changes in the nature of human society on a global scale. This theory, as I have argued in more detail elsewhere (Garnham 1998), is one of the, perhaps *the*, dominant ideology of our time, shaping and justifying the actions of business leaders and politicians and, through the media, increasingly shaping the common-sense understanding of our times. The main alternative paradigm shares many of the same presuppositions and, in spite of its critique of history and of grand historical narratives, is also based, as its stress on the 'post' implies, upon a theory of history—of something called modernism superseded—if only in thought—by something called postmodernism. Since such theories are making historical claims they can only be put to the test of history.

Finally social theory and the study of communication in particular has its own history. We can only clarify the reasons for studying communications, the questions it raises and the methods appropriate in our attempts to answer them, if we ground our enquiry in the specific intellectual and disciplinary history that brought us to where we are today. This not only saves us from reinventing theoretical or empirical wheels. Social theory is, as Marx put it 'the self-clarification of the struggles and wishes of the age'. The questions to which we respond and their prioritization are not random. They are posed by the age in which we live. But in the case of communication and the Enlightenment emancipatory project the relevant period is not merely the present. Underlying this book, that is to say, is a conviction that, contrary to the post-modernists and much of the Information Society hype, we live with the same historically posed problems of modernity as those that faced the thinkers of the Enlightenment. That the emancipatory project they initiated was precisely a project. Enlightenment was not a given state. It was a possible historical achievement. This is what Kant meant when he claimed that he lived not in an enlightened age but in an age of enlightenment. It is for this reason that he uses the metaphor of human growth from childhood to maturity to describe the search for and achievement of enlightenment. In short the arguments of the philosophical discourse of modernity, however 'old', speak to us still because they have not lost their relevance.

Before looking at the range of relevant histories we need first to clear out of the way a larger dispute as to the nature of historical explanation. We need to do this because we need to know what kinds of problems a historical approach can address and how we can legitimately mobilize historical arguments in the present. It is also important because such disputes continue to divide those studying the media, for instance the difference between the political economy and cultural studies approaches to the analysis of the media turn, at least in part, on differing views as to the nature of historical determination and the relevant determining forces.

Let me first get out of the way the post-modern attack on history. Here we must distinguish between the claims being made with regard to the subject of history—the historical record—on the one hand and claims being made with regard to the writing of history in the present on the other. The hermeneutic tradition upon which post-modernism draws makes two relevant claims. First, so far as the subject of history is concerned it focuses on the actions of intelligent historical agents and argues that these actions can only be understood and interpreted in terms of the culture, way of life, or tradition within which they are embedded. Thus on the assumption that we no longer share that culture the past is necessarily opaque to us and lessons for the present certainly cannot be drawn. In so far as it focuses on meaning it is suspicious of, if not actually hostile to, structural explanations. In so far as this alerts us to the difficulties in interpreting the historical record, and in particular in so far as it warns against anachronism, it is to be welcomed. Ironically post-modernists are in general only too free in passing anachronistic judgements on the past. But the reason they do this and defend the practice is because of the second claim of the hermeneutic tradition, namely that history is a text, and this in two senses. First, the historical evidence is a text which has to be read and, within the linguistic model with which they are working, this text then has an entirely arbitrary relation to what it signifies—the past. Second, the text written by the historian is both an interpretation which is undetermined by the text of history and at the same time a text determined by the social or political interests of the historian in the present—the so-called perspectival position. Thus history is necessarily a fiction mobilized for present political purposes. Of course those who hold this position don't carry it through to its logical conclusion, because clearly such fictions cannot be mobilized for present political purposes since their readings in turn cannot be determined. Thus the writing of history becomes a socially pointless exercise, a form of intellectual masturbation. The most objectionable aspect of such history-writing, and indeed of the 'new' anthropology that shares the same positions, is its arrogance and self-righteousness masquerading as concern for the Other, the marginal and the dominated. As Gellner has written, such theorists exhibit 'a quite special masochistic distaste for their own culture. All cultures are equal, but one of them (their own) is a damn sight less equal than the rest' (Gellner 1985: 2).

A much more substantial argument, however, concerns the nature of historical determination, and this in two senses. When examining a historical process what kind of causal claims are we making and what is the relationship between the past, the present, and the future? It is a commonplace now to tar modernity with the brush of progress, that is to say with a self-understanding as an inevitable process of historical betterment. Such a view of history is indeed still both prevalent and ideologically powerful. It is mobilized in the classic Whig theory which closely associates the development of the media with the development of the capitalist free market and of democracy as an intertwined story of human liberation. We find such a view enshrined in Fukayama's *The End of History* (1992). It is also enshrined in currently powerful technologically determinist views of the history of communications as a story of the triumphant rise of science and its harnessing to make a better world for us all.

The most powerful and prevalent example of this trope, with which I am sure you are familiar in one form or another, goes as follows: human society is on an up escalator called progress which is powered by technological development allied to the force of the free market, and which is creating, not only a more materially comfortable, but a freer and more spiritually fulfilling world. Central to this process has been the development of communication technologies. Printing began a process of liberation which the new electronic forms of communication will complete as we waft down the Information Superhighway to the promised paradise of an Information Society. Those who stand in the way of this progress have failed to read history correctly and, whether out of misguided nostalgia or spite, are slowing down the train of history and postponing the moment when human beings will come into their rightful inheritance. I only caricature slightly what is a widespread view. It is of course easy to expose the fallacies of this grand narrative. Post-modernists do it every day before breakfast. The problem, however, is that only too often they substitute another grand narrative which is as facile and misleading; namely that we are on a down escalator called Western rationalism or imperialism—the two are often not clearly distinguished—which is powered by the autonomous Kantian subject and logocentrism, and which has led to the suppression of difference in a dominated, disciplined world. This is, of course, the narrative of the Dialectic of Enlightenment dressed in a new set of clothes.

Here we need carefully to distinguish how we understand the nature and direction of historical change from its evaluation. Here I am taking it as read that we can make a valid distinction between structure and agency and that there is no contradiction between believing in the intelligence of human actors on the one hand and in structural determination on the other. The historical problem is to analyse the relationship between the two, how human agents make their history but not in conditions of their own making, and with results that they do not intend, but which then become the conditions for future makings. Many of the critiques of theories of historical determination—in particular critiques of historical materialism—still rest upon models of determination based upon a mechanistic model of cause and effect. But such models have now been widely superseded by evolutionary process models drawn from biology and Darwinian evolutionary theory. Here let me stress first that in understanding human social practices we have to take the findings of evolutionary biology extremely seriously. Since all social theories have to be based, ontologically, upon some theory of human nature and its malleability, and while recognizing that a key human species characteristic that any theory of social evolution must take into account is the extra-organic inheritance of cultural traits, at the same time we need to recognize that certain human attributes that impact on our social behaviour, for instance language capacity, have been hard-wired into us, as the evolutionary biologists say, by the evolutionary process. Evolution in this sense is a historical process but over a very long time-scale.

But more importantly, and one can find this argued at length in Runciman's *A Treatise on Social Theory* (1983–97) or in Hodgson's *Economics and Evolution* (1993), an evolutionary approach to historical development draws from Darwinian theory two very important conclusions for our purposes. First that, although the instigator of the process of change is random, these random variations under certain specifiable conditions produce self-reinforcing non-random patterns which endure unless either their environment radically changes or they come into competition with other randomly generated changes. The random instigator in biology is genetic variation. What should be seen as the carrier of variation within evolutionary social theory, and in what senses it can be said to be inherited, is precisely a matter of dispute. The second key point about this picture of historical development is that it is not deterministic in the sense that it is going in a predetermined direction, nor is it deterministic in the sense that a historical trajectory is determined by its originating conditions. In the language of evolutionary theory historical evolution is phylogenetic not ontogenetic. Development is generated from random changes and the direction of development, because characterized by complex interactions, cannot be predicted from its origins. That the pattern is the way it is can only be seen with hindsight. It is, however, what is known as path-dependent. This is a concept now mainly used in the analysis of the development of technological systems. What it means is that this is a truly historical process. It takes place irreversibly through time such that certain trajectories of development get locked in, or perhaps rather human agents get locked into certain trajectories. It can be seen in this sense as function-alist and this is the sense in which Cohen (1978) defends Marx's view of historical determinism. It is not functionalist in the sense that develop-ments are understood as taking place because they are necessary for sys-tems maintenance, since in the evolutionary perspective the system is itself always undergoing change. There is no presumption of equilibrium or op-timality. If the system were equilibriating evolution would never have taken place. On the other hand it is functionalist in two other senses. First, at any time historically created structural conditions limit the choices that intelligent agents are likely to take assuming a minimum level of self-interest, for example societies such as ours have developed a level of division of labour and social co-ordination without which the current level of population could not be sustained. It is clear that this system of co-ordination has structural characteristics which place constraints on human action and choice. Short of a widespread drive to social suicide therefore, human agents are likely to act in such a way as to attempt to pre-serve some similar level of social co-ordination. This doesn't mean, of course, and this is essential to an evolutionary approach, that they will succeed. Unwitting social suicide is always possible. Some may now even judge it to be likely. To the extent that one can be locked into paths of so-cial development, the past does indeed determine the future, but it doesn't make it predictable.

It is also functionalist in a second sense, namely that the various evolved patterns of human interaction, what we might call institutions as well as structures, are reciprocally determined. And thus one set of social struc-tures or solutions to the problems of social co-ordination may be incom-patible with another. They cannot both live in the same ecological niche without significant modification. What the nature of the reciprocal rela-tion is will always be a matter of empirical analysis and dispute, but that there is as a result only a limited range of possible social forms, and that there is therefore no such thing as a perfect or ideal society, seems from the historical record to be clear. This is a quite different judgement, I must stress, from whether members of such various societies do or do not find them good or bad, just or unjust.

Beyond the general issue of determination histories are distinguished by the nature of the determinations they identify and emphasize and the extent to which they are mono- or multi-causal, although in effect no one, even the most extreme and committed socio-biologists, actually holds to a mono-causal view; it is always a question of emphasis. For example it is often claimed that Marx's version of history makes the economic determinant. But in effect, since this is only in the last instance and it works its effects on historical evolution through the superstructure, through class consciousness and politics, the Marxist historical-materialist understanding of this process is much more complex and multi-causal. Where the emphasis is put will rest on an underlying view of social structure and process. For instance different historical accounts may place their emphasis on the economic, the political, the social, or the cultural, but in each case their explanations of the nature of historical change, of what is at stake, will depend upon how they theorize the divisions of the social structure and the relation between those spheres. Indeed one can see that a key element in the historical explanation for the rise of modernity, which is at the same time a description of modernity and is shared across a wide range of historians and sociologists, is the development of a division of labour and an increasing separation between distinct social spheres. Different historical explanations of both the origins and further development of modernity will then prioritize the impact of these spheres in different ways.

I cannot here write a substantive history of social communication. That would be the subject for a substantial book in its own right. My purpose is to outline those historical approaches to the media, or those historical approaches to social theory, which are of relevance to the questions we currently pose about the media, which are either in fact mobilized in current debates or which I find most useful for thinking about the problems within modernity posed by the media. The purpose of this outline will be to clarify what problems are being addressed and how.

But finally, before I turn to that task, I would like to stress at this point a further intellectual bias which this stress on history reveals. Much current work on communication, especially that within an Information Society perspective, as well as much current policy debate and indeed the culture of the media themselves, are enraptured by the new and the ephemeral and exhibit an almost willed amnesia that amounts to what one might call a nostalgia for the future. But one of the great benefits of a historical perspective is to stress, against the current of the age, what Braudel has called the 'longue durée', the long-term rhythms and patterns of determination within which humans have in the past and continue in the present to pursue their social lives. At the present time I think it is important to stress the slowness rather than the speed of change, the relatively restricted possibilities and range of choice open to human beings and the way these have raised over a long historical period and continue to raise the same set of questions as to how we might and should lead our lives, as we necessarily must, together.

Theories of Social Evolution: Means of Production, Coercion, and Persuasion

Let us start at the most general level, of what might perhaps more appropriately be called historical sociology rather than history, with broad theories of social evolution. Runciman has recently articulated in his three-volume *Treatise on Social Theory*, with theoretical rigour and sophistication and based upon a wide range of evidence from the historical record, a version of what is a very widely held theory—a version Callinicos has dubbed neo-Weberian. This theoretical approach argues, in Runciman's words, that 'societies are conceptualised in terms of the allocation of power among their members, for the simple and sufficient reason that non-random interaction among and between the members of any and all societies implies their capacity mutually to influence each other's behaviour'; power is then defined as 'the capacity of persons to affect through either inducements or sanctions what is thought, felt, said or done by other persons, subject to that capacity deriving from the possession of institutional, not personal, attributes—institutions being defined in turn as sets of interrelated practices whose rules, which may or may not be either explicitly formulated or universally acknowledged, apply to specifiable groups or categories of person irrespective of those persons' choice or consent' (Runciman 1989: 2). Runciman then goes on to argue that 'the range of variation between one society and another, vast as it is, is neither infinite or random; that it is only as the outcome of an institutionalised competition for power that it can be explained' (1989: 4), and that 'the structure of a society can be reported initially in terms of the relative location within it of groups or categories of person sharing a common endowment (or lack) of power by virtue of their roles. But for the researcher actually to locate them requires an answer to the question how many dimensions of structure are there—or in other words, how many kinds of power'. And the answer he proposes, and this is the crucial point for our present purposes, is 'three—the economic, the ideological and the coercive—which, although always mutually interdependent, are never fully reducible to one another . . . But it can hardly be disputed that there is a distinction to be made between access to or control of the means of production, means of persuasion and means of coercion respectively' (1989: 12). That this way of looking at societies is close to the heart of the historical definition and understanding of modernity can be seen by Runciman's admission that 'my choice of the terms "means of production", "means of persuasion" and "means of coercion" is a conscious attempt to combine what I believe to be the most valuable insights of both Marx and Weber, although neither ever put the distinction in quite this way themselves'. On this basis he then goes on to argue that

> it is the restraints on, and variations within, convertibility and congruence [between the three modes] whose study is likely to shed light on the workings and evolution of societies of different kinds. Each of the three forms of power has its autonomous rules; but at the same time, each is reciprocally influenced by the other two in at least some aspects and to at least some degree. Every society has its mode of production, its mode of persuasion and its mode of coercion, and only when all three are taken into account can different societies be assigned to one or another of the range of possible alternative modes and sub-types of the distribution of power. (1989: 16–17)

I have focused on this model at some length because I want to argue that we can distinguish various historical approaches to the media according to which of these dimensions of social power they focus upon and what ranking of and relationship between the modes, whether implicitly or explicitly, they propose in explaining social structure and social evolution. Runciman is clarifying the theoretical presuppositions of a theory of social power and its evolution that is much more widespread. For instance it underpins, although it is not derived from Runciman, Bourdieu's historical analysis of the development of the cultural field and the exercise of symbolic violence as the preferred mode of domination in capitalist societies, and is behind Gellner's analysis of the shift from traditional to modern societies in terms of a shifting relation of power between, in his terms, the *Plough, Book and Sword* (Gellner 1988). And a similar model underlies Gramsci's highly influential theory of hegemony (see also Mann 1986, 1993; Callinicos 1995). Because of the importance of this model, it is crucial to stress that the media do not in any simple way map onto the model such that they are institutions within the mode of persuasion. The practices of mediated social communication can clearly be attached to roles and the exercise of differential endowments of power within all three modes, and it is precisely the purpose of both historical and contemporary analysis to analyse the ways in which those social resources are mobilized by those occupying productive, persuasive, or coercive roles, and with what effect on the power relations both within each mode and between them.

This general model is mobilized by both Gellner and Bourdieu for essentially similar purposes. Each focuses, although their conclusions and modes of analysis are very different, on two related concerns within a general analysis of the key characteristics of the shift from traditional to modern societies. First they focus not on the media as conventionally understood but on the development of formal systems of education as the core of the mode of persuasion within the wider context of a shift from coercion to production as the key axis of domination or as Gellner, with his habitual vivacious cynicism put it, echoing De Maistre, a shift from rule by the hangman to rule by generalized bribery. Within that general picture of historical development Bourdieu has focused on the historical development in France of the intelligentsia as the dominated fraction of the dominant class and of the specialized fields of cultural production, but again with a focus on formal education, within which that intelligentsia exercises its power. The second concern of both has been, following Weber, the historical analysis and explanation for the growth of rationality and the scientific world view. This strand of historical work then links to the whole field of the historical sociology of science and the intellectuals in, for instance, the work of Gouldner (1976) and Bauman (1987).

But where this approach links back directly to media history is through that tradition which focuses on media technology and its impact on the power relations both within and between the modes. It is difficult, I think, to underestimate the influence now exercised by that version of media history which focuses on technology, and in particular by an explanation of the transition to modernity that places print technology at its centre and extrapolates from this to make similar claims for the causal impact of electronic technologies on a similar epochal shift to what is variously described as post-industrial, post-modern, or information society. Here a key work in what is now a very rich field of historical writing on the relationship between a nascent print culture and the Enlightenment is E. Eisenstein's *The Printing Press as an Agent of Change* (1979; see also Febvre and Martin 1990; Darnton 1979, 1982; Baker 1992; Chartier 1985, 1987). Here it is the lessons that have been drawn from her work by others rather than her own analysis which have been crucial. For instance Ithiel de Sola Pool, in calling print and the new electronic technologies 'technologies of freedom' (De Sola Pool 1984) allies a technologically determinist history to classic Whig theory and sees printing technology as the key agent undermining autocratic power based on monopolies of knowledge and, allied to the free market, as the basis for the rise of liberal democracy. Here the lesson he draws from history is that any regulatory curbs on the free market mobilization of new technologies is undemocratic. In fact Eisenstein herself is much more careful and nuanced in her interpretation. For instance she takes on the counterfactual example of China, and its prior development of movable type, to argue that the impact of print on the transition to modernity in western Europe can only be understood as part of a wider set of social changes. Thus she places the roots of a developing scientific world view and practice and of a growing demand for written materials that made printing economically competitive with scribes as prior to the development of printing technology, and she differentiates between the impact of printing on an elite scientific culture and its development on the one hand, and its impact via Protestantism and printing in the vernacular and via the printing of visual images on the other, on the creation of a popular print culture and a more extensive public sphere. This is an important argument and one shared with Mukerji in her *From Graven Images* (1983) because it separates the impact of printing from the simple creation of a culture based upon writing. Indeed Mukerji argues that the primary impact of printing was in helping to create a materialistic culture by creating in the form of prints and printed textiles the earliest widely circulated and mass-produced industrial commodities.

This is important because Eisenstein is clearly in part writing within a tradition that prioritizes a technological, stage theory of history whereby the nature of human consciousness was altered by the shift first from orality to literacy (Ong 1982) and then by the shift from literacy to the 'secondary orality' of electronic media (McLuhan 1964). The priority given to technological development as driver of historical change is well captured by the title of one of Ong's books, *Orality and Literacy: the Technologizing of the Word*. The most recent and influential mobilization of this broad theory of historical development is by Meyrowitz in his *No Sense of Place*, where indeed a useful résumé of this whole approach can be found (Meyrowitz 1985: 16–23).

A major influence within this school was Harold Innis (1964, 1972), but he focused on the impact of media technologies, not on the mode of persuasion so much as on the modes of coercion and production. Indeed it was a theory he developed out of more general work on political economy. Innis's argument, as is well known, was that different media technologies favour differentially the spread of control over time or space, and thus it is a theory that embeds the media within a wider study of physical transport systems and their relationship to systems of economic and political power. History from such a perspective has been widely influential recently in analysis of the development and impact of telecommunications networks which are seen as primarily determined in their development and themselves effecting changes either within the structure of economic production or within the apparatuses of the state. A typical example of this type of historical approach and its consequences for current thinking is Mulgan's *Communication and Control* (1991):

we have become used to the idea that communication systems can carry conversations, films and sounds, but it is their nature as control infrastructures that generally predates their role as media in the modern sense. The early postal networks of Persian, Roman, Mongol and Chinese empires were tools of administration, under the direct control of military and political authorities. The first global network based on electricity, the British Empire's cable network, was also a tool of extensive control as well as a medium for trade and interpersonal communication. The very first telegraph networks were designed to control movements of trains along tracks, the radio to control the movement of ships; today's computer networks are primarily used to control flows of aircraft, missiles, goods, ideas and money. At the end of the 20th century, too, it is the nature of communication networks as control technologies, as the means for co-ordinating the production, distribution and exchange of commodities, the logistical organisation of armies and missiles or the effective governance of civil populations, that is proving most decisive in shaping the direction of technological development. (1991: 2)

Another influential example of work within this tradition would be Beninger's *The Control Revolution* (1986). But this emphasis on the shifting historical impact of communication technologies on power over time and space has in its turn become central to the 'new geography' and to the work of sociologists like Giddens, who place their emphasis on explaining current developments, particularly the impact of so-called globalization upon the impact of electronic communication networks on shifts in the relations of power between differing spatial locations, both within and between countries, and on the differential power to control flows of information through both time and space (see e.g. Castells 1996; Harvey 1989).

The Media, State Formation, and Democracy

Innis's focus on the historically shifting impact of communication technologies upon the exercise of both economic and political power takes us in a number of different directions. On the one hand such an approach can be integrated into a stage theory of history, whether technologically or economically determined, such as Daniel Bell's theory of post-industrial society and developments out of it in the direction of Information Society theory such as that of Castells. On the other hand it points to histories of modernity which place a stress on state formation and bureaucracy and give primacy therefore to the role of the media within the mode of coercion and to the problem, from the perspective of the mode of coercion, of the relationship to the modes of persuasion and production. We find here, for instance, those histories that link the development of the mass media, first newspapers and then broadcasting, to the problems of running a modern state with a representative form of government. This is in part how I read Scannell and Cardiff's history of public service broadcasting (Scannell and Cardiff 1991), and one can find a similar emphasis in Williams's *TV, Technology and Cultural Form* (1974). This approach now links contemporary media developments to the problem of the decline or otherwise of the nation-state and to a change in inter-state relations, and to actual or potential shifts in both the relationship of citizens to their state (electronic democracy and reinventing government) and the modes of political identity-formation and mobilization (the media and the politics of identity). There is as always both a Whig liberal version of this story, the media as part of the story of the growth of political liberty, a version one finds even in Raymond Williams's *The Long Revolution*, and of which a certain post-modern anarchistic linking of cyberspace, new identities, and a liberation from politics is itself a variant, and a more pessimistic, Dialectic of Enlightenment version such as Habermas's *The Structural Transformation of the Public Sphere* (1989). But one can also place here more punctual studies of the growth of government information production, the relationships between the state and the media and between the political system and the media, including the relationship between the growth of commercialization of the media and the changing nature of the relationship between politicians and voters, and the nature of the political culture more generally, for instance the growth of voter apathy and the decline in participation rates. As Schudson (1998) has recently argued, current concerns about the state of political culture as a story of decline often rest upon an unsubstantiated historical view of what that culture was like before, as do similar theories of tabloidization and dumbing down. Here an important strand of historical work has been that on the creation of the structures of modern media in terms of the interrelationship of technology, economics, and politics (Horowitz 1989; Streeter 1996; McChesney 1993).

The Media and Industrial Capitalism

On the other hand the Innis approach points to those histories that focus on the media within the mode of production and which may or may not be linked to either a stage theory of history or a theory of historical materialism which gives priority to developments in the mode of production as the key explanatory variable in historical shifts in social power.

Few, I think, even those most distant from the tradition of historical materialism and any notion of economic or material determination, would deny that central to the history of modernity is the study of the development of what Weber called 'that tremendous economic cosmos' that we call capitalism or the capitalist mode of production. And so it is that central to histories of the media have been those histories which analyse and explain the development of modern media institutions and practices through the prism of capitalist development. But within that more general history a range of distinct themes can be identified which are related to different ways of conceptualizing the nature of capitalist development and the relation of the economic domain to the spheres of the social, the cultural, and the political. For the sake of analysis I wish to separate out the themes in order to clarify the kinds of argument being made, although in actual histories these themes are often and necessarily intertwined.

First there are those histories which emphasize broad structural changes. In their most influential form they link stage theories of economic development which variously interrelate a development from agriculture to industry to services, from industrial to post-industrial, from Fordist to post-Fordist, to both the stage theories of media technology—oral, print, electronic—and stage theories of media structures and practices. In some versions it is media technology that is seen as the determinant and the focus is on media as a means of production (Bell 1973). In other versions changing media structures and practices are seen as a response to shifts in the relationship of production to consumption—from mass production to flexible specialization—and in the structure of consumption itself, from mass markets to niche markets and from goods to services (Toffler 1980; De Sola Pool 1984). It is at this level of analysis that I would place histories of international communication which stress the creation of global markets whether from a positive (De Sola Pool 1984) or negative (Schiller 1992) position vis-à-vis capitalism, although they are often, perhaps usually, also related to histories of state formation and inter-state relations or in short to the general history of imperialism and the creation of what Wallerstein has called the World System.

Linked to the above but not committed to a broad stage theory of development are histories which focus on the development within the capitalist mode of forms of economic organization. Such work is often influenced by economic and business history, for instance by the work of Alfred Chandler (1977). Here the emphasis will be on the media as means of production and the ways that they have developed in response to problems of economic organization. They may focus on the capitalist firm and its use of communication systems as control systems (Beninger 1986; Mulgan 1991; Castells 1996). Here I would place histories which emphasize the development of advertising linked to retailing and mass consumption as crucial to the formation of modern media systems. Or the emphasis may be on the ways in which capitalist forms of organization have impacted on the production of media themselves—the whole cultural industries tradition (Adorno and Horkheimer 1997; Smythe 1981; Wasko 1982; Curran 1977). This approach was emphasized by Asa Briggs in his Fisher Memorial Lecture of 1960 when he wrote:

The provision of entertainment has never been a subject of great interest either to economists or to economic historians—at least in their working hours. Yet in 20th-century conditions it is proper to talk of a highly organised entertainment industry, to distinguish within it between production and distribution, to examine forces making for competition, integration, concentration and control, and to relate such study to the statistics of national income and output, the development of advertising, international economic relations and—not least—to the central concept of the market.

This cultural industry approach can and has gone in a number of directions. One approach is to focus on the general process of commodification (Mosco 1996). This can be linked to an underconsumptionist theory of capitalist development drawn from Baran and Sweezy (1968) and to conscious strategic planning on the part of corporate capitalism as in the Ewens's influential *Captains of Consciousness* (1979) and *Channels of Desire* (1982).

The Media and the History of Time

Another linked approach derives from the more general study, as part of the study of the process of transition from pre-capitalist to capitalist societies, of the social and cultural struggle over labour discipline and the control of time. The two *loci classici* are Thompson's *The Making of the English Working Class* (1963) and 'Time, Work Discipline, and Industrial Capitalism' (1967). But this general approach then focused on the creation of leisure as both a concept and a social field and on the struggle over both the boundaries and relations between work and leisure and over the cultural forms and practices that were to fill this newly created time—a struggle which produced both a specific sense of time which the media both respond to and reinforce (Scannell 1996)—to the creation of modern forms of commercial, professional sport and entertainment (Yeo 1981; Bailey 1978). What this approach importantly underlines is that this struggle was also a struggle over the control and definition of education and that contemporary forms of the distinction and opposition between entertainment and education are historical creations. From this viewpoint the history of the development of media forms and institutions is a question not of ideology, although ideologies will be involved, but of shifting social relations as an outgrowth of struggles over relations of production. Thus it includes work such as Smythe's on the Audience Commodity (Smythe 1981) as well as the more widely influential work on the shifting definitions and relations between the public and the private, a properly historical debate which underlies much of the debate on the public sphere, particularly between Habermasians and feminists like Nancy Fraser (Fraser 1989; Fraser in Calhoun 1992; Sennet 1993; Habermas 1989; Elliott 1986; Calhoun 1992).

The History of Consumption

This approach in its turn has developed in recent years away from the social control approach which views commodification as an extension of capitalist control and thus consumption as a question of class struggle to a view of consumption, drawn from Weber and Veblen and informed by anthropologists such as Douglas, as a culturally universal symbolic carrier of status distinctions and struggles over status distinction. This historical work has mainly focused on the development of consumption in eighteenth-century Britain as part also of the historical debate on capitalist take-off. The question of whether capitalist development, and in particular the development of the division of labour, can best be explained in terms of supply push or demand pull goes back at least to Adam Smith, who was ambivalent on the question. For this work see McKendrick, Brewer, and Plumb (1982), Brewer (1997), and Brewer and Porter (1993). For its application to contemporary analysis see Nava, Barker, Macrury, and Richards (1997); for a critique see Fine and Leopold (1993).

Cultural Histories

Running in parallel with these lines of analysis, and often intertwining with them, is a tradition which looks at the impact of capitalist development on the cultural field by starting with the division of labour and the specialization of social domains. Thus, contrary to the cultural industries approach, it poses the question of the nature of the development of the cultural sphere and of the institutions and forms of modern culture not from within the economy, but starting with the historical separation of the spheres of culture and economy that was part of the creation of modernity, and then examines both the resulting internal dynamics of the cultural sphere, and its often troubled relationship, both organizationally and ideologically, with the economic sphere. Here, drawing on the general fields of intellectual and cultural history, we find historical analyses of the separation such as Williams's *Culture and Society* (1958) or Elias's *The Civilising Process* (1994), histories of taste and systems of patronage such as Haskell (1980, 1981), histories of the changing structure of cultural fields and of the social position of cultural producers as in Bourdieu (1984, 1993, 1996), Di Maggio (1982), Clark (1973), Elias (1994), and Wolff (1981); histories of cultural ideologies such as Williams's *The Country and the City* (1973) a tradition which has been carried forward in much of the recent work on heritage and the enterprise culture (Samuel 1994; Hewison 1987). Here I would wish to echo Frith's regret that media history and cultural studies have been cut off to their detriment from that field of art history that derived ultimately from the engagement with Hegel and which is covered by the names of such historians as Burckhardt (1943, 1995), Panofsky (1951, 1966, 1991), Huizinga (1965) and Gombrich (1994) and their more contemporary successors Baxandall (1972, 1985), Alpers (1988, 1989), Ginzburg (1985), Haskell (1980, 1981, 1983), and Clark (1973), a tradition of historical enquiry which itself links to the Annales school and its study of 'mentalite' (Duby 1978; Le Roy Ladurie 1980) (for a useful review of this work and its general relevance for the study of the media; see Simon (1995) and Hennion (1995)).

This approach in its turn links to what in recent years has been a growing and important field of historiography which focuses on the ways in which history itself is mobilized for broadly ideological purposes. I am thinking here in particular of a general contemporary concern with the relationship of media systems and forms to the nation-state, nationalism, and globalism. Here important histories have been Hobsbawm and Ranger, *The Invention of Tradition*; Benedict Anderson's *Imagined Communities*, a study of the interrelationship between the rise of nationalism and what he calls print capitalism, and its exploitation by intellectuals as propagators of the ideology of nationalism; Linda Colley's *Britons* (1992) on the ideological creation of a British Nation; and also Weber's important *Peasants into Frenchmen* for the French case, or indeed Said's immensely influential *Orientalism* (1995).

This approach links to a more general historical analysis, often located within a historical sociology of knowledge, of the development of the intelligentsia and what Perkins (1989) has called the 'rise of professional society' (see also Bourdieu 1984; Bauman 1987; Wiener 1981; Carey 1993). Within the sociology of knowledge this approach links to the history of the development of science and as we have seen therefore to the question of the relation of that development to print. It also links to an approach derived from the study of the labour process, labour relations, and the sociology of organizations and professions. For instance I would place here histories of the development of journalistic and other media practices such as those of Schudson (1978) and Chanan (1976).

Given that I have placed my approach to media history within the more general problem of the origins and development of modernity we cannot leave the field without underlining the theme which, often implicitly, underlies all these histories and their contemporary mobilization. This is the theme posed by Weber of the iron cage of rationality and what he called the irretrievable fading of the rosy blush of the Enlightenment or what Hegel originally identified as the Dialectic of Enlightenment. For what is at stake in contemporary historical debates about the media is not just the nature of the historical development of modernity but also the normative judgement to be made of it. Thus we need to separate two related questions. First, is the historical hypothesis of modernity as an increasingly socially rationalized and alienated society actually supported by the historical evidence? And secondly if it is, or to the extent that it is, is that such a bad thing? That such a process has both taken place and is a bad thing is simply assumed by many analysts, and indeed is a key underpinning of postmodernism in most of its forms. It is indeed not easy when looking at actual historical accounts and approaches to separate the two levels. For instance, take the so-called mass culture debate. It is in my estimation a mistake to think that one can dismiss the critique of mass culture simply on the grounds of elitism. Both because that is to leave unanswered the problems of unequal cultural and economic power that arise from cultural forms that are produced by a minority for large, dispersed audiences, while at the same time failing to address the question of the theory of alienation or reification upon which the mass culture critique rests. Because the critics, by posing the problem as one of a struggle between difference and the universal, between the reasoning subject and the play of identities, in effect accepts the original iron cage of rationality argument as to the nature of the problem posed by modernity.

It is difficult, I think, to underestimate, the influence of the model of historical development and its normative evaluation enshrined in the Dialectic of Enlightenment. Apart from the Frankfurt School's model of the culture industry a similar model of the growing reification of the world is mobilized in Habermas's *The Structural Transformation of the Public Sphere* and perhaps recently most influentially of all in the whole of Foucault's *œuvre*, which is devoted to a fascinated micro-analysis of the inescapable process by which historically the bars of the cage were built and inexorably tightened around us. The problem with this perspective in my estimation is that it is built upon an ahistorical theory of alienation which in its turn is based upon an ahistorical theory of human essence which is in some way lost either, depending upon the theory, in the process of labour or in the process of linguistically based communication or through repression within the unconscious. The problem with all such theories is that the posited essence has to be pre-social. In my view this is as true of the Marx of alienation, rather than the Marx of surplus value, as it is true of the ontology of logocentrism. In both cases it cannot accept that human so-called nature is both essentially social and socially created such that we can conceive of the development of modernity as a process involving interrelated gains and losses; for instance, the process of economic rationalization through exchange relations and of bureaucratic rationalization through systems of law and administration are both a process by which human relations are increasingly mediated by abstract structures, which have to be understood and controlled as such, and also the necessary condition for greater ranges of social possibility and difference. It is not an either-or situation. There is both a higher level of social discipline, if that is the way one wishes to characterize it, AND a higher level of individuality and reflexivity. Indeed one is the condition for the other. The problem for our purposes is that this alters the way we define the historical problem.

Let me take three examples in relation to current issues within media studies. First, for instance, the problem with Habermas's theory of communicative action and the historical account of the development and the re-feudalization of the public sphere on which it rests, is that, in spite of his attempt to escape from the problematic of alienation and reification via a theory of communicative rationality and the life world, the language of colonization and of distorted communication still reproduces the original way of setting up the problem.

My second example comes from Scannell's recent book *Radio, Television and Modern Life* (1996) which adopts a Heideggerian approach to the problems of the public sphere and everyday life. Towards the end of that book he argues:

Before broadcasting public life was not 'for-me'. It was, definitionally, beyond the reach of me-or-anyone. As such it showed up then, of necessity, as anonymous, impersonal and distant: beyond the range of my concerns. Our stylised thematization of the 19th century in the preceding section was intended to bring this out, to show that the world as totality—in its parts and as a whole—was 'in practice and in principle' always beyond 'my' grasp. Lukàcs drew the correct conclusion from this—that the meaningfulness of the world could not be comprehended. The fracturing of the wholeness of the world—a real historical phenomenon, not a subjective projection onto the real—contributed to that seemingly unstanchable haemorrhage of meaning from modern life which Lukács interpreted as the phenomenon of reification. Being and Time can be understood historically in the same way—as a critique of reification and truly heroic recovery of the meaningfulness of existence in a world whose meaning was, at the time of writing, almost completely covered over. From their very beginning radio and later television have unobtrusively contributed to the recovery of the world in its meaningfulness that had become covered over in the course of societal modernisation.

Now huge claims are being made here, but they are based, as Scannell to his credit makes crystal clear, upon an interpretation of a real concrete historical development. Now in my view this reading of the history of modernity is deeply misguided. But it is subject to historical analysis. Did this process actually take place? Because if it didn't, the problem to which it is argued broadcasting offers a solution simply falls away.

My third example is the debate over the decline or otherwise of the mass audience and the whole effort, present in both Scannell and in the so-called new audience studies, to recuperate something called everyday life in an attempt to get round what this school of thought sees as the elitist or alienating view of the audience as a mass and of media content as ideology. Now it is clear that mass as a concept or attitude has its own history, but the point at issue is how we understand historically the relation between the necessarily large scale of modern social formations on the one hand and the necessarily generalized and abstract forms of mediation which ensure social co-ordination and individual emancipation on the other. Thus a claim is made for the progressive and emancipatory advantages of new media developments on the basis that they herald, or indeed may already have caused, the death of the mass audience. (see e.g. Toffler 1980; Negroponte 1995). If by this we mean that large numbers of people will cease or have ceased to consume a relatively restricted range of common media products, then empirically, as Neumann (1991) in particular has shown, this is simply untrue and, for reasons that both Neumann and Winston (1998) elucidate, unlikely to change in the foreseeable future. But the point historically at stake is that to see this as regressive or in some sense anti-human and to see new developments as liberating requires as its underpinning the historical theory of modernity as rationalization, alienation, and reification. If the theory can be shown to be false historically then both the problem and the evaluative prognosis go away and we can worry about something else.

I can pose the opposition between histories based upon different valuations of the same process by contrasting Foucault to Elias. What Foucault sees as the alienating exercise of discipline as power Elias sees as a civilizing process of increased internalized social control as self-control. Whether the thesis of rationalization stands up to contemporary evidence of recrudescent nationalism, the growth of theocratic movements, the increasing public rejection of science, and resort to mysticisms of one sort or another is certainly an important historical question. But more crucial in my view is the evaluation of the historical evolution of rationalizing processes. And in this I am firmly on the side of Elias, as I imagine would be anyone who had actually experienced what are now only too prevalent historical realities, the breakdown of viable systems of economic production and distribution and of systems of legal order.

In short what I wish to argue is that all theories of the media rest upon historical theories as to the process of the historical development of media institutions and practices and their relationship to the development of modernity and its characteristic social structures and practices. That we cannot avoid mobilizing histories. They are the narratives that make action and critique both possible and necessary. That the form of the history, the kinds of stories we construct and mobilize, will depend upon both the question we are asking in the present and how that question has been framed historically. But that such histories must, contra the postmodernists, be subject to validation both in the light of historical evidence (history is real and we get it wrong at our peril) and in the context of a rational discursive sphere of criticism (the validity of historical arguments is socially grounded).

3 | The Media as Cultural Industries

I want in this chapter to look at what is at stake in thinking about the media as cultural industries and thus studying them from a political economy perspective.

As I argued in Chapter 1 the media are systems for the production, distribution, and consumption of symbolic forms which necessarily require the mobilization of scarce social resources—both material and cultural. In modern societies such resources are largely allocated and used within the structuring constraints of the capitalist mode of production. To describe the media as cultural industries is to point to the demonstrable reality that symbolic forms are in general produced, distributed, and consumed in the form of commodities and under conditions of capitalist market competition and exchange.

To examine the media from this perspective is then to be concerned with two distinct forms of power and their effect on the structure and performance of the media system and on the relation between the producers and consumers of culture; in particular who has access to what communicative resources and what they can do with them.

The first form of power is structural. It is concerned with the ways in which a market system, co-ordinated by what Habermas, following Talcott Parsons, calls the non-linguistic steering medium of money, allocates resources and constrains behaviour in ways that are not under the intentional control of individual or group agency.

The second form of power is that exercised by economic agents within these overall structural constraints, but where the ownership or control of resources provides some room for intentional strategic manoeuvre. This form of power is often referred to as corporate power, and in particular focuses on unequal market power and its regulation. In short, the study of the exercise of economic power is a classic field for the study of social theory's central problem, the relation between structure and agency.

It is ironic, I think, that a version of cultural studies and post-modernist thinking, which is at pains to deny the economic determination of culture and the grand historical narratives of capitalist development and modernity upon which such concepts of determination rest, has come recently to dominate the study of the media and culture at just the time when theories of an Information Society, which places developments in information and communications at the heart both of capitalist development and restructuring and as then determining a total global social and cultural transformation, have come to dominate thinking and action in the field of economics itself and in the social practices of business, including the media business, and politics. In order to understand what, both theoretically and practically, is at stake in these debates it is necessary first to look at how the capitalist mode of production works and determines, within limits, the structures and practices of social communication.

Capitalism, Modernity, and Emancipation

Theorists from a wide range of positions agree that the development of the capitalist mode of production was central to modernity. Indeed, for many, modernity and capitalism are unselfconsciously coterminous. This development involved two processes. On the one hand, as part of a general process of social differentiation and specialization, the economy—the mode of production of the material means for social survival and reproduction—developed into an increasingly autonomous social realm co-ordinated through the steering medium of money. At the same time, as a result of the dynamic self-generating and self-sustaining process of economic growth set off by industrial capitalism, the mode of production and its accompanying structures of incentive, motivation, and legitimation came increasingly to dominate ever greater areas of social action, including the modes of persuasion and coercion. As a result, whatever one's evaluation of this process, one can legitimately describe the modern world as capitalist. Thus no theory of modernity and emancipation can bypass an attempt to understand the genesis and operation of the capitalist mode of production. No theory of post-modernity can avoid the question posed by Information Society theory of whether or not this mode of production is entering another phase of epochal transformation.

From the perspective of the emancipatory project of the Enlightenment the development of the capitalist mode of production raised a specific challenge. On the one hand it could be seen as emancipating humans from material necessity and thus providing the foundation for the personal autonomy and virtuous polity central to the Enlightenment. On the other hand, in a version of the Dialectic of Enlightenment, the capitalist market system, driven by the instrumental, means/ends rationality of efficiency, was the classic case of the iron cage of rationality. It had come to dominate humans and was no longer under their social and moral control. In Habermas's terms the systems world had come to dominate the life world.

The colonization of the cultural sphere by market forces then raised an especially acute problem. For Kant and his successors emancipation depended upon enlightenment, which in its turn depended upon publicity—the free exchange of ideas about the world and about social relations with fellow-citizens in order to arrive at truth and a freely chosen and shared moral community. The challenge presented by the development of the culture industries was the provision and domination of the means of publicity by the logic of things rather than of autonomous moral beings. As we shall see in later chapters, this is the core of the Frankfurt School's critique of the culture industries and of Habermas's search for unconstrained communication within a public sphere.

Thus from an emancipatory perspective we need to see the general question of the nature of the capitalist mode of production and of the difficult balance to be struck in its regulation between its genuinely emancipatory and its dominating characteristics as central. We then need to see the regulation of the culture industries as a particularly acute but special case.

The Political Economy of the Media

In order to get to grips, both theoretically and empirically, with the above issues it is necessary first to examine the ways in which we can understand the capitalist mode of production as working and as determining the structure and practices of social communication.

For present purposes we can say that the capitalist mode of production brings into a specific historically constructed set of relations the means and forces of production, capital, and labour to produce and exchange commodities (whether goods or services) on competitive markets. This system has certain defining characteristics: competition between capitals in search of accumulation which drives innovation and the search for efficiency and thus growth in productivity for the system as a whole; the separation of labour from the means of production, an increasingly deep division of labour, and thus the provision and allocation of labour through a labour market based on wages. These sets of relationships are co-ordinated across the system as a whole by money in the form of price signals on a market. Neither individual capitals nor workers have any choice but to participate in the system. Capital has to invest and workers have to sell their labour to survive. Given a relatively simple assumption about human motivation this system will produce a relatively consistent pattern of action on the part of both capitals and workers in response to the steering of the price system. As with a linguistic medium, we can distinguish between the structural relations which are outside the control of any one individual, and even social group, and the individual actions which the system produces, i.e. people do or do not invest in a certain activity, they do or do not go to work, acquire certain skills, consume certain products, etc. These are both individual rational responses and uses of the system. Thus the economy is structurally determining because it produces systemic results which no single economic actor planned or desired, from effects at the level of the national or global economy as a whole (e.g. stock market or currency collapses, the business cycle), to those at the level of a sector or firm resulting in falling or rising rates of profit, investment flows, hiring or firing of workers, bankruptcy, or takeover. It is also structurally determining in another historical sense in that the complex system of specialization of function and scale of co-ordination that the capitalist mode of production made possible is a necessary condition for the levels of production necessary to sustain societies at the size and with the complex characteristics they now have. Assuming we do not wish to commit general social suicide, we either have to try and sustain this system or we have to find an alternative that is similarly efficient. Thus from a social evolutionary perspective the development of the capitalist mode of production and the societies based upon it is path-dependent. We cannot go back without unacceptable consequences. Of course environmental disaster may force such a retreat, but the point is that human agents would not knowingly choose such a course of action. In this sense to say that the structure is determining is not to say that actors would not or do not choose it. It is to say that given the constraints it creates then their rational choice is to sustain it. It is also important to note that the kind of structural determinism involved does not deny the role of rational human agents and their strategic instrumental human action as a determinant of the operation of the system. On the contrary the system only works in the structurally determining ways that it does so long as human agents continue to act in specific ways that they see as rational and that, within the situation in which they find themselves, are as rational as any social decision can be in conditions of 'bounded rationality'. Capitalists and their managers really do make what they see as rational decisions about where best to invest, how to position themselves on markets, what to produce, etc. Workers, within much narrower constraints, do indeed decide whether or not to get trained, which jobs to apply for, whether or not they will accept a given wage, and what they will consume. But they do so within a set of constraints specific to the system, in particular in response to price signals, and with results determined at the level of the system and thus with results that they may not have in any sense planned.

We can make our first approach to understanding how the mode of production structures the field of social communication at this level of the structure. First the amount of resources made available for communication is determined by the amount of the economic surplus in general. (It is very easy to ascertain both by historical comparison and by comparison between countries that the range of different communication media and the level of output within these media is closely linked to GDP and overall levels of disposable income. Because of economies of scale, small countries can support fewer nationally produced media than large countries.) The amount of media sustainable under market conditions is in general determined both by the level of disposable income and resulting consumer expenditure and by the level of advertising support. Thus if we are to understand the present pattern of media provision and the possibilities for its future development we need to understand what drives and constrains consumer expenditure and advertising expenditure. For example many of the recent and current predictions for developments of new media, and thus both the business strategies and the public policies based upon them, have foundered on the rock of what economists call realizable demand. There is a gap in any economic system, which is a system for dealing with scarcity, between consumers' needs and desires on the one hand and what consumers are both able and willing to spend in general, and on any given good or service in particular. Similarly there is a gap between the aspirations and talents of those, whether individuals or social groups, who might want to communicate or produce symbolic forms of expression on the one hand and both the jobs available and realizable consumer demand on the other. The point to be stressed here is that the structure of the cultural labour market and the structure of cultural demand are not random. This does not mean, however, that they cannot be changed by specific public intervention—for instance the reregulation of UK broadcasting in the late 1980s significantly restructured the broadcasting labour market and thus, in analysable ways, the structures of power and control over cultural production. The structure of public consumption can also be shifted by policies of public subsidy, education, or indeed censorship. We can see this possibility and the problems associated with it in the debate over universal service in telecommunications and public service in broadcasting. But the point again is that these interventions are increasingly made on the basis of economic analysis and theory and are constrained in their effects in ways that are subject to economic analysis—assuming of course that such production and consumption is not entirely withdrawn from the economy and directly organized by the state.

A further overall structuring effect is the division between what economists call intermediate and final demand. Intermediate demand refers to those goods and services produced for use within the productive system itself. Machines, raw materials, marketing, accountancy, and legal services or industrial training. The level and structure of intermediate demand is determined by the level and structure of capital investment and the strategies and structure of firms. Final demand refers to those goods and services sold direct to consumers and is determined by level of disposable income, which in its turn is determined by the share of wages in the overall output. This distinction is important because much of the discussion of media and culture, even that informed by an economic perspective, is overwhelmingly focused on final demand. This is misleading for two reasons.

First because much of the debate on the effect of so-called new media and the Information Society is based upon the supposed implications of increased consumer choice and consumption of media, and the supposed demassification that has resulted or will result, and its consequent cultural/lifestyle and political effects. This strand of thought tends demonstrably to exaggerate the changes in consumer behaviour, when even the most cursory look at actual consumption and expenditure patterns will show the limited range and degree of change within what economists have called the principle of relative constancy, i.e. in real terms the proportion of disposable income spent on media consumption has remained relatively constant.

Second it tends also to neglect the fact that much media, much of the development of information and communication technology and their use, is primarily driven by the needs of the production system itself. Advertising is an obvious example. We know that newspapers and broadcasting in their current form would not have developed historically without advertising support and that they are still dependent upon advertising finance either entirely or for a significant proportion of their revenue. Indeed the very growth of a mass media market in the newspaper and magazine industry was dependent upon the low consumer prices and thus economies of scale that could be built on the top of advertising revenue, itself dependent upon the development of a new phase of consumer capitalism and the move to mass-market branded consumer goods. We also know that the level of advertising demand has no direct connection with the level of consumer demand for the media products and services financed by it, but is more closely related to levels of corporate profitability. Thus to understand the media economy and what is and is not sustainable within it we need to understand the nature of the advertising market. This is not to say that the structuring effect of advertising finance is everywhere the same. We know, from the differential rates of overall advertising expenditure, that this is in part a cultural phenomenon and that it is not common across all capitalist economies. It has tended historically to be significantly higher in Anglo-Saxon countries and in Japan than in the rest of Europe. We also know incidentally—contrary to the propaganda of the advertising industry and its economist supporters—that levels of advertising expenditure do not correlate with economic success.

Similarly many readers may think of the telephone primarily as a medium of personal domestic communication. In fact telephone systems, and now the Internet system built upon it, have been since their inception and remain overwhelmingly business communication systems. Personal private telephone usage, and the policy of universal service now related to it, are parasitic on this business use. This is important because many of the models for the new media, in particular the Internet, are based on the model of the telephone. How a system develops, to whom it is made available, at what cost, and for what purposes are significantly dependent upon its primary usage. In the absence of public intervention power over this development will be exercised primarily by its major users. This point is well illustrated by a presentation I heard a few years ago by a senior international telecommunications executive. He argued that for all the talk of globalization the market in which his company was primarily interested, for which it was investing and competing, extended to about 100 acres in total, i.e. the major business centres of London, New York, Tokyo, Frankfurt, and so on, and its only profitable customers were 120 multinational corporations. This is in fact an exaggeration, but it is an exaggeration that underlines a crucial aspect of the economy of the media. As Charles Jonscher demonstrated several years ago, the so-called information explosion does not primarily involve the domestic consumption of media but the use of business services (Jonscher 1983). Finally we need to remember that this is not a new phenomenon. Indeed the newspaper first developed, in the era of what Benedict Anderson has called 'print capitalism', as a business service.

Media Regulation and Models of Market Power

We have been looking so far at the general question of the capitalist mode of production as a structural determinant and the way in which Adam

Smith's 'invisible hand' works to structure the overall distribution of social resources to and across the communication sector. But given this broader system we also then need to analyse how and why economic agents act as they do and with what results. To understand how the process of capitalist market competition works, and the reasoning underlying both corporate strategies and public regulatory intervention, we need to draw not only on the still dominant neo-classical marginalist model of market competition but also on the insights of institutional and industrial economics.

There are two ways in which you can look at the operation of an economic system: as a market or set of markets within which competitive agents interact, or as a set of concrete production systems. While these perspectives are by no means necessarily incompatible—indeed they are now combined in much regulatory analysis— they do emphasize different problems of economic power, different structural constraints, and different types of actor strategies. The former perspective focuses on competition between capitals, on financial flows and profit maximization, the latter on the co-ordination of raw materials, productive technology, and labour to produce commodities with specific properties to meet specific market demands in pursuit of efficiency.

Let us then look at some of the implications of examining the media sector and media policy debates from these two perspectives.

The Media Market

Whatever the pros and cons of the market as a general mechanism for social co-ordination and economic development the media offer a challenge to the neo-classical, marginalist model of how the market is supposed to work which stems from the particular characteristics of a market in information or communication. This challenge is now central to thinking not just about how the media are organized, how they are developing, and how, if at all, they should be regulated. It is also crucial to thinking about the future of the economy in general, precisely because those who argue that we are in transition towards an information economy, and an information society based upon it, argue that what has always been characteristic of the media sector of the economy—the production of immaterial commodities— is now characteristic of the general production of goods and services throughout the economy as a whole.

To understand what is at stake we need to look first at the basic assumptions underlying the neo-classical model of the market. This is based upon fully rational economic agents pursuing utility maximization on markets where no agent is powerful enough to determine either the price of factors of production or the market clearing prices of commodities, where consumers have a choice of substitutable utilities, and where market entry and exit are costless, where the cost of production can be passed on proportionally to consumers, i.e. the costs are captured in the price or, in economists' terms, there are no externalities and there are no freeloaders. Were such a market to operate it would ensure the most efficient allocation of resources to production. No resources would be devoted to producing things no one wanted at prices they couldn't afford, and the share of output going to producers would reflect the minimum effort required to produce that output and would not include a rent unjustifiably extracted from consumers. Because competing firms face competing consumers, there is neither monopoly (a single seller) nor monopsony (a single buyer), the most efficient producers will survive and capital will shift into the most profitable, because most efficient, firms or sectors or into new markets not already saturated—where new demand can be created or where demand has not yet been fully satisfied at the lowest possible cost.

This model of markets produces the famous demand and supply curves. When production of a new product starts it requires relatively high fixed cost—the minimum costs of market entry, such that the real cost of production of the first unit of production is high, and in general therefore the product is sold at below its cost of production. Profitability is dependent upon achieving a production run of a given size over which to spread fixed overheads and thus upon a given level of market penetration. On the other side of the coin it is assumed that for any given product demand will be relatively low at a high cost, but that demand will increase as the price comes down until a point is reached where demand is saturated and no more units of production would be sold at any price. The key to the neo-classical, marginalist model is that the crucial production and consumption decisions are made at the margin. Production ceases to expand at the point where the cost of production of an extra unit exceeds the revenue that can be derived from an extra sale. It is by this marginal *tâttonment* that supply and demand are kept in rough equilibrium through time and thus the economy runs at near its maximum efficiency. It is important to note that this is a model to explain the strategic behaviour of producers and consumers. It says nothing one way or the other about distribution, or the allocation of the surplus, except in so far as labour is included within the model as a factor of production, the employment of which is dependent upon its marginal productivity—the price that can be got for the last unit of production produced by the last worker to be hired—and upon the relative cost of capital investment in machinery versus the cost of hiring labour. In this model the level of wages and thus the distribution of the surplus are determined by this market clearing price for labour.

It is important to understand the basic outline of this neo-classical, marginalist model because it is the foundation upon which are based most common-sense assumptions about how markets in general, and media and information markets in particular, work and thus debates about their desirability or otherwise and the need for their regulation or otherwise.

The Market Model and its Critiques

In order to understand what is at issue in these debates we need to understand first the general critiques that can be made of this model and then the more specific critique of its applicability to information and communication markets.

The first and crucial critique, with particular importance, as we shall see, for communications, is that the assumption of rational, fully informed economic agents is unfounded. In the real world information is not a cost-free good, and for this reason the costs of acquiring the information necessary for economic decision-making and problems of differential access to that information need to be factored into the model. From this perspective possession of scarce and by definition costly information may provide competitive advantages which are not easily overcome. For instance, British Telecom has information about customers and their telephone usage and BSkyB about subscribers to satellite services which are not available to potential competitors. Any incumbent in a market will tend to have information about operating costs or may have privileged contractual relations with potential suppliers, ignorance of which raises the risks of competitive market entry. It is also for this reason that it may be more rational for a firm to protect and enhance its share of a market it is already in and knows, rather than attempt to enter a market of which it has no knowledge or experience. These factors make industrial structure much stickier than neo-classical theory would assume. On the demand side consumers cannot afford to make a full trawl of available choices. Their actual purchasing decisions are much more likely to be determined—and given information costs quite rationally so—by habit—sticking with the devil you know—thus by brand loyalty, or by advertising, where the search costs are borne by the seller not the purchaser. In pure theory consumers are supposed to be faced by a range of products or services which are near-substitutes and between which it is possible to make easy trade-offs between quality and price. But in fact, while this may be relatively easy when buying fruit in a street market, in most transactions it is not. It is difficult to judge the real 'quality' of one product compared with another. Indeed much marketing effort by corporations goes into trying to make products different from one another, if only marginally so, such that they are not substitutable, and by muddying the waters of price comparability by various pricing strategies.

Secondly the model assumes that factors of production and products are homogeneous, so that shifting investment or purchasing power from one to another is relatively costless or frictionless. But again in the real world this is not so. From the production side this problem is addressed particularly from the perspective of fixed costs. Capital investments are in fact in the form of specific production technology or labour skills which cannot simply be switched to another form of production as and when marginal cost signals indicate. The plant would have to be written off and the skilled work force, built up over time, would be lost altogether or lost to competitors. Thus there is path-dependent inertia in the system. It will be in the strategic interest of management to run an operation at less than maximum profit rather than exit altogether, particularly because the process is taking place in time and in conditions of bounded rationality. It may be perfectly rational to put off the evil day: the market might make an upturn; your competitors may exit the market before you do, and so on.

Thirdly the model assumes that both investment and purchasing decisions are discrete—in economists' terms divisible—each decision can be taken in isolation in the light of the market information then available. This may be true of very simple forms of production: when demand increases an extra worker with already available skills is taken on; when there is a downturn the worker is sacked. If I decide to satisfy my food needs today by buying a loaf of bread I can easily satisfy the same need tomorrow, for whatever reason, by buying a pack of spaghetti. But most decisions in a developed economy are not of that type. From the production point of view investment is lumpy—you either invest in a production facility, say a broadcasting network, and hire or train workers with the necessary skills to run it, or you don't, and that investment will only pay at a given level of output even if market demand fluctuates around it. Thus given the initial investment it may well pay over an extended time period to maximize output and sell at below the cost of production—what is known as dumping. There is also the problem of joint production. Oil refining is the classic case whereby the process produces a range of products for which the market conditions may be very different, but the production of one entails production of the other. The same is true of a broadcasting channel—

given the investment in running the channel—the individual production costs at the margin of the each discrete element in the schedule—a news service, light entertainment, soap operas, game shows, etc.—and even more of any individual programme, are unlikely to make any difference one way or another as to whether to continue production. This is why many seek the holy grail of pay per programme as a way out of this dilemma, enabling the assumption of more efficient allocation of production resources across programmes. Similarly with telecommunications networks. They may initially be installed to provide telephone services. But substantially the same plant can then be used at small extra cost to provide data services. Or local cable networks may be able to carry both television signals, telephone calls, and data. The problem for the neo-classical model is how then to allocate the joint costs between these two services such that marginal costing could produce most efficient outcomes. In effect it cannot be done. All results will be arbitrary and will produce the result those making the allocations wish to achieve for whatever reason. Many of the dilemmas of regulating communication networks and media markets turn on this problem.

On the demand side the same problem arises. Let us take television as an example. If I purchase or rent a television set or a satellite dish I do so because I expect to be able to consume a service. Indeed the service may not even be provided by the same person who is selling the TV set and the price for the service is certainly not related to the price for the TV set by a system of market competition. There is a chicken-and-egg problem here which is central to the problem of the development of communication networks. Without the service the TV set is worth nothing. Unless a significant number of people have purchased sets it is not worth broadcasting the service. But unless the set manufacturing and retailing industries are in the same ownership as the television broadcasting industry there is nothing in the market mechanism that will ensure this co-ordination. Indeed this is precisely why broadcasting began as an outgrowth of the radio-set industry. The service was provided free to persuade people to buy sets. Unless this co-ordination is underwritten by the government it presents real problems for launching new network and services and for the appropriate role of competition regulation within that process, as we can see from the launch of digital television. There is also on the demand side the problem of what economists call externalities. A purchasing decision may have impacts on other consumers for which they do not pay if they are positive or for which the purchaser doesn't pay if they are negative. Pollution is one classic case. The tension between public transport and the private car is another. Externalities can be seen as another example of joint production. But here a production process produces the product or service which a set of consumers purchases and, at the same time, a polluting by-product.

The Industrial Economics Approach

But any system of production can also be seen from the perspective of industrial economics not as a frictional system of capital flows, but as a material social process. The industrial economics approach focuses on the specificities of a production system as a concrete cycle bringing together fixed investment in plant, variable investment in raw materials, and labour, within a production system with specific costs and functional characteristics depending on the available technology, labour skills, market size, and consumer demands. This will be a variable geometry system primarily driven by the search for efficiency rather than profit maximization. In short, while capital in its abstract monetary form can circulate freely, once it is invested in real processes of production, which to accumulate it has to be, it is locked into a specific structural dynamic. Whether the two coincide or approach one another will depend on the characteristics of that specific system of production. As against a generalizing view of the market this perspective sees the economy as divided into what Storper and Salais have recently dubbed 'worlds of production' (Storper and Salais 1997) or distinct value chains.

The classic example of this approach to the corporate economy in the twentieth century is Chandler's *Scale and Scope* (1990), itself an expansion of his classic *The Visible Hand* (1977), in which he argues that the major explanatory factor of market structure and corporate behaviour, in particular the economic dominance of large oligopolistic corporations on a global scale, has been the exploitation of economies of scale derived from mass production systems allied to mass marketing and distribution. The post-Fordist argument is in essence that shifts in production technology related to information and communications technology and in consumer demand (fragmentation, specialization, higher value) has shifted this mass economies of scale dynamic towards flexible specialization. This argument has then been applied to the media in terms of a shift from mass media or broadcasting to niche media and narrowcasting.

In the field of media a classic version of this industrial economics approach is that of Bernard Miege (1989), who identifies three different forms of media organization whose differences stem ultimately from differences between the types of commodity they are producing. Miege distinguishes between editorial, press, and flow models. Editorial produces individual cultural goods—books, records, films, etc.—financed largely by direct sale to the end consumer where the problem is (a) the management of highly skilled creative labour working under artisanal conditions, and (b) the uncertainty of demand. Because the nature of the product demands constant renewal—new books, new recordings, new films—for which demand is highly unpredictable, it is necessary to exploit economies of scope through managing what Miege calls a catalogue. In an economy of hits and flops you can only survive if you produce a range of products wide enough to ensure high enough statistical probability of achieving the one in ten hit. It is control of the catalogue and its distribution that is crucial, and much of the direct labour can be subcontracted to 'freelancers'. The press model is that of the newspaper industry which typically employs large industrial workforces of the mass production type to produce and rapidly distribute a single, highly perishable product—the newspaper. Its perishability requires rapid production and distribution but ensures repeat consumption. The repeatable form ensures brand loyalty and helps to mitigate uncertainty of demand. The financial problem is managing the relationship between subscription and advertising revenue. The flow model on the other hand is that characteristic of broadcasting where uncertainty is dealt with by producing a constant flow of product as a packaged service and where speed and range of distribution are crucial, and thus the strategic point in the value chain is control of access to appropriate distribution systems. The financial problem has been, until the advent of efficient subscription systems, how to ensure revenue where the end consumer cannot be charged. What all these models show is that concentration is, in different forms, the essence of survival in the media sector, since it alone ensures the necessary economies of either scale or scope, and that the crucial competition issue is where within the value chain strategic market power lies. Faced by convergence—the migration of both the production and distribution of all types of media goods or services to the digital mode and thus in principle the sharing of a common distribution infrastructure—many now argue that two potential or actual strategic bottlenecks can be identified where rents or supernormal profits can be raised. One is technical bottlenecks in networks arising from the natural monopoly characteristics of either the network itself or of the market information generated by the network. Hence the regulatory battles over the local distribution loop between telephone, cable, and satellite companies and over the set-top box. Another is rights to the few types of content which possess a high probability of success—feature films and high-profile sporting events.

This view is important for current policy debate because the debate over the impact of digitalization and so-called convergence within the media sector, and its impact on both the media sector itself and on the wider economy and society, turns in large part, as we shall see in a moment, on whether one sees the problem as one of competition for end-user markets or as one of a restructuring of the value chain and a relocation of strategic power within that chain.

The Institutional Approach

In part because, contra the neo-classical market model, all economic agents operate with inadequate information, there is now a whole school of economics dealing with the problem of decision-making under conditions of 'bounded rationality' devoted to game theory and informational economics. This approach focuses in particular on the important question first raised by Coase (1937) as to why if the market is so efficient we have firms at all since firms are institutions within which market relations do not operate. It secondly raises the question, which has long been central to debates about the locus of power within capitalist economies, of whether it is shareholders or managers who really control firms and their strategic actions. One can for instance read the reforms to the regulatory system of UK broadcasting in the 1980s as an attempt, through the auctioning of franchises, to shift power from managers, supposedly undisciplined by market forces because protected from takeover, to shareholders through the operation of the capital market. Of course in the case of media moguls the manager and shareholder may be one and the same.

An important version of this approach for our purposes here are the new institutional theories of the firm based upon transaction cost theory (Williamson 1975, 1985). This approach argues that all market transactions carry two types of risk derived from the necessarily partial information held by participants: first they have inadequate information about the market because searching for such data is both costly and time-consuming; secondly, they have inadequate information about other participants' intentions because all market transactions are subject to strategic deception. Two conclusions follow from this. First that firms can be explained as envelopes within which transactions can be shielded from the market and from the costs and uncertainties that the market inevitably brings with it. Where a firm draws its firm boundary, what it internalizes and externalizes, will depend both upon the costs of information search in relation to the costs of non-market co-ordination and upon the costs of ensuring compliance with contractual agreements. For regulatory purposes this in its turn will determine the relationship between a particular firm structure and market efficiency and the costs and efficiency of regulation itself, since regulation entails not only defining the specific target of and rationale for regulation, but also ensuring compliance in ways that are no more harmful than the abuse being regulated. It has two other important consequences. It means that the means of communication themselves and the cost of their provision, because they directly affect both information search costs and co-ordination costs, may affect firm and market structures throughout the economy. This is one of the key arguments of the information economy and post-Fordist theories (see e.g. Castells 1996; Cairncross 1997; Coyle 1997). It also means that the social setting, including the regulatory setting, will affect the overall efficiency of economic activity by the extent to which it does or does not promote trust. Thus efficient firms and markets rest, as economists are becoming increasingly aware, upon structures of social solidarity or cultural norms external to the mode of production *per se*.

The Economics of Media Policy and Regulation

Let us now turn to look at the ways in which these economic models and arguments are mobilized in debates over media policy and regulation. Whichever model is used, at the heart of such arguments lies a notion of market failure as the justification of regulatory intervention. While other public interest arguments are raised, they are very much at the margin. In current media policy debates it is in general assumed that a properly operating competitive market will maximize public benefit, or as it is sometimes called welfare, in the field of communications.

Within this competitive market model the media present, as is widely recognized, particular problems of market failure stemming from their very nature. These problems are of three sorts. The problem of concentration, the problem of public and merit goods, and the problem of networks.

Concentration

Concentration is a general problem for those in favour of competitive markets because it leads to oligopoly or monopoly where a small number of firms accumulate sufficient market power to manipulate the market in their favour at the expense of consumers. It presents a particular problem in the field of media because of the ideology of pluralism that underpins the desirability of the marketplace of ideas, and thus the very legitimacy of the provision of media by private economic interests. It is recognized within the neo-classical model that both economies of scale and scope can lead to concentration—economies of scale being the situation where the unit costs of production decline as production increases (a natural monopoly being a special case where the entirety of demand for a given product or service can be provided more cheaply by one supplier than two or more—or technically where the returns to economies of scale are continuous) and economies of scope being the situation where two or more products or services can be produced more cheaply jointly by one supplier than separately by different competitive suppliers. These, as I have said, are general problems within the market model. But the media are special because of the immaterial nature of the symbolic forms being circulated and of their use value. It is precisely because it is now argued that the centre of gravity of capitalist economies is shifting from the production and circulation of material goods to the production and circulation of symbolic values, even when these, as with a motor car, are embedded in a material good, that the model of the media market and its regulatory problems is being applied more generally to the analysis of the so-called information, post-industrial or post-Fordist economy.

Here we need to make a distinction within the media between production and reproduction. The relationship in media between the production of the original prototype—what in a normal industry would be covered by research and development—and its production in multiple series for distribution to consumers is very different from that in a normal industry. In the media the costs of producing the original artefact, be it the edition of a newspaper, a film, or a television programme, is high relative to the unit costs of then reproducing that original—what in the newspaper is called the first copy or in the film industry the negative cost. This means that the marginal cost of an extra reader, viewer, or listener is extremely low. In broadcasting it is in effect zero. Thus there are continuous returns to economies of scale and no economic barriers to maximizing audiences. These economies of scale dynamics are then reinforced by economies of scope dynamics. The use value of the information industries, unlike other industries, is based on the production of novelty. If I already possess a piece of information, by definition I no longer need to purchase it again. It also means that I don't know if I want to consume a given information product until I have consumed it. My decision to buy cannot be based on previous knowledge of the product. This means that unlike most industrial production demand is very unpredictable. In most consumer goods industries this is not true. Loaves of bread or motor cars have embedded within them definable and repeatable qualities which are in turn related to known production costs. It is the job of industrial engineers and cost accountants to design products with features which they know from research and market testing consumers want at a price they can afford. While new products may do better or worse on competitive markets this is within controllable limits, and products rarely fail. Competition takes place through the continuous innovation of product quality within known patterns of use and demand and by improving productivity in order to compete on price with market rivals within the same product market. None of this applies within the media. Products routinely fail producing the prevalence of the hit-and-miss phenomenon. Misses don't just fail, they fail abysmally, while the major proportion of the revenues is captured by the small proportion of hits. The problem is that no one in the industry, whatever they may claim, can predict the hits. This has several important consequences. First it favours economies of scope, because if you only produce a single product your chances of going bankrupt are very high. In order to make a reasonable return it is necessary to spread the risk over a range of products. Thus the ability to produce, and even more important distribute, a significant product range is crucial. In the medium to long term the large operator will always defeat the small. Second, it means that in general the media do not compete on price, since there is no calculable relationship between costs of production and revenues received for any one product. Nor can the consumer make a trade-off when making a purchasing decision between price and quality. They are simply incommensurable. This links to economies of scale because the unit cost of the individual consumer product—a book or a record or a newspaper or a video—may be so low that there is little margin within which to make meaningful price discriminations. Thus in general media are sold as products within broad standard price categories; to illustrate the point a book publisher or film producer cannot adopt a market-entry strategy of competing against established bestsellers by offering a cheaper film or novel. Price signals may to some extent determine—indeed demonstrably do determine—whether a consumer will enter that market, i.e. will buy books or go to the cinema at all. They do not determine purchasing decisions as between products within a given category. (We may now be witnessing partial exceptions to this with the predatory pricing strategy of Murdoch within the UK newspaper market (Sparks 1998) and, since the abolition of the Net Book Agreement in the UK, the sale of bestsellers at reduced prices as loss leaders.) Examples of economies of scope that may not at first sight be obvious are the newspaper and the television schedule. The purpose of both forms is to capture on average over time a readership or viewership by presenting, not individual items of information or entertainment, but a range of items that will satisfy enough of the people enough of the time. As becomes clear if one considers the arguments of the Peacock Committee

(Home Office 1986) in favour of pay per view as the preferred model for the provision of television programmes, or by advocates of newspapers tailored to individual needs by search engines on the Internet (Negroponte 1995) the newspaper and television channel model of economies of scope, because its economics is based on the bundling of programmes or items of information, is a form of concentration which presents a problem for advocates of market competition as the route to consumer freedom and the maximization of efficiency in production. It is for this very reason that much current regulatory attention is being applied to the anti-competitive effects of the sale to subscribers of cable and satellite channels in packages.

Public Goods

This characteristic in turn links with another key feature of media products. They are what economists call non-rival in use or public goods. When I consume a loaf of bread I am in competition with other potential bread-eaters for scarce resources, since once I have consumed the loaf it is not available to anyone else. Broadly this is true of other material commodities, and indeed of services where the scarce resource is the time of the person delivering the service. If a doctor is treating me he or she cannot be treating someone else, and the doctor's time is finite. None of this is true of media or information. When I watch a television programme or read a newspaper it doesn't stop anyone else consuming the same piece of information. In such a situation it has long been recognized by economists that the market model of provision has serious problems. First, where there is no scarcity there is no justification for rationing by price. Secondly, the erection of a price barrier will lower total welfare since it will exclude those who would have consumed the good or service if free without raising the utility of those who continue to consume. The problem, however, is how to avoid the free-rider problem or, to put the matter in another way, how to raise the revenue necessary to pay for production. That the free-rider problem is a serious one is illustrated by the prevalence and extent of piracy in media industries (the record industry has calculated that 15 per cent of global turnover is accounted for by pirates; academics will attest from personal working experience that policing photocopying is not easy). This has been 'solved' in a number of ways. First and most paradoxical is by means of copyright. In effect against a background of a general belief in the desirability of free competitive markets, and of the general political and cultural desirability of a marketplace in ideas, the state underwrites a monopoly and the producers' right to a monopoly rent. This is done in the peculiar circumstances of markets in information to provide an incentive to production in the face of free-riders. The second solution is advertising revenue—selling audiences to advertisers rather than selling products or services to ultimate consumers. But again this produces major market distortions which may require regulatory intervention. The third solution is to erect the artificial barriers to consumption we have come to know as box offices, and thus turn, *de facto*, a public into a private good. As we can see from the example of the shift of sports coverage from free over air to subscription or pay per view television this, it can be argued, does not increase consumer welfare. It does, however, massively raise the monopoly rent extractable by those—whether sports teams or broadcasting companies—who control the rights. The problem here arises from the fact that the product—the sporting event—is, like in effect all media products, a monopoly. Such products are valuable to the producers and distributors in so far as they are unique. There is in effect no substitute which the relevant consumer will accept. These monopolies are socially created, and this is a process eminently worthy of study. For instance, while individual football clubs attempt to exploit their popularity via pay per view services, and while Bernie Ecclestone is attempting to turn a collaborative agreement between motor-racing teams into his private property through the contractual control and exploitation of television rights, it is clear that what is being sold—the attraction to a public of football matches or motor racing—depends upon a collaborative non-market social arrangement. However good and attractive a team Manchester United is, it is nothing without a football league of some sort. Indeed this is precisely why in the United States it is the league franchise in baseball, basketball, or American football which is the valuable asset, not the team or its historically arbitrary geographical location. The same is true for motor racing. What these examples illustrate is that one of the factors which is economically crucial to understanding how power is exercised within the media industries, and thus how regulation should be applied, is the identification of those positions in the value chain where barriers can be erected such that monopoly rents can be extracted from the total revenue stream. The reason why the media present a constant regulatory problem from the point of view of concentration as market failure is that their economic survival under market conditions depends upon the exploitation of monopolies, in the sense of the unique defining characteristics of pieces of information. The only question then is who should be allowed to exercise those monopolies and under what conditions. (For further discussion of the above issues see Collins *et al.* 1988; Congdon *et al.* 1995; Graham and Davies 1997; Collins and Murroni 1996.)

Networks

This question of barriers or bottlenecks where the product flows and thus the financial flows through the system can be controlled and exploited brings us to the issue of networks. The media are primarily distribution networks, not units of production. The media have been largely defined in terms of, and constructed around, technologies of reproduction and the systems of distribution based upon them. Networks present major problems for the neo-classical model because they are essentially collaborative social institutions. Network economics is all about sharing resources rather than about exchanging discrete, substitutable, and therefore competitive, products or services. A network optimizes its value when everyone is connected, and it can be used by anyone to connect to anyone.

All economic activities are networks for social co-ordination and collaboration which manage flows of commodities and money between economic agents. How these networks are structured and why, and how differential power may be exercised within these networks is thus crucial to understanding how economic power is exercised and to what ends. Within the field of communications these networks of distribution are of particular importance, since communication is primarily about the exchange of meanings within a flow of symbols. Precisely because the media industries have developed as exploiters of the economies of scale to be derived from rapid reproduction and mass distribution of what is often a highly perishable product in competition for very scarce consumer time, the development and control of distribution networks has been crucial historically to the structure and development of those various industries. This aspect of their activity is for the most part hidden from the view of the ultimate consumers, and similarly neglected by analysts, who focus understandably on the symbols circulating rather than on the networks through which they circulate. This is a serious mistake. If we were studying a country's diet and eating habits today we would, within the total food chain, focus our attention, rightly I think, on the role of supermarket chains rather than on either the food producers or on an ethnography of family eating habits, important as both those might be. But it is the supermarkets' buying-power, distribution logistics, location policies, stock control, and marketing which determine the pattern of what is made available, the ways in which shifting consumer tastes are channelled, broad patterns of consumption, and above all where in the chain the major profits are taken. Media systems are at their core, just like supermarkets. They are systems for packaging symbolic products and distributing them as rapidly and cheaply as possible. In the field of communication there are broadly two types of network in operation. The one which is most familiar to media students is the top-down, one-way network upon which the classic mass media were and are based, whether a network of railways and kiosks for newspapers and magazines, film distribution and exhibition chains, or radio and television transmission networks. The other form, a form which is now, because of digitalization and so-called convergence, becoming dominant right across the media, is the interactive switched telecommunications network originally developed for the telephone. Such networks are designed to connect all users with all other users for two-way communication.

Networks have always presented problems for an economics based upon the assumption of the market as the ideal form because they are shared resources. But from the perspective of the economics of regulation two points are crucial. First networks are designed as traffic concentrators. Because they involve high levels of fixed investment, and because each individual end user's capacity utilization and economic contribution will be low, networks are designed to ensure the maximum shared use of the invested resources. Take a telephone network as an example. In principle it is technologically possible to join every individual subscriber to every other subscriber by a separate cable so that each time I make a telephone call to a different person I use a different two-way dedicated link. But such an arrangement would be totally uneconomic. None of us as individuals makes enough telephone calls to pay for so many copper cables. The solution to this problem was the hierarchical switched network. The calls of individual subscribers are gathered at a local exchange, and then all use a common connection to another regional exchange which in turn uses major high-capacity connections between major exchanges to distribute calls out again in the same way at the other end. This hub-and-spoke system is a common one for communication systems. It has recently become familiar as a name in relation to the planning of airline routing and the resulting competition for slots at major hub airports. But it was probably first systematically developed by Roland Hill in his reform of the British postal service in the 1830s. It was this rather than the flat-rate penny post that was crucial. But the flat-rate postage stamp is illustrative of an important resulting aspect of the economics of a network as a traffic concentrator. The flat-rate stamp is significant for three reasons. First, given that the name of the game is to maximize the sharing of the sunk investment, a flat rate both emphasizes the shared cost element and at the same time encourages maximum usage by spreading the cost, thus encouraging maximum use at the margins. The reasons why this may be acceptable to all users, even if some appear to be subsidizing others, are the so-called network externalities. The value of a network to its existing users grows as each additional user joins the network, both because it spreads the unavoidable fixed costs across a larger number of users and because it increases the numbers of people existing users can contact. Thus a network needs to be seen as a club rather than a market. The problem, as has been discovered in both broadcasting and telecommunication, is what happens when this coalition of mutual interest breaks down (Noam 1987). Because of network externalities and the traffic-concentrating economics of network design, networks are classic examples of natural monopolies. They are more efficient run as monopolies. This being so the problem arises as to how to control access to and pricing of these monopolies, particularly when, as is the case with the switched telecommunications network, they become increasingly important as a way to do business generally. Thus getting the regulatory structure of the network right may have very wide economic, not to mention social, implications. Many of these problems are common both to the switched, interactive networks such as the telephone and to one-way networks such as broadcasting, whether by terrestrial analogue or digital, satellite or cable. The reason that network economics are central to understanding economic power in communication and the debates over regulation is because it is claimed that the so-called digital revolution is establishing the model of distribution and its regulation, developed within telecommunications, to the distribution of all information on the model of the Internet (see European Commission 1997b).

These issues have now become of more general interest than simply to those interested in media and media regulation. First because it is claimed that the economics of the network is now central to the political economy of the global information society—a centrality well illustrated by Castells's use of the title *The Network Society* (1996) for his recent major analysis of current global political economic trends towards an Information Society. It is also because it is claimed that the whole global economy is moving towards what has been called the 'weightless economy' (Quah 1994; Coyle 1997) or the 'economy of signs' (Lasch and Urry 1994), whereby all production is becoming in effect the production, distribution, and sale of information and therefore the issues that have bedevilled media economics and regulation become issues for the economy in general. In particular it raises the question of transaction costs in a new and more general form. Efficient markets depend upon widely distributed information and on trust as necessary infrastructures, or upon what Andrew Graham has called common knowledge. What then happens when the availability of this common knowledge is itself threatened by the very market system for the efficiency and justice of which it is supposed to be a necessary foundation? Thus, increasingly, how systems of information and communication are regulated, who controls them, and for what purpose are central not just to culture or politics but to the operation and legitimacy of the economy itself.

4 | The Media as Technologies

Gains in technics are never registered automatically in society; they require equally adroit inventions and adaptations in politics; and the careless habit of attributing to mechanical improvements a direct role as instruments of culture and civilisation puts a demand upon the machine to which it cannot respond. . . . No matter how completely technics relies upon the objective procedures of the sciences, it does not form an independent system, like the universe; it exists as an element in human culture and it promises well or ill as the social groups that exploit it promise well or ill. The machine itself makes no demands and holds out no promises: it is the human spirit that makes demands and keeps promises.

Lewis Mumford, *Technics and Civilisation*

Throughout the world, information and communication technologies are generating a new industrial revolution. It is a revolution based on information, itself the expression of human knowledge. Technological progress now enables us to process, store, retrieve and communicate information in whatever form it may take—oral, written or visual—unconstrained by distance, time or volume. This revolution adds huge new capacities to human intelligence and constitutes a resource which changes the way we work together and the way we live together.

Bangemann Report

The Internet revolution has challenged the corporate-titan model of the Information Superhighway. The growth of the Net is not a fluke or a fad, but the consequences of unleashing the power of individual creativity. If it were an economy, it would be the triumph of the free market over central planning. In music jazz over Bach. Democracy over dictatorship.

Christopher Anderson , *The Economist*, 1 July 1995

The new media and information devices that are currently being tried out or discussed around the world are additional evidence of a wholly new stage through which the economies of the West are passing. A great shift is taking place from producer to consumer sovereignty in Western democracies, a shift that is bringing in its train a change in values and in systems of economic management. In the field of information such devices as teletext, viewdata, cassettes and cables and videodisks all fit the same emerging pattern: they provide opportunities for individuals to step out of the mass homogenised audiences of newspapers, radio and television and take a more active role in the process by which knowledge and entertainment are transmitted through society.

Smith, *Goodbye Gutenburg*, 22

No one studying the media can avoid the question of technology. Within the general problem of the nature and effects of social mediation we can identify three distinct types of mediation. There is the mediation by other human agents, the problem raised for modernity above all by the social division of labour and which I examine as regards the mediators in Chapter 5, and as regards the more general problem of political representation in Chapter 8. Second, there is the mediation by systems of symbolic representation, the implications of which I examine in Chapter 7. Finally there is the mediation, both between humans and nature and between humans themselves, by means of tools. This third form of mediation has been the central focus of that tradition of social thought which sees labour as the defining characteristic of the human species and sees the development of tools rather than of speech as the defining break between the animal and the human and thus the foundation of human culture.

From this perspective to study the history and social consequences of the development of the systems and processes of social communication I am calling media is to study the development and deployment of technologies for the production, distribution, and consumption of symbols. Indeed both in everyday parlance, in the academic division of labour and in sectoral distinctions between businesses, the media are defined, named, and distinguished one from another not on the basis of the symbols they carry but on the basis of their underlying technologies of production and distribution. We thus talk and think about the media, research the media, invest in, manage, and regulate the media in terms of film, records, the press, radio, television, and telecommunications. As we have seen when examining the political economy and regulation of the media in Chapter 3, the differences between these underlying media technologies matter. They in part explain why this particular medium seen as a business operates in the way it does and is regulated in the way it is.

Emancipation from Nature

Central to the emancipatory project of modernity has been the search for emancipation from the constraints imposed by nature. Humans, as embodied creatures, were necessarily embedded within the natural world. And this embedding took two forms. On the one hand humans were dependent for their physical survival on interacting through labour with nature in the sense of the physical material world. On the other hand human reason and self-consciousness had to come to terms with what were seen as the instincts, drives, or passions of its own inner animal nature. There were then two responses within Enlightenment thought to the problem posed by nature.

In the early, largely French, phase of the Enlightenment, as it developed out of theological thinking, nature was seen as ultimately benign, as the equivalent of God's will, and the purpose of reason was to understand both outer and inner nature so as to live in harmony with it. Natural philosophy, or science, took on the task of theology in revealing the mysteries of the divine dispensation that nature represented, knowledge of which, and thus human action in harmony with which, was blocked by ignorance and superstition—the new versions of sin. This way of thinking then developed into the positive tradition in social science represented by Saint-Simon and Comte from which much modern policy research stems. It is a way of thinking about nature that remains important when thinking about technology, but in a paradoxical sense. It underlies versions of technological determinism which see technology not just as the expression of nature's laws but as the inevitable improver of the human lot, and thus sees those opposing technological developments as Luddites and conservative barriers to human progress. But it also lies behind the thinking of many, for instance in the environment movement, who mobilize scientific evidence to oppose technological development on the grounds that it is interfering with or blocking a more 'humane' and natural relation between humans and both their natural material environment and their inner natures.

The second response was to seek emancipation from the constraints imposed by both external and internal nature by controlling them. Human culture and freedom were now seen as anti-nature. The exercise of reason, and science and technology as its finest products, were now seen as the escape route out of the realm of necessity and into the realm of freedom. However, as the critics of the new social, economic, and cultural order built upon the foundations of this scientific and technological revolution, whether from a Romantic or Dialectic of Enlightenment position, soon began to point out, the problem was that what had been created was a new nature. This new nature, in large part created by the harnessing of science and technology in machino-manufacture and the huge leap in productivity, deepening of the division of labour and extension of the realm of bureaucratic social administration that it produced, had put in place a new systems world that dominated humans and restricted their freedom as effectively as nature had previously done. At the same time this new nature, far from being subject to the critical investigative gaze of scientific reason, was obscured by a new mythology of scientific rationalism itself. This is the core of the critique launched by the critical theorists of the Frankfurt School and which underpins their analysis of the culture industries.

Thus the dialectical tension within the philosophical discourse of modernity between emancipation and constraint, between agency and structure, between life world and systems world, between the human and the animal, culture and nature, doubt and knowledge, continues to be played out on the field of technology. As we go on to examine contemporary debates about technology in general, and media technology in particular, we need to remember that it is the relation between these poles of thought that is at stake.

Technological Determinism and the Information Society

In spite of the assaults of critical theorists, Romantics, and postmodernists and growing popular suspicion, science and technology, and the technologically determined view of progress linked to it, retains high prestige and currency, perhaps particularly at present in relation to information and communication technology, at both a popular and elite level.

Thus, as we saw in Chapter 2, an extremely influential way of thinking about the history of the media and their social impact is in terms of the successive development of key technologies—writing, printing, information technology—linked to a stage theory of human social development. Many of the crucial contemporary debates about the media mobilize such histories and can only be understood as part of wider debates about technology, technological development, and the modern world. Debates on media economics and policy or on the social and cultural impact of the media are in fact often largely debates about technology. Whether these debates concern the impact of so-called convergence on the future of the media industries and their regulation or the wider question of the nature of the so-called Information Society, they work with assumptions, often implicit, about how technologies come into existence and their impacts, whether positive or negative. Above all, underlying these debates is a debate over technological determinism. Is technology the prime mover in social change, a fate which we simply have to accept and adapt to, whether we judge its results to be positive or negative? Examples of this type of thinking are widespread. You can find them in both the academic and popular literature about the Information Society and the so-called information and communications revolution upon which it is based (for examples see Negroponte 1995; Toffler 1980; Bell 1973; and Castells 1996; for a good, if now somewhat dated, critique of this literature see Webster and Robbins 1986; for a more general critique of this view of information and communication technology see Winston 1998). It can be found deeply embedded in recent regulatory thinking and policy documents both nationally in the UK and internationally. For instance in the policy documents from the Peacock Report onwards that led to the re-regulation of UK broadcasting in the late 1980s, in the documents from Oftel on the regulatory impact of convergence (Oftel 1995) and for example in the Bangemann Report (European Commission 1994) and the recent EC Green Paper on convergence (European Commission 1997b). Indeed I would suggest that an important exercise is to read the recent literature on media policy, the future of the media industries and the information society from this perspective. Is a technologically determinist argument being put forward and if so in what form?

The Work of Art in the Age of Mechanical Reproduction

There is one particular version of technological determinism that has been particularly influential in thinking about the media. The most celebrated exponent of this position is McLuhan who argued famously that the medium was the message—that is to say that there were explicit effects embedded within a given medium, defined as a particular technological system for communicating, whether oral, print, or electronic. While McLuhan's development of this thesis is both extreme and now widely discredited, versions of the argument still circulate and have powerful influence. Indeed one formulation of it, which was at one period canonical in media studies courses, is Walter Benjamin's 'The Work of Art in the Age of Mechanical Reproduction' (1970). Benjamin's thesis, derived ultimately from Marx's idea of a potential contradiction between the forces and relations of production, was that mechanical production *per se* had altered the relationship of the audience to cultural artefact in such a way as to destroy its aura, and introduce a more 'scientific' way of seeing the world. This intervention was a useful counterweight to the Romantic reaction, linked to notions of originality and genius, against technologically produced art as inauthentic. But Adorno was correct in his original criticism when he pointed out that first a distinction needed to be made between technologies used to reproduce works created under premodern craft conditions, for example a record of a symphony orchestra or a printed book from an author's manuscript, and cultural forms that were themselves created technologically and thus required different relations of production, such as a newspaper, film, or television programme, and that a second distinction was needed between the technology of reproduction and the relations of production and exchange within which the cultural form of audience relation was embedded (Adorno 1977). While Benjamin had seen Vertov's documentaries as the future of a mechanically reproduced cinema, Adorno more realistically pointed to the aura of the Hollywood star system. Within this tradition, and equally influentially in some circles, Brecht argued (demonstrating his technological ignorance) that it was a mere capitalist conspiracy that radio sets were not designed and marketed as transmitting as well as receiving devices, without realizing that he was talking about the telephone, which already existed on the market, and that radio as a means of cultural production and dissemination is a particular set of hierarchical relations that the technology enables but does not determine. In this sense the difference between the theatre, Brecht's chosen medium, and either radio or film is one of scale not one of technology. The only reason for dwelling on these ancient arguments is that a similar productivist romanticism now surrounds hypertext and the world-wide web and underpins the constantly forecast but constantly postponed death of the book.

Social Shaping

In response to technological determinist explanations of the role and impact of technology a range of what have come to be called social shaping approaches has been developed. These approaches can be distinguished in terms of the level of generality at which they operate and the aspect of the technology/society relation upon which they focus. What is at issue is what is being shaped, where, and how. And in each case from an emancipatory perspective we can also distinguish approaches in terms of the degree of transparency, and thus of the actual or potential willed human intervention in the shaping process. This is important because to argue against technological determinism in the name of social shaping is not necessarily to argue for increased human agency. It may just represent a flip from technological determinism to social determinism.

We can see such a flip, I think, in that version of social shaping that lies at the extreme opposite of the society–technology spectrum to the technological determinists. This approach, sometimes dubbed the strong programme in the sociology of science, argues that all science, and thus the technologies built upon it, is like religion or ideology, simply a set of beliefs as to what counts as truth, that is developed, negotiated and sustained as part of the cultural repertoire of a given social group. Thus the truth claims of science, and so its social prestige and power, are culturally specific, but epistemologically arbitrary. It is totally socially shaped (Latour 1987; Wolgar 1996; for a brief critique of this position see Sokal and Bricmount 1998). One important strand within this school is the feminist one which argues that the version of reason upon which Western science has been based since the Enlightenment is male and thus that science and technology as currently conceived and practised are inevitably complicit with the power relations of patriarchy and neglect and suppress the interests of women (see Harding 1991; Calhoun 1995: ch. 6 for a discussion). The problem with this position from my perspective, is that it solves the emancipation problem by epistemological fiat. The relation with nature is no longer a problem, because nature is totally malleable. Its characteristics are simply the projection of socially constructed beliefs. Thus ironically the social shaping has nothing to shape.

Technology or Technologies

A problem with certain versions of social shaping is a tendency to take a very general view of technology as if it was a single thing or process. Thus the problem is thought of as the analysis of either technology in general or a very general species of technology such as new media technologies or information and communication technologies, which are indeed shortened to ICTs so that they can more easily be thought, written, and spoken about as though they were a single phenomenon. This is then often linked with a very general view of the social level at which shaping takes place such that, for instance, it is capitalism or the West which is seen as the shaper.

We need I think on the contrary to deconstruct the idea of technology. First we need to distinguish, as for example Winston (1998) usefully does, between the underlying science and its actualization in artefacts and processes, and then between the various ways in which the scientific potential is realized in prototypes as possible uses, from what Winston calls inventions, which are those potentialities which are actually taken up and socially deployed. These distinctions have two values. First they allow us to decouple the question of scientific truth, and the prestige and legitimacy attached to science, from a judgement of the value and impact of a technological exploitation of that science. It is important, however, to stress that this does not allow us to disregard the underlying science. It is, in my view, a weakness of the social shaping approach to technology, a weakness prevalent in much alternative thinking about technology and its impact, in the social sciences in general, and within media studies in particular. It is no doubt attributable not just to the general lack of scientific background among its practitioners, but more generally to an anti-scientific and anti-technological bias within the field that stems from an attitude deeply embedded in post-Enlightenment thinking about the arts and culture as opposed in its values to science. The result is that it sees technology as totally malleable and thus cannot take seriously the constraints that nature places upon human action. To take some examples: what you can do with the radio spectrum is in part determined by the laws of physics and the propagation characteristics of radio waves. Any serious discussion about the social possibilities and consequences of the development of radio-based technological processes needs to take place in the full knowledge of what constraint that places on contemporary practice and future development. These may of course be a matter of genuine scientific and engineering debate. While the actual uses are determined by a particular configuration of political and economic power the range of its possible uses and the trade-offs to be made between them, for instance between mobile telephony and broadcasting, are not infinite. Similarly with thinking about so-called cyberspace. A failure to take technological constraints seriously leads to a form of idealist thinking whereby cyberspace is seen as flying free of the limits placed upon its use by the engineering characteristics of the telecommunications networks and software protocols upon which the Internet runs, and on the real material economic constraints blocking alternative configurations and patterns of use. In short the danger of this approach to technology is that it leads to an idealist disembodiment which can then as easily flip into a paranoid distopian, as utopian, view of its impact. Any serious student of the media, their future impact and development needs, therefore, to take seriously the cost-benefit, means-ends thinking of engineers. Indeed the specific visions of technological use and development that such engineering thinking may at any time favour and propagate can only be critiqued if it is first understood.

Devices and Systems

The second distinction we need to make is between stand-alone technological devices, for instance, a PC, a Sony Walkman, or a radio receiver, and technological systems, for instance a broadcasting or telephone network. In particular, their diffusion characteristics will be different. A stand-alone device can be developed and launched on a market speculatively. If it responds to some human need, even if it is not one envisaged by its designer or the firm marketing it, it can be pushed along a normal curve of diffusion. It can also be modified in response to early patterns of use. It doesn't require standardization and there is room for a range of alternative competing versions of the technology. In short the market can be used as part of the research and development process. It is thus much more amenable both to a classic market analysis of technological innovation and deployment and to a social shaping approach. Technological systems, on the other hand, particularly physically networked systems, require a far higher level of diffusion and interoperability of components to operate. With systems you either have them or you don't have them. They thus suffer economically, as we saw in Chapter 3, from a chicken-and-egg problem. For instance the launching of a new system of broadcasting, such as the current launch of digital broadcasting, requires, if it is to offer a realistic alternative to the current system of analogue broadcasting, large up-front investment and an assumption that a large proportion of potential users will actually use it. It is thus subject to natural monopoly characteristics and in general requires strong institutional support from the state in order to make the risk acceptable. It also has a high level of built-in inertia. Once people have invested in one system or standard they will be unwilling rapidly to change to another system with different and competing technical characteristics. This is why to date the introduction of high-definition television has been a failure in spite of high-level economic and political efforts and why, in spite of other high-value uses for spectrum capacity, it will only be possible to phase out analogue broadcasting over a long time-scale. For this reason there is little room at the level of the system for social shaping by consumers. The key technological decisions in designing the system will have necessarily been taken before there is a single consumer. Thus how those decisions are taken and within what interplay of power and interest becomes a crucial question.

Of course the relationship between stand-alone devices and systems is not a simple one. The dependence of stand-alone devices on underlying systems ranges across a spectrum from minimal to almost total dependence. Thus devices require, at a minimum, systems such as electricity supply or a maintenance network or a retailing system. This is not a trivial question in some instances. For instance early attempts to develop educational broadcasting in less developed countries often foundered on the lack of an electricity supply and trained maintenance engineers to keep the necessary sets running. Hence the importance of the development of the wind-up radio in countries where a supply of batteries cannot be assumed. Thus identifying and analysing this relationship is always important and is a corrective to the more euphoric and simple-minded projections of the future uptake and speed of growth of new systems. For instance Internet usage depends upon PC penetration. One of the things overlooked in attempts to launch high-definition television was that the sets were too big, and required a viewing distance that was too great, to fit into most people's homes. Attempts to launch a combined television and telephone foundered on the fact that most people didn't want to use the telephone at the same time and in the same place that they watched television. Attempts to link digital television with Internet shopping may founder on the same problem.

Technology and Technics

A further distinction needs to be made between technology and technics: technology is a technique embodied in a physical tool, whereas technics are the underlying institutional forms, cultural values, and socially developed skills which a technology expresses and within which technologies are developed and put to work. Thus, for instance, we can distinguish a technics of symbolic communication within which technologies of writing—alphabetic, cuneiform, or ideographic were developed and deployed. This is important because it allows us to distinguish between a technology of communication—for instance television transmission and reception—and the socially invented and learned skills, such as programme-making, schedule construction, advertising, or licence finance, patterns of interpretation and consumption which the technology itself doesn't summon into existence. As we shall see, technological possibilities may be unexploited or produce results quite different to those envisaged by their 'inventors', and we know they can and do differ as between different social formations; broadcasting technology does not determine the institutional forms of either advertising-financed commercial or licence-financed public service broadcasting. This is important for two reasons. First because when we examine technology from the perspective of power and its distribution it may be the technics rather than the technology that is crucial. To take an obvious point, the invention and deployment of the technology of writing was clearly of epochal significance, as Innis argued, for the increased scale of social organization and for the huge increase in the potential for non-organic, intergenerational cultural inheritance it made possible, but the power relations of this technology were carried by literacy and the shifting relations between the mode of persuasion on the one hand and the modes of production and coercion on the other. And these sets of relations and the levels of literacy accompanying them differed significantly between different societies. Secondly, it is important, because in contemporary debates about the development and control of so-called new media, for instance centrally at the present moment the Internet, or about the transfer of technology between firms and countries, it may well be the barriers to the transfer of 'know how', for instance the relevant working population's skill levels, that are crucial and not the technology *per se*. In the current battles around the future of the Internet it is not the routing protocols, which are the Internet's underlying technology, which are crucial, although they create the field of battle, but the differing models, and thus rules, for its operation. The clash is between the libertarian technics of its founding inventors and their 'Californian ideology' on the one hand and the norms of the corporate sector with its structure of private property relations on the other. Crucially for the argument here the outcome of this battle is not determined by the nature of the technology.

Techno-economic Paradigms and Path Dependency

Two influential approaches to the analysis of the technology–society relation which combine a concern with technological systems with a concern with the technics within which they are embedded have been the so-called neo-Schumpeterian and path-dependency approaches. Both these approaches have been extremely influential in debates about the impact of information and communication technology and appropriate policy responses to it. Both are located within the wider debate within economics about the nature of the innovation process and the sources of the comparative competitive advantage of firms, nations, or regions within the global market economy. What both approaches underline is that apparently technologically determinist arguments are in fact often arguments about economic processes of which, in Raymond Williams's phrase, the technology is symptomatic.

Neo-Schumpeterianism

This approach is represented by the work of Freeman, Dosi, Perez, and Soete and is reflected in the recent report of the Experts Group on the Information Society (European Commission 1997a). They argue that the capitalist mode of production is characterized by long waves of development, of around fifty years, each linked to the development and deployment throughout the economy and society of a core techno-economic paradigm—steam power, electrical power, and now information and communication technology. Each paradigm works by making a step change in the productive potential of the economy. As the potential of a given paradigm is exhausted the process of technological innovation is driven by the entrepreneurial search for new sources of growth in both new production technology and new products. Three aspects of this approach are crucial. First it is entrepreneurial competition which drives the process of technological development and application. But, second, it takes a long period for the advantages of the new paradigm to work its way through the social system, since it has to combat both investments in existing technological systems and the set of institutional structures and learned practices associated with the previous paradigm. Thus, third, societies or economies may be more or less capable of adapting to this process of change and thus reaping the productive advantages of it. And this process of adaptation is susceptible to conscious policy intervention, whether in science and research and development policies, in skills training, in labour market restructuring, in company and regulatory law, or in tax policies. From this perspective, for example, changes in the structure of the broadcasting and telecommunication industries and their regulation are driven by the simultaneous economy-wide impact of ICTs on both production and consumption. On the one hand the operation of 'Moore's law'—the doubling of capacity on microchips every twelve months—has made possible and, by massively lowering costs, created a market for, a hugely expanded range of products and services. On the other hand this has created new skill requirements and working patterns which in their turn contribute to the formation of new patterns of consumption. While I think it is true to say that this school, in the classic Enlightenment liberation from nature tradition, sees these changes as ultimately beneficial, it does not argue that this process of change is conflict-free. The social changes involved will, at least in the medium term, involve winners and losers. In policy terms there may be more or less socially just and efficient ways of managing this change process. The argument then becomes one as to whether, for instance, given the imperatives of the techno-economic paradigm, there are alternative models of broadcasting and telecommunications regulation and market structure which are equally efficient while offering more or less equal social distributions of resources and power. Thus technology is seen as determining because of its sheer productive potential, but the technics can, and indeed have to, be socially shaped. There are more or less transparent, intelligent, and socially just ways of utilizing the potentials that the techno-economic paradigm makes available (Dosi *et al.* 1988; Freeman 1996; European Commission 1997a).

Path Dependency

Path dependency is a closely related approach to the relation between technological systems and social shaping, but it operates at a lower level of generality and focuses on distinct technological systems, in particular in the form of technological standards, whether *de jure* or *de facto*, for instance the AC/DC standards for electrical current, the computer-operating system MS-DOS, or the VHS standard for video-recorders.

This path-dependency approach has been associated in particular with the work of Paul David and Brian Arthur (David 1975; Arthur 1994). It was developed as a response to the dominant views of technology and their policy implications within economics. It is a powerful critique of that combination of technological and economic determinism which is currently so influential in thinking about media development and which argues that the market, if left to itself, will produce the optimum technological solutions. That the technologies which have stood the test of market competition are what people want.

Neo-classical economics regarded technology as a black box, the specific characteristics of which were irrelevant. It was produced exogenously to the market system of supply and demand. All that needed to be known about it was that a new technology would be deployed by capital when its costs for a given output were lower at the margins than the cost of employing extra labour. In economies driven increasingly by technological competition this seemed to be a less than revealing analysis. At the same time the alternative Hayekian view was that the market not only served to drive innovation in the search for efficiency but also acted as the only possible efficient search mechanism between rival technological solutions. Thus for Hayek and his followers the problem facing economic agents was not that of arriving at supposedly rational decisions (this was for Hayek by definition impossible because the information necessary could never be gathered—the problem of so-called bounded rationality). The virtue and function of the market was to take this responsibility off our shoulders by aggregating the necessarily partially informed decisions of boundedly rational economic actors. For Hayek, our needs, and our definition of them, may differ and our assessment of the future will certainly differ. Only the market can aggregate this uncertainty into some semblance of a desirable social outcome. From this view stemmed the doctrine central to technology policy and the regulation of communications in the 1980s, namely technological neutrality. Central planners or policy-makers, it was argued, could never have enough information to make rational decisions as to the best technology or path of technological development. Thus they must not attempt to pick winners among firms or branches of technology. They must not back national champions in what were regarded as strategic technologies, nor must they attempt to steer technological development by means of regulation. In the event I would argue, at least for the UK case, that such technological neutrality proved impossible. Since technological choices had to be made, and since control of certain key technological systems would determine market power, at least over the short run, any regulatory policy tended to favour one technical solution over others, for instance, by continuing to allocate spectrum to different specific uses and thus not allowing broadcasters to use their spectrum for mobile telephony or vice versa; by stopping British Telecom integrating its fixed and mobile networks and services; by favouring the development of cable networks, and so on.

Path-dependency theory undercut this whole approach. The classic article is by Paul David on qwerty (1985). The problem posed is that it is well known that the layout of the qwerty typewriter keyboard, which we still all use today as a computer interface, is not the most efficient. It was developed to solve the particular problem of sticking keys in a particular early typewriter design. There were other competitive rivals which, it could be argued, were equally if not more efficient in the early days of the typewriter market and there have been attempts since, one backed by the considerable weight of US navy investment and training, to introduce a more efficient configuration. They have not succeeded. Similar cases can be seen in the rivalry between AC and DC current in electricity supply and, in the field of media, in the triumph of VHS over Betamax in the home video recorder market. David's argument, which is supported by the complex mathematical probability theory of Arthur, is that for those technologies where there is an advantage in sharing a common system there is a point in the diffusion of a new technology, even if you start with a range of equally good competitive technological solutions, where the spontaneous decisions of individual users lock in one technology and drive out the others. The source of the advantages of sharing may be various: they may be the advantages of a common technical standard, for example MS DOS; they may be due to what are called network externalities, as with a telephone network where users want to be able to talk to the maximum number of other users. In the case of qwerty they were due, at least in part, to the advantages to secretaries of only needing training for one type of machine. The implication of Arthur's work is that they may be essentially random and unpredictable. This process is path-dependent in three senses. First, that small and possibly random differences in the early stages of diffusion will determine the future path of development. Second, that it is a process of lock-in: once that path is determined it may be difficult if not impossible to break out of it. Third, that in economic terms the development and sale or deployment of such technical systems exhibit increased returns. The whole neo-classical theory of market competition producing optimal equilibria is based on the idea, derived ultimately from Malthus and the analysis of agricultural production, that all processes of economic production are subject to decreasing returns. There is a point where it is not either possible or profitable to expand production. Thus market dominance is self-righting, and monopolies must by definition be inefficient. What Arthur and David show is that, at least for certain high-tech systems, this is not the case. First, as classic natural monopoly theory argues, under conditions of network externalities a sole supplier is more efficient than any combination of competitive rivals, i.e. there are increasing returns to economies of scale. Secondly the lock-in process allows the dominant supplier, at a certain stage in market development, not only to make super profits but to reinvest them in further developments along its now favoured technological trajectory. Thus lock-in is further reinforced. Essentially this is the explanation for Microsoft's dominance and why it presents such a problem to US anti-trust authorities. The implications of path-dependency theory are (a) that across a range of technologies monopoly power is both likely and is likely to be sustained without regulatory intervention; (b) that the outcome is not, as the Hayekians would argue, the technically most efficient system, and (c) there is potential for public intervention to steer the lock-in process in desirable rather than undesirable directions, for instance to ensure that your national technology wins out against a rival system or that a technologically, socially, or economically superior technical solution is favoured. The problem, however, as David candidly admits, is that because of the randomness of the process and because, according to the mathematics of chaos theory that underlies it, very small differences of choice in the early stage can make all the difference to the trajectory taken, the choice and timing of intervention becomes in effect an insuperable problem. Public policy-makers are just as likely to lock into the 'wrong' solution as the market. Finally what this line of analysis underlines is, for better or worse, the high level of inertia that exists in technical systems, a point constantly underlined by Winston, although Winston bases his argument on different premises, namely that what he calls the law of the suppression of radical potential ensures that existing social power-holders and social habit and custom ensure that new technical developments are held back and only developed in such a way as not to radically undermine the status quo. You can of course read this either positively or negatively depending on your view of the nature and desirability of 'radical' change. In Winston's case he uses it as a valuable, powerfully argued and historically based corrective to the general hype surrounding the rapid and radical changes the so-called communication revolution is going to bring us.

Technologies of Production and Technologies of Consumption

The differences between the various social shaping approaches derive either from the nature of the question they are asking or the problem they are responding to or from the level of generality at which the shaping is deemed to take place. One can, in general, see a stress on the shaping power of the users of technology as opposed to its producers. But then one can distinguish various approaches in terms of how they define the users and the uses to which technology is put. Here we can see a broad divide between the social shaping analyses that focus on the general problem of the relation between the 'invention' and production of a technology on the one hand and its social diffusion and use generally on the other, those that focus on technologies of consumption, and those that focus on technologies of production.

Thus for instance both Winston and Webster and Robbins are concerned to counteract the technological determinist hype propounded by the advocates of a communication revolution and its supposed creation of an information society. In response Webster and Robbins stress the ways in which technological development and use are determined by the general structure of capitalist relations of production and exchange and focus on contradicting the claimed trends in employment, in the nature of work and corporate organization, and in leisure and cultural consumption supposedly caused by this technological revolution. Winston on the other hand is concerned to undermine the image of rapid technical change and to demonstrate the ways in which forces of social inertia are both intentionally mobilized, in the case of corporate power, and unintentionally mobilized in the case of deep-seated and slowly changing cultural patterns.

Flichy (1995), on the other hand, is more concerned to show the relationship between essentially malleable technological development, particularly of systems, and wider patterns of social, economic, and cultural development within which technologies became specific patterns of social use. In particular he is concerned to examine the way the dominant communication systems were successively moulded, first by the needs of the state and its military, then by the developing needs of corporate capital, and finally by the development of new forms of private life and private cultural activity, by new forms of sociability. In Flichy's approach to social shaping there are two distinct processes involved. The first, at the level of the development of a technology, may involve the shift between two forms of social imaginary, for instance, in the development of a broadcasting system and the technology upon which it is based, the translation of a technological and organizational paradigm developed for telecommunications and the transmission of messages between people to one derived from thinking about entertainment and the desire to allow large numbers of people to participate in a given cultural event or performance.

The road from wireless telegraphy to radio was also highly complex. The inventors of radio broadcasting circulated between four different spheres. They came from Marconi's wireless telegraphy tradition. They sought new receivers for Herzian waves and found them in thermionic lamps. They were also part of a research trend experimenting with free communication. Finally, they bathe in a social movement, that of a turning inwards of the family to the private sphere, of the organisation of entertainment at home. By circulating between these spheres, they were to link up the different contributions . . . Radio broadcasting necessitated mass production of receivers and the required expertise was developed during the war. The commercial form had to be given to this new social use. It was through the combination of several traditions—those of telecommunications, mass industry and the press, that the radio was finally to find its economic base. On their long road from Hertz to NBC waves were in a sense transformed. At each stage of this movement there was a new contribution, an enhancement. The main actors in this process all 'captured' an innovation and integrated it into their own technological or social project, until a stable system was finally attained. A medium was born; its shape changed little afterwards. (1995: 114)

And secondly a social learning process whereby the development and take up of communication technologies as both commodities and modes of consumption, the passage from science to invention to production to social diffusion and use, involves a complex process of interactive trial and error, at each stage, on the part of both the producers of the technology and its users, such that technology and its social use are involved in a process of mutual shaping.

Technology and the Labour Process

One important social shaping school developed out of Marxist labour process theory. It has been concerned to argue against the view that technologies of production could be explained within an explanatory model that stressed the benefits of technology as freeing humans from material want and responding to consumer demand for better products. This school then reads the history of technological development as the history of a struggle between capital and labour to control production, or, in its more revisionist form, as the history of the development and management of a corporate economy. Here, for instance, drawing on the work of theorists such as Braverman (1974), issues of de-skilling and of the power relations within corporations become central. Here we are concerned with issues such as the impact on labour relations and conditions in the press of the introduction of computer typesetting and the electronic newsroom, with the impact on broadcasting production practices of digitalization and miniaturization in production equipment and the resulting spread of so-called multi-skilling. Whether a process of de-skilling is taking place and/or whether this is also related to a shifting balance of gender power within media production is a matter for dispute and debate. The point at issue is the kind of questions we ask about the impact of technology and the kinds of dynamics we can establish in its development and introduction. One crucial point to come out of this line of work—a classic case can be found in David Noble (1979)—is that technological change may have nothing to do with improving the products or services to final customers, although opposition to such changes will often be condemned by management in just those terms. Selfish, conservative workers are standing in the way of a better life for users. This is not to say that there is not a powerful strand of thinking about production technology that is either naively utopian or nostalgically conservative. The former can be found in the view derived from Bell that the new electronic technologies of production enable a more decentred, human work environment when the reality may be the increased hours of work, anti-social shift patterns and lower pay that have been witnessed in both the UK broadcasting and press industries or the isolated exploitation of homeworking rather than the liberating bucolic vision of the telecottage. The more revisionist line of argument sees the development of information and communication technologies as a response to problems of co-ordination in large corporations (Beninger 1986; Mulgan 1991). The strength of this tradition is that it underlines the ways in which communication and information technologies and systems, for instance the telephone, have been driven not by the demands of consumers, but by the demands of the corporate sector, and that other social uses have developed as almost accidental by-products of this demand. This is important for how we think about future developments and debate access to, for instance, the Internet. Why should we expect it to respond to the needs of individual domestic users? That is to say, an unreasonable expectation of a technology or technological system can too easily lead either to a paranoid conspiracy theory (it is evil capitalists or the military who are blocking the peaceful or social use of this technology) or to unreasonable demands (in the name of universal service we should cable all households with broadband).

5 | Media Producers

A major organizing theme of post-Enlightenment social theory, perhaps *the* organizing theme, has been the division of labour. A wide range of theorists are in agreement in seeing the development of modernity as centrally an increase in social specialization with the necessary accompanying increase in social complexity. It is the division of labour that raises the need for and problem of social mediation. This in its turn creates the social need for the institutions and processes that I have called media. From this perspective it is important to stress that the problem for social theory arose from the dialectical nature of this process. On the one hand the growth of social specialization created the conditions for, and up to a point the reality of, greater individuality and reflexivity as the potential roles, careers, and identities open to individuals proliferated and the range of social interactions increased. On the other hand this also led to what Mulgan has recently called 'greater connexity' as we all became more deeply embedded in a range of social interdependencies, the very range and complexity of which lead to the development of the relatively abstract structures of social co-ordination of the systems world.

One aspect of this problem upon which this chapter focuses is as follows: both our individual survival, or at least quality of life, and that of the social formation itself depend at least in part on the process of symbol production and circulation that I have called the media, while at the same time that process, because of the more general process of social specialization itself, has come under the control of a specialized cadre of what within social theory have come to be called intellectuals. Our knowledge of and relation to both the natural and social world and to ourselves is increasingly mediated through a specific group of people. The question is then raised of how that group is chosen and trained, why it acts as it does, and how it relates to other social groups.

Marx saw the division of labour as the producer of alienation and exploitation, and saw the future communist utopia that would replace capitalism as a social world in which specialization of roles and functions would no longer be the rule. As he famously put it in *The German Ideology*,

As soon as labour is distributed, each man has a particular, exclusive sphere of activity, which is forced upon him and from which he cannot escape. He is a hunter, a fisherman, a shepherd, or a critical critic, and must remain so if he does not want to lose his means of livelihood; while in communist society where nobody has one exclusive sphere of activity but each can become accomplished in any branch he wishes, society regulates the general production and thus makes it possible for me to do one thing today and another tomorrow, to hunt in the morning, fish in the afternoon, rear cattle in the evening, criticise after dinner, just as I have a mind, without ever becoming hunter, fisherman, shepherd, critic. (Marx 1963: 22)

Weber saw the division of labour as part of the process of social rationalisation leading to the rule of instrumental reason in pursuit of efficiency and to the disenchantment of the world. If for Marx the exchange relations of the market are the dominant expression of the set of social relations resulting from the division of labour, for Weber bureaucracy fulfils the same role. Durkheim, on the other hand, was more positive, and in this he is followed by Elias in *The Civilizing Process* (1994). For Durkheim the division of labour leads to a replacement of the mechanical solidarity of pre-modern society by the organic solidarity of modern society, whereby the very density and complexity of necessary social interactions breeds the norms necessary for a more collaborative form of social existence and thus makes socialism the appropriate 'form of religious life' for modern society.

Within this general perspective on social development the position within the division of labour of specialists in symbolic production and transmission has been a focus of special concern. As we have seen, historical sociologists like Gellner and Runciman see social evolution in terms of the shifting relationship between three basic social functions or roles, and the groups that carry out those functions or fill those roles—in Gellner's words between the plough, the book, and the sword, in Runciman's between the modes of production, persuasion, and coercion.

For those working within the post-Enlightenment emancipatory project the problem of the division of intellectual or mental labour was particularly moot because at the core of the Enlightenment vision of human emancipation was an emancipation of the mind, a cultural revolution. In Kant's essay 'What is Enlightenment?' (Kant 1991), mature emancipated people not only have a duty to think for themselves in order to free themselves from dogma; they also have a duty to share those thoughts with others through publication. Indeed, as we shall see in Chapter 8 in more detail, the very definition of autonomous thought, and of the truth, justice, and beauty which are its aim, depends upon public communication. For Kant, enlightenment is a social not an individual process, dependent on a process of social communication. Thus to accept that modernity creates a social group possessing *de facto* if not *de jure* monopoly of that process is to strike at the very heart of the project. Habermas's theory of communicative action and the public sphere, for instance, is, as we shall see, an attempt to return to this Kantian project. But is it sustainable in the face of the division of labour that is at modernity's core?

This problem is part of the more general problem posed for the Enlightenment project by mediation in general. Emancipation depends upon a notion of potential social transparency. Emancipation is produced by reason revealing the truth of things, including the truth of social relations. When this reality is directly present to our own perception and experience within the life world, rational emancipatory analysis may be difficult enough, as we can see both in the problem of the direct observation and measurement of natural phenomena and in the problems presented for self-understanding by unconscious drives. In the social realm, where reality must of necessity be mediated by other social actors, with, as they say, their own agenda, the problem is even greater. Indeed it is the problem that makes the question of ideology both central to social theory and of continuing concern.

Given this central problem there are two issues. How do the specialists in symbolic production relate to knowledge itself? Can they in any sense be said to speak a truth which is valid for others as well as for themselves, or on the other hand can they only speak from the position of intellectuals as a social group relative to other social groups? Second, how do intellectuals as a social group relate to other social groups? Do they speak for others? Do they provide people with the information and cultural resources and pleasures that they need? Are they producers of cultural and informational commodities?

The problem of media producers has been neglected in recent media and cultural studies—indeed in social theory generally—because of the general linguistic turn and the supposed death of the author that has accompanied it. If the author does not exist or has no intentional power, why study her or him? From such a perspective they only retain an interest in so far as their claims to intentionality or truth are seen as moves in a discursive power game. I will return to the general problems with this position in Chapters 6 and 7. Here it is sufficient to note that the approach being adopted here is that the producers do exercise some power over the symbolic forms produced and distributed and that the nature of that power is worthy of analysis in its own right.

There are broadly three ways of defining the specialists in symbolic production whom I will call intellectuals. First they may be defined as a class whose power, sometimes called symbolic power, derives from monopoly control over the production of knowledge and cultural legitimation through the possession of socially accredited power to define what counts as either true, right, or beautiful. By analogy with industrial or financial capital this defining power is sometimes called, for instance in the work of Bourdieu and his school, cultural capital. The possession of such capital is also linked to a process of creditation through the educational system, and thus intellectuals may be defined as those who have received a given level of education, usually higher education. Secondly they may be defined functionally as information workers, those whose specialized position within the division of labour is the manipulation of symbolic forms. Thirdly they may be defined normatively as a vocation, as representatives of a critical, emancipatory tradition appealing to universal values. It was against this normative role that Benda's 'clercs' had famously committed treachery.

These definitions are not, of course, mutually exclusive, but each focuses on a different set of social problems. Class analysis tends to focus on the interests that unify intellectuals as a social group vis-à-vis other social groups and, in recent theory and analysis, has tended to stress not their potential as a new emancipatory universal class but a cynical view (for instance in both Bourdieu and Gouldner) of the ways in which the normative ideal is merely an ideological front for the pursuit of their own selfish class interest, either as the dominated fraction of the dominant class or as the operators of a repressive 'regime of truth'. Functional analysis has focused, as in the now widely influential post-industrial, Information Society thesis of Daniel Bell and his epigones, on the restructuring of the mode of production, the accompanying recomposition of the labour force and the possible economic, social, and cultural consequences of this process. In terms of the argument of this book this mode of analysis has particular relevance since it can lead to either a pessimistic or optimistic assessment of the social consequences of information technology. For the optimists the development of an information society which results from harnessing the full potential of information and communication technology is liberating because it leads to the general democratization of intellectual work and critical discourse. Everybody becomes an intellectual and participates in the new electronic *agora*. For the pessimists these same developments place increased powers of manipulation and control in the hands of a new technocratic elite, leading to widening knowledge gaps and a widening gulf between the information-rich and the information-poor. Finally the normative approach, unless linked to the class or functional approaches, is condemned to either the ivory tower or the wilderness. However attractive its vision, it is unable to face the crucial questions of how such critical intellectuals might be socially produced and in what ways their critical judgements might be made socially effective.

But whatever mix of approaches one chooses to adopt it is best to start from the Gramscian position that all human beings are intellectuals in the sense that they are not creatures of pure instinct but constantly apply their innate powers of rational analysis and imagination to those everyday interactions with their material environment and their fellow humans that constitute their identity and project. They are, as Marx put it, architects not bees. The analysis of intellectuals *per se* is then the analysis of what Gramsci called 'the system of relations in which [intellectual] activities (and therefore the intellectual groups who personify them) have their place within the general complex of social relations' (Gramsci 1971: 8). Or as Zygmunt Bauman puts it, 'the category of the intellectual [is] a structural element within the societal figuration, an element defined not by its intrinsic qualities, but by the place it occupies within the system of dependencies which such a figuration represents, and by the role it performs in the reproduction and development of the figuration' (Bauman 1987: 19).

The great advantage of such a perspective from the point of view of media studies is that it enables us to avoid the fetishization to which media studies is only too prone. It tends to focus on things—institutions, such as television stations or newspapers, the varied forms of media content or the situated practices of audiences—rather than the whole social process which lies behind them—the process by which those shared meanings, on which social maintenance and reproduction depend, are created, circulated, and appropriated. We can then see newspapers or broadcasting or whatever other instance we wish to study as special cases of this general and always historically shifting process. In particular a focus on intellectuals enables us to place the system of education in its proper place at the centre of media studies and to study the significance of the shifting relation between the education system and the media, understood as the modern systems of mass communication. It is from such a perspective that I refer to the intellectual fraction that works within the educational system, particularly higher education, as either the traditional intelligentsia or academics, and to the intellectual fraction that works within the media as media intellectuals. This usage is purely functional and implies no normative evaluation. The second advantage of approaching media studies from the vantage-point of the intellectuals is that it focuses on the agencies involved in the process of social communication and cultural reproduction and at the same time shifts that focus from the consumers, the overwhelmingly dominant concern of recent media and cultural studies, to the producers, thus striking a more appropriate balance between the autonomy of the reader and authorial intention. It enables us to ask who, within the existing structure of the division of cultural labour, are the producers, what are they trying to achieve, and why do they think and act in the ways that they do. This then enables those of us who are not entirely happy with the status quo to at least ask whether successful interventions in production and circulation are possible, rather than relying on audience resistance alone as a possible force for change.

In 1993 Edward Said gave the BBC Reith Lectures under the title *Representations of the Intellectual* (1994). This was a highly symptomatic moment of convergence. The Reith Lectures supremely symbolize a vision of broadcasting as an 'intellectual' enterprise in the sense of recognizing the social importance of broadcasting's pedagogic role. They grant an accredited intellectual largely unmediated access to the means of modern mass communication to talk to a general audience, using a classic mode of academic address, on an issue of contemporary intellectual importance. The test of worth, both of the speaker and of the subject, is not that of popularity, the normal currency of the mass media, but of peer recognition within the intellectual milieu itself, now largely concentrated within universities and specialized publishing. The value of thus allowing the general public to participate in the discourse of an intelligentsia, and by so doing legitimating that intelligentsia's role in national life and culture, is seen as self-evident.

This view of the media's role is now, and has been for some time, deeply unfashionable. And yet, I want to argue, Said's choice of topic was not accidental. For reasons I want to try and explain, the question of intellectuals, their social genesis and role, is very much back on the agenda. It provides a particularly illuminating perspective from which to examine some of the central problems now occupying media studies, but with much wider reverberations in the general polity and culture.

Said argued for the continuing relevance of one particular definition of the intellectual's role. Taking his cue from Sartre's famous distinction between 'intellectuals' and 'technicians of practical knowledge', a distinction Said rephrases as that between amateur and professional intellectuals, Said firmly allies himself with the former and identifies them as individuals:

endowed with a faculty for representing, embodying, articulating a message, a view, an attitude, philosophy or opinion to, as well as for, a public. And this role has an edge to it, and cannot be played without a sense of being someone whose place it is publicly to raise embarrassing questions, to confront orthodoxy and dogma (rather than produce them), to be someone who cannot easily be co-opted by governments or corporations, and whose *raison d'être* is to represent all those people, and issues that are routinely swept under the rug. The intellectual does so on the basis of universal principles: that all human beings are entitled to expect decent standards of behaviour concerning freedom and justice from worldly powers or nations, and that deliberate or inadvertent violations of these standards need to be testified and fought against courageously. (Said 1994: 11)

This is a restatement of the classic post-Enlightenment view of the intellectual and as such is touchingly and boldly old-fashioned. It is a view that has in recent years been deeply undermined in almost every respect. In particular two key aspects of this definition of the intellectual have been challenged. It has been argued that intellectuals cannot and do not represent anything except either the interests of their own class or status group or the interests of power more generally. The very existence of universal truths or a general humanity to which intellectuals might appeal has been profoundly questioned from a position of post-modernist scepticism.

Nonetheless, I want to argue, the question of the intellectuals will not go away and is a question central to the study of the media and culture. As Ernest Gellner has put it, 'at the basis of the modern social order stands not the executioner, but the professor'. Gellner has also remarked that modernity marks a shift from societies characterized by generalized physical violence (i.e. the executioner) to a system of generalized bribery. One of the central questions, therefore, about intellectuals is what is their relation to this reward system and to the structure of economic and political power based upon it. It raises in short the question raised by both Sartre and Said of the rise of the professional intellectual and their position and role within the structure of economic and political power. The question from Said's perspective, therefore, is whether the structural conditions have ever existed, and whether they now exist or might exist, to produce a social group, a set of discourses, and institutional structures answering to Said's description. Namely a group that represents a wider public and holds the status quo normatively to account in terms of a set of shared universal values.

The Intellectual and Alternative Historical Narratives

The terms 'intellectual' and 'intelligentsia' have never entirely lost, in English and in Anglo-Saxon culture, the aura of suspicion attached to their foreign origins. Both still carry the marks of their originating context. The intelligentsia in Russia saw themselves as the heirs of the Enlightenment leading the common people out of the darkness of tsarist political repression and cultural obscurantism. Intellectuals in France were the writers and academics who supported Dreyfus and were so dubbed by their anti-Semitic right-wing opponents. It was a word of disdain, heir to the Napoleonic coinage 'ideologist', indicating a mixture of subversion and other-worldliness. To this original denigratory meaning has been added, in its passage into English, the culturally deep-seated, chauvinist suspicion of Continental theory—a suspicion famously voiced by Burke as 'an insuperable reluctance in giving my hand to destroy any established institution of government, upon a theory, however plausible it may be'—a suspicion which fuelled Burke's opposition to the French Revolution and still fuels the opposition of his epigones such as Conor Cruise O'Brien to the whole Marxist tradition which they see as stemming inevitably from it, what O'Brien has called secular utopianism:

throughout the nineteenth century, and up to the Russian Revolution, the French Revolution was seen, by revolutionaries, everywhere, not exactly as a model, but as a measure of what had to be surpassed or—as far as the French were concerned—completed. The French Revolution had been betrayed: by the Thermidorians, by Bonaparte, or—as Michelet believed—by priests and women. Next time, there must be no betrayal. In the meantime, the French Revolution remained as the great demonstration that it is indeed possible for people with ideas to seize power and put their ideas into practice. It was thus the licence, the model, and the comfort of Utopians of every description. (O'Brien 1993: 606)

This narrative of a linked political and philosophical history—in O'Brien's version an extreme intellectual determinism which sees the gulag as the inevitable result of Rousseau's thought—has been given a powerful vindicating boost by the recent collapse of the Soviet communist experiment and the 'I told you so's that have accompanied it. How closely tied this narrative is to the question of the historical role of intellectuals is well illustrated by Isaiah Berlin's response to O'Brien's attempt to recruit him to the anti-French Revolution, pro-Burkean camp:

one more word about the French Revolution and my feelings—that is all they are—about it. My views, I think, such as they are, are shaped by tentative British empiricism (for which I was duly attacked by left-wing American sociologists, etc.) and the traditions of the Russian intelligentsia. Now the latter really were deeply influenced by, if not the events, then by the slogans and the ideas disseminated by the French revolutionaries. It does seem to me that it inspired people to attack prejudice, superstition, obscurantism, cruelty, oppression, hatred of democracy, and to struggle for various liberties—of speech, of belief, the celebrated 'inviolability of the person', which is one of the five principles enunciated by Russian liberals and contemptuously thrown aside by the Bolsheviks—and that kind of thing: the anti-Dreyfusard tradition, in short, which does go back to the French Revolution. In France the ideological divisions were, as you know, largely pro- and anti-the French Revolution; and the antis were genuine reactionaries—Barres, Drumont, Deroulede, and, of course, Maurras and his disciples, Pound, Eliot, etc.

Hence, if I have to line up, I line up with the Revolution—despite all the fallacies and the horrors, which are certainly there—against the *Infame*. (O'Brien 1993: 617)

Thus in approaching the question of the intellectuals one is confronted not just with alternative definitions or theories, or even bodies of empirical evidence, but with alternative historical narratives with profound political resonances. It is these alternative narratives that are at stake in current debates between modernists and post-modernists and that have their distinct influences on how we approach the study of the media and culture today.

There is a narrative of progress, emancipation, and civilization which propagates a positive vision of the intellectuals' role and there is a narrative, if not of decline, then of a false turning and of repression and barbarism which propagates a negative vision. Walter Benjamin has taught us that every monument to civilization is also a monument to barbarism, but we can nonetheless clearly distinguish these two narratives and their respective implications for how we approach the question of intellectuals.

Thus one of the reasons the question of the intellectuals is back on the agenda is that it is inextricably bound up with the definition of modernity and thus with any discussion of a transition beyond modernity to the condition of post-whatever.

The positive vision is a mixture of the functional and the normative. It is the classic modernist, post-Enlightenment story of intellectuals as a product of a division of social labour and the carriers, in alliance with progressive political movements, of the emancipatory rationalist critique of tradition and of the harnessing of scientific enquiry to human material and social betterment.

As Halsey puts it in his recent discussion of what he calls 'the decline of donnish dominion', or the proletarianization of academics:

the decline of donnish dominion was written in the stars from the moment that the ancient civilisations of the Near East began to form an abstract alphabet (Goody 1968). Literacy thereby became potentially a democratic possession. Access to human capital became intrinsically available to all. Nevertheless a long and incomplete evolution has been needed to turn potential into reality. The history of popular communication from usable alphabet through the printing press to modern information technology has been a very slow process, albeit accelerating in our own time. The process has been slow because to democratise communication also requires transformation of virtually every aspect of social structure. People are bound together by power and authority, by interest and sentiment, by habituation and learning, as well as by words and numbers. Vast changes of human society are therefore required to work out all the implications of this original linguistic revolution. (Halsey 1992: 258)

However, Halsey goes on to argue, drawing in particular on Gellner, that lying behind this process is another more general one which creates the central paradox around which debates about intellectuals and the role of the media revolve. On the one hand historical evolution creates the possibility for general democratic access to the means of cultural production and dissemination, while on the other the division of labour places control over these resources in the hands of a group of specialists. We have here the source of the tension which underlies post-modernist populism in media and cultural studies, between a vision of organic intellectuals participating in a direct cultural democracy and a vision of a necessary division of labour and thus of intellectuals as 'representative'.

There are broadly two versions of the historical evolution of intellectual labour, both stemming from Weber. One, as expressed for instance by Gellner, stresses rationalization, and grants intellectuals, as professionals within the division of labour, a broadly progressive role within the development of modernity. Focusing on the necessary development of what he calls 'exo-training' ('it may be useful to distinguish between one-to-one, intra-community training and call it acculturation, and specialised *exo-training* (on the analogy of exogamy), which calls for skills outside of the community, and call that education proper' (Gellner 1983: 31), he argues that:

A society has emerged based on a high-powered technology, and the expectancy of sustained growth, which requires both a mobile division of labour, and sustained, frequent and precise communication between strangers involving a sharing of explicit meaning, transmitted in a standard idiom and in writing when required . . . The level of literacy and technical competence . . . required of members of this society, if they are to be properly employable and enjoy full and effective moral citizenship, is so high that it simply cannot be provided by the kin or local units. (Gellner 1983: 34)

And this is why he claims that the modern social order is based on the professor. But for Gellner, and those who argue like him, the universality to which Said's intellectual lays claim is not only an inherent product of the evolution of modernity. It has produced a social order to be defended, however hesitantly, in the face of its post-modernist critics, as superior to the available alternatives.

On balance, one option—a society with cognitive growth based on a roughly atomistic strategy—seems to us superior, for various reasons, which are resumed without elegance; this kind of society alone can keep alive the large numbers to which humanity has grown, and thereby avoid a really ferocious struggle for survival among us; it alone can keep us at the standards to which we have become accustomed; it, more than its predecessors, *probably* favours a liberal and tolerant social organisation . . . This type of society also has many unattractive traits, and its virtues are open to doubt. On balance, and with misgivings, we opt for it; but there is no question of an elegant, clear-cut choice. We are half-pressurised by necessity (fear of famine, etc.), half-persuaded by a promise of liberal affluence (which we do not fully trust). There it is: lacking better reasons we will have to make do with these. (Gellner 1984: 258, as quoted in Bauman 1987)

The alternative version of this historical evolution, as expressed for instance by Bourdieu and Bauman, places its stress on the move from societies based on shared and implicit doxa (tradition in its purest sense) to ones characterized by a struggle between orthodoxy and heterodoxy. This version takes a broadly negative view of intellectuals and stresses their role as the ideologists of power, the priesthood propagating and defending orthodoxy, bargaining with its monopoly control over the means of communication for a share in the fruits of power. For this tradition the claims of intellectuals either to truth or the representation of general interests are merely moves, even if not understood as such by the participants, in the game of power.

But one can see within this version a potential contradiction which lies at the heart of much debate over the intellectuals. If intellectuals, as a social group pursuing its own interests, propagate orthodoxy, where does heterodoxy, or the critical tradition come from? Does this, unlike orthodoxy, not require a specialized group of intellectuals for its development and propagation? Does it spring newborn from the 'people' themselves, from the life world as a spontaneous reaction to everyday experience? We can see here a theme that runs through much thought on the relation between intellectuals and political and cultural opposition. Is the problem seen as one of getting rid of intellectuals and their corrupting influence so that the people can be free to express their inherent intellectual powers, or as one of harnessing in some way the powers of specialized intellectuals in the service of oppositional movements?

In Bourdieu's own work, as in that of Gouldner, there is a way out of the dilemma that is close to Gellner's position. The argument is that intellectuals, in their struggle for monopolies of distinction with the holders of economic and political power, develop what Gouldner dubs 'a culture of critical discourse' which is objectively critical and progressive. That is to say the internal rules of the intellectual field require the development of structures of debate and argument, appeals to evidence, transparency, which become a self-generating critical project. From this point of view Said's intellectual is the sociological product of the historical evolution of the intelligentsia itself. The problem, however, remains as to whether this culture of critical discourse is necessarily tied to a progressive political project.

At this point we need to return to various interpretations of the relationship between the intellectuals and the post-Enlightenment project. All parties agree that the two are closely intertwined and it is of course for this reason that the various current assaults on the Enlightenment and modernity are also assaults on intellectuals.

What I have described, in my discussion of Said's position, as the classic view of the post-Enlightenment intellectual, argues that the intelligentsia was a historical product and prime mover in the assault on tradition in the linked names of reason and progress that was the project of the Enlightenment. The intellectual was the creator and carrier of a culture of critical reason potentially open to all humanity and the grounds and means of general human emancipation from tradition and exploitation. From this point of view the true intellectual is inherently progressive. The defence of intellectual freedom is inherently democratic. And the problem is the means for the general propagation of this culture of critical reason, and thus the centrality of education, such that all humans become intellectuals, and the linkage of intellectuals to political movements for change.

The alternative interpretation of the post-Enlightenment intellectual, now widely current, argues a diametrically opposed interpretation of the same development. For this school, for example Conor Cruise O'Brien, or Zygmunt Bauman, or in some interpretations Foucault, the Enlightenment broadly represents a process of social rationalization within which intellectuals are the complicit operatives of regimes of truth. Far from being the unmaskers of ideology they are, as Napoleon first described them, ideologists. Post-Cartesian theories of critical reason become the warrant for totalitarian systems of power, for the increased domination of the life world by the systems world of which the intellectuals are the operatives. Intellectuals are the carriers of instrumental reason. It is in their class interest to develop ever more extensive and controlling intrusions into the lives of ordinary people. This, in Horkheimer and Adorno's phrase, is the Dialectic of Enlightenment.

For Bauman the intellectuals in western Europe, far from fulfilling an emancipatory role, became complicit, from the seventeenth century onwards, with a new form of power. They became what he calls 'legislators'. This role, in his definition,

consists of making authoritative statements which arbitrate in controversies of opinions and which select those opinions which, having been selected, become correct and binding. The authority to arbitrate is in this case legitimised by superior (objective) knowledge to which intellectuals have a better access than the non-intellectual part of society. Access to such knowledge is better thanks to procedural rules which assure the attainment of truth, the arrival at valid moral judgement, and the selection of proper artistic taste. Such procedural rules have a universal validity, as do the products of their application. The employment of such rules makes the intellectual professions (scientists, moral philosophers, aesthetes) collective owners of knowledge of direct and crucial relevance to the maintenance and perfection of the social order (Bauman 1987: 5)

He goes on to argue that intellectuals, deploying this regime of truth, acted as gardeners, controlling and repressing the people in the name of the superiority of culture over nature. In the words of Jacques Revel:

the people were seen as carriers of this fossilised trace of a social and cultural archaism; it was both an indication of their subservient status and its justification. Popular practices, therefore, represented a bygone age, nothing more than a repository of the erroneous beliefs of humanity and the infancy of mankind . . . The domain of the popular was now the negative world of illicit practices, odd erratic conduct, unrestrained expressiveness and nature versus culture. (Revel, as quoted in Bauman 1987: 58)

He then goes on to argue that:

the most crucial consequences of the passage from the wild culture of pre-modern times to the garden culture of modernity; of the protracted, always ferocious, often vicious cultural crusade; of the redeployment of social power in the sense of the right to initiative and control over time and space; of the gradual establishment of new structures of domination—the rule of the knowledgeable and knowledge as the ruling force [was that] traditional, self-managing and self-reproducing culture was laid in ruins. Deprived of authority, dispossessed of its territorial and institutional assets, lacking its own, now evicted or degraded, experts and managers, it rendered the poor and lowly incapable of self-preservation and dependent on the administrative initiatives of trained professionals. The destruction of pre-modern popular culture was the main factor responsible for the new demand for expert 'administrators, teachers, and "social" scientists' specialising in converting and cultivating human souls and bodies. The condition had been created for culture to become conscious of itself and an object of its own practice. (Bauman 1987: 67)

I have quoted Bauman's argument at length because it is perhaps the clearest current version of the negative narrative and one which makes its links to current debates in media and cultural studies crystal clear. As he goes on to argue, post-modernism appears to mark the end of this narrative and to strike a sundering blow at the very foundations of the intellectuals' historical role:

the pessimism and defensive mood of the intellectuals, which presents itself as the crisis of European civilisation, becomes understandable if seen against the difficulties the intellectuals encounter whenever attempting to fulfil their additional role; to wit, the role which, with the advent of the modern era, they were trained—and trained themselves—to perform. The contemporary world is ill fitted for intellectuals as legislators; what appears to our consciousness as the crisis of civilisation, or the failure of a certain historical project, is a genuine crisis of a particular role, and the corresponding experience of the collective redundancy of the category which specialised in playing this role. (Bauman 1987: 122)

This approach to the historical role of the intellectuals has been powerfully reinforced by the collapse of 'really existing socialism'. Since one strand of the argument is that the Jacobin intellectual leads directly to the vanguard party and the apparatchik, and that substitution of instrumental reason for tradition was the warrant for the totalitarian social experiment unleashed in the Soviet Union and its satellites, the collapse of this system it is argued finally, and thankfully, discredits that tradition. But this argument has a wider currency in the form of New Class theory. This theory stresses the rise of the professional intellectual, the cadres of bureaucratic and economic rationalization. One strand in this tradition has focused on the particular situation of the communist regimes in eastern Europe and the Soviet Union. The argument was that two trends were leading to a new form of class power. On the one hand there was a congruency between the founding ideology of the communist regimes—secular social perfectibility through the planned application of instrumental reason—and the values represented by intelligentsia. On the other, the bourgeoisie had been removed and the means of production had been placed in the hands of a state bureaucracy entry to which was increasingly dependent on formal technical qualifications. Some analysts (e.g. Szeleny, and Martin 1991; Kennedy 1991) have then gone on to analyse the collapse of these regimes in terms of the strategies of this New Class and the characteristics of the new regimes in terms of the strategies and fate of this New Class in the face of the new situation in which those countries find themselves, in particular in relation to the positioning of the intelligentsia in relation to economic reform on the one hand and nationalism on the other.

But for my purposes the application of New Class theory to Western capitalist societies is more interesting. This tradition of analysis goes back to Weber, Veblen, and Trotsky. It sees the key to understanding the creation and role of intellectuals in the social production of a cadre of professional information workers to answer the needs of the corporate economy on the one hand and the bureaucratized state on the other. This school of analysis, which includes thinkers as diverse as James Burnham, Daniel Bell, and Galbraith, saw a convergence between the Soviet and capitalist roads converging in a model of a rationalized industrial economy and a bureaucratic state run according to the norms and increasingly in the interests of a new technocratic class. This line of analysis then leads in two, sometimes intertwined, directions. One leads to the theory of the Information Society with its broadly positive view of information workers as possessors of a new and crucial economic power based upon the centrality of knowledge exploitation to the reproduction of capital and as carriers of new, less hierarchical, cultural attitudes and lifestyles. In this view the spread of information technology, for instance in the form of the Internet, leads to a general democratization of the means of intellectual production and of access to the culture of critical discourse. The other leads to a New Left version of New Class theory which focuses on the repressive power of welfare state bureaucracies and their allies in the bureaucracies of trade unions and political parties. This version of New Class theory has been very influential, I would argue, on cultural studies. It makes common cause with Information Society theory in the analysis of New Times. In an American version, in the pages of *Telos*, it now makes common cause with the new communitarian populism. For this version of New Class theory as applied in the capitalist West the enemy has not been capital, but the welfare state bureaucracies, not economic exploitation but the culture of dependency and the hegemony of the caring professions.

Critical Media Studies and the Figure of the Intellectual

Critical media studies, at least in Britain, has always been founded upon an ambivalent narrative of the intellectual. Raymond Williams and Richard Hoggart, in their early careers, both shared a view of the media analyst as a classic critical intellectual, judging the performance of the media against universal cultural standards and participating through education in the production of a critical audience capable of resisting the blandishments of the cultural industries. Throughout his career Williams attempted to hold in balance a view of 'the culture of art and learning' as the possession of all the people, and of a broadly progressive general democratic and cultural development, with an analysis of the class bias of actually existing British culture and in the fields of both education and the media through a critique of the ways in which the members of the professional intelligentsia acted as cadres of a highly and unusually closely intertwined political, economic, and cultural elite, a social formation which closed off the space for the development of a critical intelligentsia on the Continental European model. This specificity of national histories is important, and I will return to it. As Paul Jones (1995) has recently and rightly pointed out, Williams refused the turn to a class-reductionist, anthropological interpretation of culture, and this allowed him to advocate the democratization of culture as the access of all the people, both as producers and consumers, to these cultural resources and thus the creation of an 'intelligentsia for the people' (Williams 1983). The narrative of cultural studies, and with it much of media studies, then modulated through a number of stages. Starting with Williams's critique of the Coleridgian notion of a clerisy and of Arnold and Leavis's adaptation of it, cultural studies combined a New Left critique of the New Class, particularly in its Fabian form, with the Gramscian concept of hegemony in an attempt to construct an organic intellectual practice of cultural analysis and political activism. For a time two conflicting tendencies and their supportive narratives were at play. The first was a vanguardist tendency which, under the influence of Althusserianism and the Frankfurt School, saw avant-gardist cultural practice and a critical pedagogy as key revolutionary interventions, subverting the dominant codes upon which hegemony depended. This, although understandably attractive as an ideology of specialized intellectual practice, was only tenable in a context of temporary left-wing political optimism and soon lead into the pessimistic and socially isolated cul-de-sac in which the Frankfurt School had itself ended up. It was therefore not surprising that, under the gathering influence of the Reaganite and Thatcherite right accompanied by a deregulated expansion of the cultural industries, and a crisis in education and the demoralization of the left which was the result, the other tendency won out. This was based on a critique of the elitism of high culture, the cultural judgements based upon it, and its repressive uses in a class society, linked to the concept of experience, from which cultural studies never fully broke free, and of versions of feminism and the analysis of ethnicity within which the category experience played a crucial role. This eventually led, via New Times and post-modernism, and underpinned by a narrative close to that of Bauman's, but adapted from Foucault, to a populist communitarianism within which only the most etiolated role for an organic cultural intellectual remained, that of bearing witness to popular forms of resistance.

This development, of course, played into the more general development of post-modernist thought. It is often forgotten that one of the founding texts of post-modernism, Lyotard's *The Post-modern Condition*, originated as a report for the provincial government of Quebec in Canada on the likely impact of new information technology on the universities. It was Lyotard's analysis of the ways in which the applications of this technology broke the knowledge monopoly of university academics that led him to his wider analysis of the end of modernity. At the same time Rorty's assault on the epistemological foundations of post-Cartesian philosophy radically undermined the basis for the critical intellectual's claims to either rationally based truth claims or universal standards of critical judgement. In a world of inherently relativistic cultural difference the best role intellectuals could now claim was that of, in Bauman's words, interpreter, oiling the wheels of inter-cultural exchange and understanding. With the rise of neo-Aristotelianism, an intellectual could claim to speak, at best, for her or his local cultural community as representative of a way of life. With the announced death of the author even that would be claiming altogether too much.

This widespread defenestration of the intellectual—at least in her or his amateur mode, the professional intellectuals of course proliferated regardless—has had four linked results within media and cultural studies. First, it leaves no ground for critical judgement of media performance on the basis of either truth, beauty, or right. Second, while it allows agency to audiences—for what is resistance but agency?—it tends, since the notion of authorial intention and its effect is suspect, not to allow it to cultural producers, and thus has no interest in studying intellectuals, who they are, what they think, how and why they act. Third, because of the above, it provides no ground for policy intervention in the processes and institutions of cultural production, and tends increasingly to evacuate the field of established national representative democracy in favour of identity politics and communitarianism. Fourth, it leaves little if any room for a pedagogy, whether critical or not.

The concept of the intellectual is, like the rest of the symbolic armoury upon which the power of intellectuals rests, two-faced. On the one hand it can designate an objective sociological category, however defined. But on the other it still carries with it from its origins a sense of distinction, in Bourdieu's sense, that can be mobilized, both negatively and positively, within cultural and political struggles. And the nature of these struggles, and thus the social effects of the designation, will differ from country to country and from period to period as the participants and stakes in these struggles change.

I want to illustrate this by showing how the media in Britain have participated during the last decade and a half in a mobilization of concepts of the intellectual and in the development of certain intellectual practices which cannot be explained only in terms of shifting power relations between traditional and media intellectuals, but are part of a wider pattern of cultural and political struggle. The very public, and unprecedented, refusal of the dons of Oxford to grant Margaret Thatcher, an alumnus, an honorary doctorate in 1984 has been seen as symbolic of an opposition between the traditional academic intelligentsia in Britain and the Thatcher government. Certainly Halsey has shown how the progressive prole-

tarianization of British higher education, itself part of a wider international trend, has lead to a marked move to the political left on the part of
British academics. But this has been part of a wider cultural and political
story. Thatcherism was never merely a political movement. It was a *Kul-
turkampf.* Central to the ideological foundations of the political project of
the new Thatcherite right in Britain was a narrative of national decline in
which intellectuals were cast in a key role. The story, drawing on Wiener
and Corelli Barnett, was that humanistic education, enshrined in the old
universities, had propagated an anti-entrepreneurial ethos. Drawing on
the Burkean tradition within British conservatism, the Thatcherites also
linked this intellectual ethos to the propagation of socialism—seen as
'government upon a theory'—which it was their express purpose not just
to defeat politically, but to root out culturally. Hence their attack on teachers and academics in general and on progressive education in particular as
key contributors to British failure. (A detailed analysis of the media discourse on education from this perspective would be valuable.) Hence their
attempt to bring the universities under more businesslike management.
Hence their attempt to abolish the Social Science Research Council and
the change of its title to that of the Economic and Social Research Council
on the grounds that sociology was not science but ill-disguised left-wing
propaganda. This policy thrust ended with a government which was os-
tensibly against central planning attempting to plan all university research
from the centre, largely judged on its contribution to wealth creation.
Hence also the consistent attacks on the BBC, seen as a prime site for the
propagation of these subversive humanistic intellectual views and attitudes and, the government's support not just for the privatization of public broadcasting but its public support, for instance by the symbolic award
of knighthoods, to the editors and proprietors of the aggressive tabloid
press who enthusiastically propagated these anti-intellectual views. A new
vocabulary entered popular discourse. Critical intellectuals became 'the
chattering classes', whingers, hand-wringers (at the more robust end of the
market, wankers), who when not actively subversive were out of touch
with economic and social realities. In their place as the arbiters of public
taste and the judges of the politically just the media placed themselves,
and their allies in advertising and marketing, who 'knew what the public
wanted'. As part of this cultural struggle tabloid popular newspapers pro-
moted a specific breed of public intellectual, such as Norman Stone, then
Professor of Modern History at Oxford, who was given regular space to
attack progressive views from a position of robust populism, wherever he
could find them. In parallel, a new genre of books adding to the culture of
blame appeared. Paul Johnson, an ex-left-wing intellectual and now frequent columnist in the conservative popular press, in *The Intellectuals*

(1988) indicted a range of celebrated Western intellectuals for the moral awfulness of their private lives, in the tradition of Burke's critique of Rousseau, and succinctly expressed the new populism, 'a dozen people picked at random on the street are at least as likely to offer sensible views on moral and political matters as a cross-section of the intelligentsia', without apparently recognizing that if this were true it certainly applied equally to his own views. John Carey in *The Intellectuals and the Masses* (1993) indicted British literary intellectuals for their contempt for the people and popular taste. The point is not whether one or other of these critiques was justified or not (Carey's critique shared many of the features of the well-established, and justified, left cultural studies critique of the elitism of mass culture theorists), but the general amplification by the media, in support of a political crusade, of a populist culture of philistinism and of a culture of scapegoating and blame directed at intellectuals. The media held themselves up as uniquely in touch with the people and therefore a repository of standards against which to judge intellectual production and, in general, find it wanting. This anti-intellectual campaign gained extra power from the fact that it chimed with the whole New Class analysis of the New Left and with the post-modernist populism which shared many of these anti-intellectual instincts and indeed analyses. Thus a major potential source of opposition was disarmed. This was seen most clearly in the British left's ambivalent attitude to the BBC and the defence of public service broadcasting.

The purpose of telling this story is not just to stress the national specificities of debates about the role of the intelligentsia and the media's role in those debates, but also to underline the ways in which those debates are not just about sociological categories but about wider political and cultural issues. In Britain this particular narrative has, for the moment, run its course, if only because the intellectuals and the socialists with whom they were linked are no longer a credible scapegoat for continuing national failure. But the challenge remains to construct an alternative narrative in which, inevitably I would argue, an image of intellectual practice will play an important role.

One such narrative is that of the public sphere and it is, I think, no accident that the question of the public sphere now occupies a central position on the media studies agenda. In the face of a demonstrable crisis in the forms and practices of democracy in Western capitalist polities and of the attempts to reconstruct forms of democratic politics in the ex-socialist countries, it has taken over the central role previously occupied by the question of dominant ideology or hegemony. The bourgeois public sphere was classically the creation of and ground for intellectuals. The project of the democratic generalization of the public sphere is a project to make everyone an intellectual. To defend the concept of the public sphere is to defend a protected realm for the exercise of critical discourse and, in so far as this critical discourse holds power effectively to account, a social totality ruled by reason. More specifically the general extension of the public sphere, in parallel with the general extension of democratic politics, poses the problem, which has always dogged critical intellectuals as well as elected politicians, of representation. On what grounds can those who enter the public sphere claim to represent any values or interests except their own? Does the very mode of rational critical discourse misrepresent in repressive ways the hopes and desires of that suffering and exploited humanity it claims to represent? In any possibly realizable version of a contemporary public sphere these questions are then posed of the mass media and of those who work within them. What structures and forms might be both truly representative and at the same time foster rational, critical discourse? From this point of view those who work in the media are endowed, whether they choose the role or not, with the role of a critical intelligentsia, and we can and must hold them to account for the ways in which they carry out that function.

The relationship of the media and intellectuals goes back to the very historical roots of the category of intellectuals and the close relationship between their rise and that of printing. One doesn't have to go along with a technologically determinist view of the history of the relation between printing and the Enlightenment to recognize that intellectuals, while they may have been born in the conversational mode of the salon and coffee-house, soon formed their collective identity and based their access to social power on the ever-widening circulation of printed texts as the carriers of their critical discourse. But as the narrative of the development and decline of the public sphere claims, an increasing specialization of intellectual labour lead to a growing split and struggle for intellectual hegemony between an increasingly industrialized and commercialized mass media and the traditional intelligentsia, with its base in education and specialized cultural production for an elite. This lead to a range of problems which have been at the centre of the debate on the cultural and political role of the media and on the relation between traditional, critical intellectuals and the media ever since. On the one hand, as C. Wright Mills put it, 'the means of effective communication' upon which intellectuals depended were being expropriated. This, in Mills's view, had serious general political and cultural repercussions:

The independent artists and intellectual are among the few remaining personalities equipped to resist and to fight the stereotyping and consequent death of genuinely living things. Fresh perception now involves the capacity to continually unmask and to smash the stereotypes of vision and intellect with which modern communications swamp us. (Wright Mills 1963: 299)

This then leads to a prescription for intellectual intervention which Said describes as 'disputing the images, official narratives, justifications of power circulated by an increasingly powerful mass media . . . by providing what Mills calls unmaskings or alternative versions in which to the best of one's ability the intellectual tries to tell the truth' (Said 1994: 22) This then leads not only to a strategy of intervention in the media as a public intellectual but also to a parallel strategy of critical media pedagogy. The problem with this strategy is the closing of access to the media for these public intellectual interventions, the result both of economic developments internal to the media themselves and of overt political intervention and the delegitimation of education itself, which an entertainment-dominated consumerist media propagates.

On the other hand the media institutions themselves, and the media intellectuals, draw an important part of their legitimacy, particularly in relation to politics, from that tradition of the critical intelligentsia and its role in the public sphere enshrined in the image of the free press and of the journalist as a tribune of the people holding power to account. Thus at present we can see both media owners and governments mobilizing the ideology of a free press in their regulatory struggles and policy disputes. However cynically it is deployed, this ideology places real limits on media capital's room for manœuvre. At the same time the increasing proletarianization of media workers within global conglomerate media empires and an increasingly casualized labour market creates the conditions for potential fissures among media intellectuals themselves around their differing roles as either the professional cadres of media capital or as representatives of the Fourth Estate. At the same time there would appear to be a growing concern among the public at large about media standards—whether in terms of sex and violence, or invasion of privacy, or the coverage of politics, in which implicitly the media are being held to account by their audiences against standards which are not purely those of the market but which derive from the critical intelligentsia and public sphere. To retain the credibility upon which their legitimacy in large part rests, both media institutions and media intellectuals must respond to these concerns.

We can find one such response, involving an alliance between academics and journalists, in the United States, in the Project on Public Life and the Press that Professor Rosen, its director, describes in *Critical Studies in Mass Communication* (Rosen 1994). It is ironic that Rosen starts his account from a recent intervention in public life by Rorty, one of the high priests of post-modern relativism. Rorty noted (Rorty 1991) that a 'belief that democracy has not been working lately, that the ordinary voter is being tricked day and night, is almost universal among us', meaning by us 'we well-educated people, the intellectuals', and urged intellectuals to assume their responsibility for public intervention. We regularly observe, he argued, democracy falling short of its ideal. We criticize the schools and the media for their assorted failures. But 'we usually take no blame ourselves'. 'He went on to criticise', as Rosen puts it, 'the tendency in cultural studies to academicise politics, abandon a public language, fetishize difference, and treat "issues of race, class and gender" as a universal mantra'. 'The press and the professoriate', Rorty wrote, 'are acting as if both believed not only that democracy has not been working lately but that there is no longer any point in trying to make it work . . . By redefining the scope of their own professional activity and their relationship to democratic politics so as to legitimate this hopelessness, [journalists and academics alike] are in danger of falling into the role of cynical outsider—some one who always knew, deep-down inside, that democracy was not going to work' (Rorty 1991: 46, 490). In response to these concerns the Project of Public Life and the Press is attempting to return to that vision of the public intellectual which is embedded in Deweyan pragmatism. This is part of a wider movement of concern in the United States at the steady debauching of the political process in which the media and politicians have been complicitly involved, especially in recent presidential elections and, for instance, the effort, funded by the Markle Foundation, to create on television non-partisan, informational public interest coverage of campaign issues during presidential elections.

Lying behind this project, as Rosen describes it, is a specific vision of the public and of the relation of intellectuals and journalism to that public derived from Dewey. As James Carey, quoted by Rosen, puts it:

The god term of journalism—the be-all and end-all, the term without which the entire enterprise fails to make sense—is the public. Insofar as journalism is grounded, it is grounded in the public. Insofar as journalism has a client, the client is the public . . . The canons of journalism originate in and flow from the relationship of the press to the public. The public is totem and talisman, an object of ritual homage . . . But for all the ritual incantation of the public in the rhetoric of journalism, no one quite knows any longer what the public is, or where one might find it, or even whether it exists any longer. (Carey 1987: 5)

He goes on:

The real problem of journalism is that the term which grounds it—the public—has been dissolved, dissolved in part by journalism. Journalism only makes sense in relation to the public and public life. Therefore, the fundamental problem for journalism is to reconstitute the public, to bring it back into existence. How are we going to do that? (Carey 1987: 14)

The answer of Rosen and his project is by a process which combats the separatist tendencies that the professionalization of intellectual life breeds and that brings journalists and professors together in a common project to create what Dewey called 'an intelligent state of social affairs'. As Rosen describes this process,

Professors enter into a partnership with journalists because neither group, operating alone, can turn evident facts into public truths. These scholars become what Walzer (1988) calls 'connected critics', addressing themselves (and their intellects) to the American people, to whom they feel a natural loyalty. In negotiating this partnership they must emerge from their own discipline to find a common language with reporters and editors, who in turn must find a common language with readers. It is through this process—groups finding each other through public dialogue—that the public may find itself as a grounding principle of political life. To pursue a public identity as a scholar is not simply to 'apply' advanced knowledge to social problems, or to translate scholarship for a lay audience. The point is to produce a kind of knowledge that can be had in no other way. Intellect alive in public life is itself a form of inquiry . . . Here then is 'the public' at work in a busy society where no one can grasp public problems in their entirety. Knowledge becomes 'embodied intelligence' (Dewey 1927: 210) not all at once through some magic medium of public communication, and not all in one place, through some all-embracing public sphere, but via many encounters with many publics at many levels, all governed by rules of engagement that constitute the society's shared public ethic. (Rosen 1994: 368).

From this position Rosen derives what seems to me to be an admirable antidote to both the post-modern frenzy in academia and the cynical commercialism in the media in his definition of the role of critical media scholar as critical public intellectual:

'Public service' in communication studies begins with an intellectual act: conceiving of an environment where 'there is real uncertainty and contingency' and thus real hope. By taking this conception public, so to speak, scholars perform an act of public service. Academic understanding earns public credentials when it engages others as they struggle to arrive at understandings that 'work' for their purposes. Communication studies succeeds at being critical when, in the company of others, it fashions a 'we' language that speaks to common values, common problems, a common heritage, a common sense of the historical moment and its possibilities; here 'common' doesn't mean common within a professional discipline, but *shared across the boundaries that divide intellect from public life*. (Rosen 1994: 369)

The ways of doing this will differ between cultural situations. The Project on Public Life and the Press is clearly founded in a long tradition in the United States of the local press's relation to a communitarian politics, in the deeply embedded cultural status of pragmatism, and in a specific social location of journalists. The involvement of journalists and their newspaper companies was also clearly in part motivated by the search for a new role and thus a market base in their local markets in the face of competition from the proliferation of electronic media. But it is to both the desirability and possibility of the general aim to which I think it is now important to point as what Rosen calls 'the political responsibility of the media intellectual'.

Central to Rosen's analysis and the project based upon it is an attempt to create a new relationship between the media and media intellectuals on the one hand and the expert on the other, which is not a mere competitive struggle for cultural supremacy. As we have seen it is common, in discussion of intellectuals, to make a distinction between intellectuals and what Sartre called 'technicians of practical knowledge' or between what Said calls amateur and professional intellectuals. The figure of the professional intellectual speaks to the functional definition of the intellectual and the historical production through the division of labour and the needs of an increasingly technological and bureaucratic modern world, of specialist knowledge workers of all sorts. In such a world of increased social fragmentation and specialisation we are all dependent on experts. But the figure of the expert is now a deeply ambivalent one in our culture. The romance of science and its application to the creation of a better world was intimately linked to the legitimation of intellectuals in both their critical and technocratic roles. Indeed the two were originally closely linked. It was the discourse of critical reason, or so it was successfully argued, which enabled the harnessing of nature and the application of social engineering (a pregnant phrase) to the betterment of human life. In the Western heartlands of industrial capitalism at least enough of this promise was realized to make the more general claim credible and thus to enhance the social prestige of the expert, particularly the natural scientist and engineer. There was of course from the beginning a parallel Romantic critique of this view, which saw this social love-affair with the scientist as a dangerous Faustian bargain. But an important ingredient in the general post-modern critique of reason has been a widespread shift in social attitudes to the expert, whether as a result of the demonstrable destructiveness and frequency of war in the twentieth century or of the decay of the environment. The critique of the domination of instrumental rationality and the association of the professional intellectual with that rationality now has very widespread popular reverberations. But such a reaction is, in my view, highly ambiguous. And the media play to and amplify that ambiguity in ways that require careful examination. In the struggle for legitimatory power between the media professionals on the one hand and the traditional intelligentsia on the other the media need experts, because their relative autonomy and the source of their intellectual 'distinction' rests upon the twin legs of a claimed transparent and objective presentation of the 'real' (thus they cannot be held accountable for this knowledge—they are just reporting) on the one hand and a claim to represent the public rather than truth. Of course all critical intellectuals claim to speak in the name of some public, if only humanity at large, which is hardly in a position to dispute the claim. But it is the form of representation of that public that is crucial. The dethroning of the expert, including the politician as the expert in politics, and the ways in which their relations to the public and to public discourse are now mediated, can be taken as a healthy democratizing process, as the decline of deference. In this account the media are amplifying the reasonable public distrust of experts and, as tribunes of the people, are unmasking their pretensions and holding them to account. The growth of the so-called people show, such as Oprah Winfrey's, as a major television genre illustrates, however, the ambivalence of this development. In such shows experts are summoned to contribute to a live audience discussion of issues of both public and private life. That experts are invited at all indicates that both the media professionals and their public think they have some standing in the matter. Their views are somehow relevant. Indeed, particularly when problems of private life—sexual and psychological—are at issue, the very nature of the problem is increasingly defined in a sort of caricatural science speak. On the other hand the shows are so constructed as to actively militate against rational, critical discussion and to place the personal experiences of the members of the audience (presented as representing, although in no structured sense so doing, the general public) on the same level as or even above the analysis based on accumulated intellectual experience and training of the expert. Attempts to adopt the mode of rational, critical discourse are placed and condemned by the form as, by definition, out of touch, ivory-tower, academic, or even perhaps evasive and self-interested. The attempt to extend the boundaries of public discourse in the slogan 'the personal is political' has become the radical narrowing of those boundaries in the enactment, orchestrated by the media, of 'only the personal is political'. As I say I think these forms of mediation and the media's relation to the accredited expert are ambiguous, and such examples can be read positively, but the dangers here of demagogic populism, and its relation to a growing range of concerns about the effect of contemporary media practice on the exercise of democratic politics, are clear.

The alternative to a strategy of intervention as public intellectuals is that of a critical pedagogy. These are not by any means mutually exclusive. A critical pedagogy immediately raises the question of 'quality', by which I mean the standards by which we, as both members of publics and as media scholars, might judge the performance of the cultural producers. This goes to the heart of both the project of media studies and research and advocacy in media policy. Much of media and cultural studies is no more, however stylishly expressed, than the observation of the passing scene. Such scholars have become the *boulevardiers* of contemporary culture. But if we are to do more than this we must believe, and I believe that a significant proportion of those who study the media and culture do so believe, that the media have some influence and that some measure of critical judgement on the media's role and performance is thus unavoidable. The exercise of such critical judgement is, of course, intellectual practice. The problem is the legitimation of the standards upon which judgement might be based. In fact cultural producers, audiences, and policy-makers make such judgements and act upon them every day. It seems that only their theoretical self-consciousness inhibits media and cultural studies scholars from playing their proper role as critical intellectuals and joining in. These inhibitions stem from those powerful currents in post-modern theorizing about intellectuals in particular and culture processes in general to which I have already referred. Theories of epistemological and cultural relativism have undermined the philosophical foundations of a critical intelligentsia, while socio-historical theories of intellectuals as the manipulators of cultural judgement in pursuit of their class interest have fuelled populist and communitarian impulses which undermine the social grounds for such judgement even within the academy itself. The problem, as I see it, is that this in principle denies all claims to either truth or beauty, however defined, and leaves the field free either to consumption choices in a market as the only test of value or to the untrammelled exercise of the critical judgement of cultural producers themselves, often of course in the name of a notional audience or public, but apparently not subject to the same critique as their sister and brother intellectuals in other fields of cultural production. I will examine this problem in more detail in Chapter 7.

In conclusion, therefore, I would wish to argue that media intellectuals are irrevocably split between two identities—that of the professional and that of the amateur intellectual. On the one hand they are the cadres of an expanding industrial sector responsible for both the direct production of surplus-accumulating commodities and for servicing, through advertising and marketing, other sectors of the economy. Their work merges with that of the growing body of other information professionals servicing the information demands of corporations and governments. From this perspective questions as to this new petty bourgeoisie's economic status (are the information professions being proletarianized and if so with what social and political consequences?) and as to whether their work and social status give them a unified ideology or cultural disposition merit attention. On the other hand, in mediating between knowledge creation and its publics and between the private and the public they are involved in the creation and circulation of public meanings to publics they in part create through their chosen modes of address. They are therefore ineluctably responsible as, in some sense, intellectual representatives of both knowledge and the public. It is from the exercise of their power to make these links that their identity and legitimacy as media intellectuals in the end derives. It is against those standards that we should judge whether, and if so how, they commit treason against their vocation as amateur intellectuals whose duty it is, in Sartre's words, to meddle in what doesn't concern them.

6 | Audiences: Interpretation and Consumption

John Corner has written that 'the consequences of media systems for the consciousness and actions of the audience/public remain the most important goal of media inquiry' (Corner 1991). In other words the study of effects, unfashionable as that term currently is, remains at the heart of media studies. By 'effects' I mean a behaviour or a thought, whether of an individual or a group, which would be other than it is in the absence of some example of media use or reception. I would argue that a nil effects hypothesis, to which some of the more extreme examples of the 'active audience' reception studies come close, is untenable within media studies because it would render the whole enterprise futile. Moreover, in both the milieux of the media industries themselves, and among the general public, the question of effects is consistently posed. Whatever academic analysts may wish to claim and whatever their sophisticated theoretical and methodological critiques of traditional effects studies, on the grounds of its methodological individualism, its simplified behaviourist linear cause–effect model, the decontextualized unreality of its research methods—particularly the psychological laboratory—the reification of its statistical methods, and even its unproductive results, a nil effects hypothesis will simply not be seen as credible. It is also the case that a nil effects hypothesis lets media producers off the hook of any responsibility for what they do.

The study of the audience, or reception studies, is motivated by an attempt to answer two major questions stemming from the Enlightenment's emancipatory project. The first is the epistemological or cognitive question of how our ideas about the world are shaped. How, in a world in which our relations to both the natural world and other people are mediated—that is to say our knowledge of them comes to us, not directly through our senses, but via the social systems of symbol production and circulation I am calling the media—can we avoid false ideas and escape from the unreflective acceptance of the ideas of others and thus think for ourselves as the

Kantian Enlightenment definition of freedom requires? The second is the problem of what Hegel called *Sittlichkeit*, the social question of how social co-ordination can be ensured culturally, and thus by means other than direct physical coercion.

Reception or effects studies, then, involves three distinct problems, which can also be a way of looking at distinct schools of audience research and disputes between them. We need to define the audience—the individuals or groups who are on the receiving end of media processes. We need to specify the nature of the relationship between that audience or audiences and the media. Finally, we need to have a view as to the relative power of audience and media within this relationship. This issue of relative power is usually thought about these days, misleadingly as I shall argue, in terms of an active versus passive audience.

Cognitive and Behavioural Approaches

In defining the relationship between audience and media we can identify a broad divide between a cognitive and a behavioural approach. The cognitive approach focuses on reception as an interpretative process; on how people's ideas, whether individually or in social groups, are or are not shaped by the symbolic forms the media circulate. The behavioural approach focuses on reception as a social practice and on the ways in which media use constrains, determines, or contributes to more general patterns of social behaviour.

This distinction is complicated by the fact that many in the behavioural tradition work, whether wittingly or unwittingly, explicitly or implicitly, within a symbolic interactionist framework which argues that patterns of behaviour, increasingly conceptualized as lifestyles or identities, are themselves motivated by and created out of symbols and thus via a process of interpretation. As Thompson has recently put it, the Self 'is a project that the individual constructs out of the symbolic materials which are available to him or her, materials which the individual weaves into a coherent account of who he or she is, a narration of self identity' (Thompson 1995: 214).

It is further complicated by the fact that cognitive approaches also of necessity work, but usually implicitly and unreflectively, with theories of the ways in which ideas motivate actions. Indeed studying ideas for their own sake is of no interest whatsoever. It is actions that in the end we are interested in, although this is in its turn complicated by the fact that the production of further symbols is itself an action.

We need to make a further distinction common within sociology between behaviour and action; behaviour being habitual and unreflexive while action is consciously intentional. When I referred above to the behavioural focus I intended to cover both. Indeed a key distinction, and matter for debate within the field, is the extent to which the behaviours identified are or are not reflexive rather than habitual. In my view this is a much more useful distinction than the one widely mobilized in disputes over the nature of the audience–media relation between passive and active. The point, as we shall see, is that habitual and non-emancipatory behaviours may be very actively pursued, and repressed and constricted identities actively constructed. Indeed it is central to the analysis of at least one important school of ideology critique, the Frankfurt School, which is often ignorantly pigeonholed in the passive audience slot, that, as Hegel classically analysed in the Master–Slave dialectic, domination and active consent are entirely compatible, resistance and the active by no means coterminous. Indeed this is a key lesson of Gramsci that the active audience/popular resistance school seems to have forgotten. The key problem precisely, from this perspective, is how the non-coercive but active acceptance of domination is achieved.

Defining the Audience

In reception studies the definition of the audience fulfils three functions. First it tells us who is actually consuming the media and thus is susceptible to any effects the media may have. Second, a clear historical trend in thinking about the nature of effects has been away from a concept of effects as the impact on the individual seen as a *tabula rasa* to a stress on the ways that such effects—whether interpretative or behavioural—are mediated by social location and group filiation. As John Corner puts it, 'That the various interpretations made by audience members were not purely individualistic but had a strong group character was a necessary factor in any sociological perspective on "reception" and a precondition of any attempt to explain why interpretative variation occurred' (1991: 289).

Defining the audience from this perspective is part of the general problem of analysing the relationship between individual agency and social structure and dynamics. The defining characteristics we choose, whether class, gender, age, geographical location, and so on, will depend upon our more general social theory and upon the kinds of effects we are trying to identify or analyse. To give brief examples, much recent audience research, for instance Morley's classic nationwide study (Morley 1980) and the work that has developed out of it, as well as the work of the Glasgow Media

Group (Glasgow Media Group 1976, 1980, 1995; Philo 1990), is concerned with the ideological effects of the media within what is theorized as a society characterized by social stratification and unequal relations of power. It is therefore concerned with whether, and if so in what ways, interpretations of the media differ according to class or gender location. The work of Bourdieu, on the other hand, is concerned with the ways in which cultural consumption is determined by class location. In both cases what is crucial are the forms of social determination external to the media, which are then seen as filters of media influence or determinants of patterns of media consumption.

Third, recent developments in audience studies which look at the role of the media in identity formation focus on the definition of audiences in terms of their differing relation to the media themselves and the ways in which that relation creates different identities or structures of social filiation. Here the audience may be defined in terms of heavy or light viewers, for example in 'cultivation studies', in terms of the audiences for different media or media genres—for instance the audience for soap opera and its gendered characteristics or in terms of small, mass, and diffused audiences (Abercrombie and Longhurst 1998).

The Audience as Real or Constructed

Thus, as Grossberg *et al.* put it, 'the concept of the audience is a social construction, a concept that can mean and be made to do many different things. Yes there are real people out there watching a television programme, or reading a newspaper or buying an album, who can be said to be in the audience for a particular media product. However, the idea of the audience is never merely an innocent description of the sum total of individuals' (1998: 208). But it does not follow from this that, as they go on to state, 'The fact of the matter is that the audience does not exist out there in reality apart from the ways in which it is defined by different groups, or for different purposes' (1998: 208) or, as Hartley claims more strongly, that audiences are fictions (Hartley 1987).

This version of social constructivism is very prevalent in contemporary reception studies. It should be noted in passing that it is quite incompatible with a notion of social identities as constructed by individuals in the active process of media consumption, with which it is often coupled.

There are three issues here. First, whether we start in our definition of the audience from ways of thinking about social groups generally or from ways of grouping the individuals who receive or consume given media or a given programme. Second, the question of the validity of any sociological generalizations about individuals. Third, whether any proposed grouping has to be recognized as such by its members to be a valid description of reality (the old problem of the class in or for itself).

It is I think the case, and I will return to this, that the stress on the everyday and the ethnographic in current audience research derives in part from a long tradition, stemming ultimately from the Romantic counter-Enlightenment, which rejects generalization and scientific enquiry as inevitably complicit in the rationalizing and therefore dominating process of modernity and in the colonization of the life world by the systems world. I might as well be straightforward. I think this refusal of generalization—and, particularly in our field, of statistical measures of probability—as inauthentic and reifying and in some way not real, but simply the construct of the researcher imposed on empirical reality, is deeply obscurantist. First the audiences as defined, for instance by the audience research or marketing departments of commercial media companies, exist in two senses. They tell us something real about the regularities of the behaviour of the individuals who go to make up these audiences, and, as the basis for product development, scheduling, and marketing, they have real effects upon both media production and consumption. Whether those effects are positive or negative is a separate evaluative issue. Second, in many cases these 'constructed audiences' are recognized as relevant by the individual members themselves. Because members of such audiences are in what Sartre called a serial relationship to one another—they experience the relationship as purely statistical—doesn't mean it is not experienced as a real membership which is actively chosen. It is precisely for this reason that bestseller lists and charts influence consumption and enable individuals to construct that sense of sharing with others, however etiolated, that the consumption of bestselling media products carries with it.

Audiences, Modernity, and Organic Solidarity

In fact to see the audience as purely an unreal social construct to be judged, as it is in recent embedded audience studies (Ang and Hermes 1996), against the 'reality' of the immense heterogeneity of individual audience members is to fall back into the ontological trap from which social constructivism was supposed to be an escape and to avoid the central problem which created audience studies in the first place, namely the historical shift from mechanical to organic solidarity and the move from audiences and other social groups as entities concretely and directly graspable both by their members and by external observers (i.e. the audience for a theatre as a given number of concrete individuals in a specific location) to social groups typically characterized by distant, mediated relations.

Thus the audience first has to be defined at the broad historical level of social structure and stratification. The development of the media and the analysis of their social significance has to be seen within the context of a move from societies within which the dominant mode of social co-ordination was based on direct interaction to ones characterized by the increased centrality and scope of mediated interactions. The audience as a social category and problem for research and analysis has been socially constructed by this historical process of the separation, within the circuits of social communication, of the moment of the production of symbolic forms from the moment of their reception, and thus both the separation of producers from audiences and the separation of audience members from one another. This is important because one pervasive reaction to this historical process, with roots deep in Romantic counter-Enlightenment thought, has been to decry this move as alienating, as one part of the more general process of social rationalization, and to then both analyse and/or normatively judge the media's relation to their audiences in terms of dia-logic interaction. We can see this both in the ethnomethodological ap-proach to media adopted by theorists such as Meyrowitz and Scannell as well as in Habermas's theory of the public sphere and the communicative rationality which supposedly legitimates it. In general, processes of social communication involve asymmetrical and distanced relationships be-tween the originator and receiver of the message which can be contrasted with the situation in face-to-face dialogue where, while there may indeed be, perhaps usually is, an unequal relation of power, the interchange of meanings is constantly reciprocal and immediate. While a dialogue will be initiated by one party, once it has started neither party is the originator or the receiver. They are both one and the other, in turn, in a constant and subtly managed shifting interplay of roles. This is indeed why, contrary to the position of ethnomethodology, the face-to-face dialogue is not a good model upon which to base the analysis of mediated social communication.

Indeed I would wish to argue that a major motivating thrust behind the current trends in audience research influenced by post-modern thinking which favour the ethnographic study of an 'active' audience embedded within everyday life is this very old nostalgic reaction to modernity and the search for the authentic direct experience of the real, non-rationalized, non-socially constructed human essence, an essence previously and vari-ously sought within this tradition of thought in the artist, the insane, the vagabond, the primitive, the unconscious.

The very development of mediated forms of communication which separate hierarchically a small number of producers from a large number of receivers constructs participants in the social communication process as audiences rather than as dialogic interlocutors. Thus at a primary level audiences are constituted as social facts by the separation between production and reception, by the difference in scale between producers and receivers, one-to-many rather than one-to-one, by the resulting separation between, and differential power of, transmission as opposed to feedback. Audiences are also constructed differentially by different media, their scale and speed of dissemination, the extent of their interactivity, whether they are publicly or privately consumed, etc. It is this approach to audience construction that is foregrounded in what Meyrowitz has called medium theory—McLuhan *et al.* (Meyrowitz 1985: 16–23). But these forms of audience construction are structural. They are the result of general historical processes rather than being intentionally willed by any human agent.

The Construction of Audiences: Patterns of Consumption

We can study patterns of consumption created by and within this general historical process from two perspectives. On the one hand we can be interested in the ways in which factors exogenous to the media—income level, education, gender, or age for instance—affect patterns of media consumption. This may be very important if we are judging, for example, claims for the democratic potential of the Internet. Or we may be interested in the ways in which the consumption of particular media are related to and perhaps cause different patterns of social action or identity formation.

As we saw in Chapter 3, the media can in part be understood as systems for the economic production and distribution of cultural goods and services. In my view this must remain under contemporary circumstances the point of departure for analysing reception. It does not mean that it explains or determines everything we need validly to know about that process within a general emancipatory theory. But it does place important determining constraints on what is consumed by whom under what circumstances, constraints which cannot be wished away by pointing to the relative freedom of interpretation. In particular we need to see the media as a process of production and consumption within which both the representations circulating and the audiences for them are mutually constructed such that neither the patterns of representation, symbols, or meanings, nor the specific audiences or markets for them, are random.

Audiences

So under conditions where the structural separation between producers and audiences is governed by market relations, the first level of analysis of the audience is an understanding of the constraints placed on cultural production and audience formation by patterns of disposable income. Within a commercial system symbols are only circulated in the quantities and forms for which sufficient people, including advertisers, will pay sufficient money to ensure the profitability of production. This is demonstrably not the same as satisfying all the cultural needs or desires of individuals or necessarily, as in the case of political communication, the expressed social communication needs of society. Thus audiences or publics are first and foremost conceived by producers, measured by audience research and marketing departments as markets, and in turn media products are tailored to the known desires and spending patterns of those markets. Thus we always need to start by studying the ways in which those markets are constructed and their effect as a social structuring mechanism. While pleasure is derived from consumption, it is not a free-flowing pleasure but a carefully channelled pleasure. While aberrant decoding and so-called resistant forms of sub-cultural identity construction through consumption are undoubtedly possible, it will always be easier to go with the flow and thus select from the range of identities constructed for one. One needs to start analysis not with the ethnography of a household but with family expenditure surveys and with the studies of demographics and consumption patterns used by advertising agencies and marketing departments. These reveal the foundations upon which the work of audience construction and related identity construction is based. Although advertisers and marketers are now constructing, in response to market fragmentation, more complex maps of the consumer, it nonetheless remains the case that patterns of media consumption remain closely tied to income levels.

But these structural effects are themselves mediated through other social structuring effects. It is this structuring of cultural consumption that has been one of the major thrusts of the work of Bourdieu. His analysis aims to demonstrate the ways in which class position structures audiences by structuring not only the economic resources available for cultural consumption (the massive popularity of television can still best be explained in terms of its relative cheapness) but also the cultural resources, what he terms cultural capital, largely determined by educational level, which in their turn structure dispositions, i.e. our willingness to consume and our expectation of deriving pleasure and benefit from, a given mode of cultural consumption. The crucial point here is that pleasure, which is seen in much current 'active' audience ethnography as the necessarily positive source of resistance or of the interpretative and identity-constructing free-

116

dom of 'bricolage', is on the contrary seen by Bourdieu as itself socially constructed and a source of the willing but unwitting acceptance not just of hierarchical judgements of taste but of the social positions associated with them.

Audience Construction by Media Institutions

But institutions also construct audiences intentionally. The effect of income patterns, both direct and as mediated by age, gender, and education in particular, are then in their turn mobilized by advertisers and media producers to measure and then segment markets with the socially divisive effects well analysed for the United States case by Thurow in his recent book *Breaking Up America* (1997).

As Gitlin (1994) has argued, the very separation of production and reception produces high levels of uncertainty in producing institutions as to the nature of the audience they are addressing. But since, in order to construct any communicative artefact at all, but more importantly in order to construct ones which will actually be consumed, they need to be designed with an addressee in mind, media-producing institutions are forced to construct some idea of the audience. As Gitlin puts it in his study of the US TV networks, while the numbers produced by this process of construction in terms of demographic categories may be unreliable, they are the best decision-makers have to work with (1994: 84). While these are partial and criticizable pictures of the audience, it does not follow that the audiences they depict are not 'real', for two reasons: (a) because they do indicate (they do not explain—that is a secondary level of analysis which in general is no concern of the producers) some of the social characteristics by which patterns of media consumption, and perhaps also patterns of media interpretation or use, can be differentiated, and (b) because these categories are the basis for the construction of texts which in their turn will—if we take a symbolic interactionist or social constructivist perspective—construct the very audiences previously constructed and measured within the research categories. Thus, however 'unreal' the original categorization, it becomes self-reinforcing within the process of production and consumption. Again as Gitlin puts it (1994: 29), we can envisage a process whereby a whole set of potential cultural desires, attributes, identities, around which audiences could coalesce, can be imagined as in suspension in the fluid of social and everyday life, but the construction of certain types of programming only crystallizes out a limited range of that potential and thus only constructs a limited range of the potential audience positions which consumers could and would willingly and actively adopt. Thus, and

I will return to this, the point at issue is not whether the audience is active or passive but rather the fields of action which are opened up or closed down, the identities which are made available or repressed.

The End of the Mass Audience?

A key issue in current studies of the media is whether the mass audience is dying. The argument is constructed by writers like Alvin Toffler in *The Third Wave* (1980) or by Negroponte in *Being Digital* (1995) within the broad framework of a post-industrial, post-Fordist argument. It is argued that the mass audience was a product of a particular stage of economic development corresponding broadly with the era of the mass production and mass marketing of consumer goods. That this stage of capitalist development was characterized by the dominance of economies of scale and the satisfaction of basic, undifferentiated needs. What became known as the mass media, focusing on producing a restricted range of products for large audiences, of which network television was the classic case, was a product of this era in two senses—it produced for and thus at the same time worked to produce mass audiences and it was heavily dependent upon advertising revenue derived from a small number of producers of mass consumer goods (it is still important to look at the type and range of firms who dominate as buyers of media advertising), advertisers who in their turn helped to construct audiences for the advertising and thus markets for the mass-produced goods they were trying to sell.

Now it is argued the economy is moving into a new stage of so-called flexible specialization where it is the consumer, not the mass producer, who is king. The market for basic needs having been saturated, rising incomes allow consumers to indulge a range of tastes and construct through consumption a range of lifestyles, and producers are engaged in increasingly intense competition for often rapidly changing niche markets. This shift in the nature of the market, it is argued, has been accompanied and reinforced in the field of media by the development of new technologies which in particular have removed the constraints of spectrum scarcity on the number of audio-visual services that could be delivered and have at the same time lowered the costs of distribution, thus making the targeting of these niche markets both technically possible and economically viable. Thus, it is argued, whatever one's position on the question of whether mass audiences were in the past manipulated and controlled by producers we now no longer need to worry because it is consumer choice that reigns and every individual or group can satisfy their desires from the cornucopia of capitalism. If one producer doesn't deliver what they want another rapidly will. There are two issues here. First, whether the mass audience is in fact dead, and second whether the new fragmented market does in fact liberate cultural consumers from the domination of producers. So far as the first question is concerned Neumann's *The Future of the Mass Audience* (1991) remains the best available study. It is based on now somewhat dated US evidence, but since all commentators see the United States, for good or ill, as the future so far as the media landscape is concerned, if the mass audience is not dead there it is unlikely to be either dead or dying elsewhere. Neumann comes to the unequivocal conclusion that for all the hype about new media the mass audience is far from dead. More recent evidence from the United States and elsewhere continues to support this view. This issue and the more general study of patterns of media consumption is of central importance because debates on the social impact of new media and policies based upon them often largely rest upon estimates of the actual or forecast uptake and use of these new media and/or the resulting decline in old media. This is also true of shifts in the attention of academic researchers, with the result that the continuing mundane effects of newspapers or network television are in danger of neglect as researchers rush to the judgement of new media based on dubious extrapolations from necessarily small samples. It has been frequently joked of research on telework, for instance, that there were more researchers than teleworkers.

Media Effects

While studying the nature of the audience, whether as structured by economic and other social determinants or by the media themselves, is a starting-point, it is certainly not sufficient. Establishing the nature and boundaries of a group to be studied as an audience tells us little or nothing about the nature of the relationship between that audience and the media. It tells us nothing necessarily about how media reception affects the thoughts or actions of members of that audience. The matter is complicated, however, because how we think about the audience may itself be determined by the kind of audience–media relation that we are hypothesizing, the kind of effect we are interested in. To take obvious examples, if we are interested in the levels and causes of social violence then we will be interested in the media use of those who commit, as against those who do not commit, violent acts. If we are interested in the ways in which relations of unequal power are legitimized or resisted in class-based societies we will be interested in the class characteristics of audiences. If we are interested in the mechanisms by which patriarchy is either maintained or undermined we will define the audience in gender terms. If on the other hand, as some current approaches to media consumption now do, we start from a position of a media-saturated society and see patterns of media use as a crucial defining variable of social identity construction then we will wish to define the audience in terms of those patterns of use. Our model of the audience may be that of the fan and of the audience–media relation that of fandom (Abercrombie and Longhurst 1998).

The History of Audience Studies

The history of audience research is now often presented, if only implicitly, as one of progress from a concept of a passive to that of an active audience, and from a conceptualization of the relationship between audience and media as the impact of the media upon the audience, whether upon its attitudes or its actions, to one of the audience using the media to gratify its needs and to construct identities or lifestyles.

I want to suggest that this way of reading the history is misleading and serves to disguise the issues which are at stake. It is more accurate to read the history as an oscillation along a number of dimensions motivated both by problems raised within the research itself and by wider socially determined shifts in what are seen as the interesting and important problems. Indeed seeing the history as a multidimensional oscillation allows us to avoid a certain proneness to fashion which causes a narrowing of vision, both substantially in terms of the problems addressed, and methodologically, and thus to a constant danger of reinventing the wheel, and to agree with Curran (1990) that it is better to read recent developments in audience research as a revisionist return to pre-existing problems and models of research rather than a revolutionary new dawn. This may be boringly unglamorous, but it does I hope induce a certain modesty and the search for small gains in the understanding of deep-seated problems rather than radical paradigm shifts.

This is important because it allows us to draw on the full range of what we have learned about the audience and both its use of the media and the effects of the media on it and avoids the trap of thinking that study of the ways in which the media contribute to attitude change or the maintenance or undermining of hegemony is necessarily incompatible with studying the ways in which people use the media in the construction of their identities; or that the study of the possible influence of types of media content and exposure on selected patterns of social behaviour, whether the consumption of given products, say tobacco, or violence, or sexual behaviour, is incompatible with attempts to study the links between the media and wider patterns of social change.

What then are the key issues at stake and along what dimensions has this oscillation taken place? First, there has been an oscillation between strong and weak media. This is often seen as the same as an oscillation between a passive and active audience. But this is, in my view, a misleading way of seeing things, because it is possible to argue that the media work their relatively strong effects through an active audience. It is also important to stress that this is only one dimension. It is therefore possible to support a powerful media hypothesis in one area and a weak one in another. For instance, we can argue that the media have a powerful influence on identity construction, but a weak one on attitude formation, or that they have powerful general behaviour effects, for instance in a decline in deference, but weak specific behavioural effects, for instance in a link between violent images and violent behaviour. Second, there has been an oscillation between seeing the media–audience relation as one of the impact, however mediated, of the media on the attitudes or actions of the audience on the one hand and, on the other, seeing it as one in which either the audience uses the media to satisfy its needs, however those needs may be formed, or within a broadly symbolic interactionist perspective, as one, for some the major, contributor to the construction of its identity. Third, there has been an oscillation between the ways in which effects are defined, whether cognitive or behavioural, whether at the individual or group level or at the macro social level. These three dimensions of oscillation then relate to another dimension, that of the mediations involved in the analysis of either the effects or uses of the media.

There has been a general tendency in audience research to discover an increasing number of filters through which any media influence has to pass. But there is a broad divide within the field between those who focus on the cognitive filters, whether these are conceived in terms of psychologically, socially, or culturally determined interpretative frames or in terms of interpretative freedom vis-à-vis the polysemic text, and those who focus on socially determined behavioural constraints. In both cases there may also be a distinction between and dispute about which sources of social determination are the most appropriate or the most powerful—whether class, gender, age, geographical location, educational level, occupation, or whatever. And the choice of social determination for the purposes of analysis or measurement will itself be determined by wider social considerations. of social theory or relevance.

From Individual Effects to Social Effects

We can see the complexity of these oscillations if we trace out one possible line of development through the history of audience research. There is little question that early audience research within United States sociology and social psychology began with a definition of effect as the stimulus of a media message causing a direct behavioural response in individual audience members, whether an act of consumption or a vote. These individual effects could then be aggregated statistically to measure a social effect. But the research itself soon showed that this was an inadequate model. Two problems arose. First, far from the anomic, socially disembedded audience that social theory assumed, it soon became clear that neither attitude changes nor behavioural effects could be directly correlated with media exposure or message content but were mediated via exogenously determined social structural effects. Secondly it was quickly realized that the relation between audience and message was not one of stimulus/response but of interpretation, and that there was similarly no direct relationship between an interpretation or attitude change on the one hand and any resulting action on the other. Again there was clearly a process of psychological and social mediation involved. The end result of this general development in audience studies was an account of highly mediated, weak media effects which, in so far as they had an effect, was to reinforce established norms and patterns of behaviour. As Schramm famously summed up the results of years of studies on the effects of media consumption on children's behaviour, 'for some children, under some conditions, some television is harmful. For some children under the same conditions, or for the same children under other conditions it may be beneficial. For most children, under most conditions, most television is probably neither particularly harmful nor particularly beneficial' (Schramm *et al.* 1961: 11). Or as Cumberbatch has more recently put it, 'research which has examined audiences is rarely able to demonstrate clear effects of the mass media' (1989: 1). But it is important to stress in the current intellectual climate within media studies that this tradition, which has continued to make more sophisticated both its identification of mediating social and psychological variables and its definition of effects, continues to provide us with real knowledge about real problems. It does tell us something that active, ethnographic audience research does not about the effect on voting behaviour of political campaigns and the more general agenda-setting function of media coverage, or about the effects on children, their cognitive development and socialization, of differing media diets, that have real and potentially emancipatory policy consequences.

There were, however, then two developments out of this mediated, weak, and reinforcing assessment of media effects. One was uses and gratifications research, which argued that people had been looking at the wrong thing and there was a need to reconceptualize the audience–media relation as one, not of the impact or effect of the media on the audience, but of the ways in which the audience used the media to gratify preexisting needs for information, entertainment, and so on (McQuail *et al.* 1972). An early critique of this approach then argued, correctly in my view, that it was functionalist, i.e. that any media use was assumed actually to gratify a need and thus it was by definition good, and that the needs were seen as both exogenous to the media and as mentalistic, as existing in the minds of the audience (Elliott 1974). It thus neglected the question of how these needs were created, including the possible role of the media themselves in creating these needs, and whether some needs, were therefore more emancipatory than others. The uses and gratifications approach and its original critique is important because we can see some of the recent developments in 'active' audience studies and the relation between media consumption and identity construction, not as a radical new move, but as a return to this approach and with many of the same problems.

The second reaction, famously marked by Hall's 'two paradigms' critique of what he called the Behavioural/Functional approach (Hall 1982), was a focus on society-wide ideological effects and on the media's role in the creation and maintenance of hegemony. This shifted the focus from the ways in which, within a society conceived as made up of competing pluralistic interest groups, the competing media messages caused attitudinal or behavioural change, and from the problem of deviant behaviour from social norms, to the ways, on the contrary, in which media messages were constructed and interpreted in such a way as to reinforce hegemony within societies conceived as divided along structural lines of unequal class power and where the general problem was seen as one of how to overthrow existing social norms rather than maintain them. This approach undoubtedly addresses two real problems which most of its critics simply avoid. Society is demonstrably unequal in its distribution of both material and symbolic resources and the life chances associated with them. Thus there is a permanent problem of explaining how such a society is legitimized. It is also the case that no social entity can be identified as such, let alone actually maintain its social existence, without some body of shared norms, values, and ideas about the world. Thus the mechanisms by which such shared norms are created, propagated, and maintained is always of central significance. The problem with much recent audience research which focuses on audience freedom and resistance is that it simply avoids this problem. It can account for and even worship social difference

123

and alternative readings and all the things that separate us. But it cannot account for those dominant readings and 'normal' patterns of behaviour which, for better or worse, unite us and make a society a society rather than a random collection of monads.

However the ideological turn in audience studies soon came up against problems of its own, which in spite of its differing theoretical starting-point drove it in the same directions as the effects and uses and gratifications approaches it had started by defining itself against. Because it combined a theory of unequal social power with a cultural or hermeneutic turn, the focus switched back to cognitive rather than behavioural effects. This immediately faced this approach with the old problem of differences of interpretation, now renamed decoding, of the same message and drove it, since it was primarily concerned with the relationship between ideology and class consciousness and action, to try and limit the range of interpretations on broadly class lines. This was the state of play with Morley's seminal nationwide study. The problems then became twofold. First it was difficult to establish a clear general link between social position and interpretation. Second, the appropriate social positional variable to use, both in selecting samples and in attempting to identify broad patterns of interpretative variation, became a matter of dispute, particularly between those who privileged class divisions and others, particularly feminists, who naturally preferred to focus on gender divisions. Another problem was the failure to incorporate any theory of motivation, that is to say of the relation between any given interpretation and a subsequent action—whether a vote or the joining of a political party or going on strike as opposed to strike-breaking etc. Before turning to the two most influential reactions to these theoretical and empirical dilemmas it is important to note that the assumed openness of the text and lack of fit between interpretation and relevant external social determinations are neither of them as great as many new active audience researchers assume. As the continuing work of the Glasgow Media Group within a broadly dominant ideology, class politics perspective shows one can establish a clear, long-lasting and commonly held relation between a given media message and the interpretations made. The fact that it is long-lasting, that is to say a consistent interpretation can be reconstructed by audience members from memory, means that it is derived from a consistent interpretative framework and is not simply the random response to given media stimuli; the fact that it is shared by others means that it is likely to be motivated in the same way by the same message. This then enables the Glasgow group both to establish a consistent relation between such interpretations and responses determined by social position and experience and at the same time to identify a relationship between media messages and changing attitudes and ideas. In short media messages do affect our understanding of the world, but how we then interpret or act upon that understanding is related to social position and experience.

The Embedded Audience

Leaving that to one side, the first major reaction to the dilemmas of ideology research was to dig deeper into the pit of interpretative variability and to end up with Fiske's dissolution of both text and audience into an endless process of ungrounded semiosis which was defined as resistant by fiat (Fiske 1989). Not only was the problem of the impact of messages dissolved, but also at the same time was the problem of the social determination of both interpretative frameworks and associated patterns of behaviour. I will look at the problems associated with the particular model of language and representation upon which this particular version of the undetermined reader is based in the next chapter. For our purposes here we need to point to the way in which this move within interpretative theory in its turn drove a parallel move away from an interpretative focus and back to uses and gratifications. Thus the second reaction to the dilemmas of ideology research was a turn on the one hand to a revived form of uses and gratifications research and the study of the so-called embedded audience and, on the other, a turn to consumption rather than reception as the preferred descriptor for the audience–media relation and to a focus on the ways in which consumption, far from being determined by production and an inauthentic and repressive form of social behaviour, was a liberating form of identity construction. Here the term 'bricolage' paralleled the polysemy of the interpretative approach.

Within this general trend the approach of Radway (1988) and Ang (1985, 1990) has been to stress the uses and gratifications of media and then to move in the direction of the embedded audience as an escape from the question of social determination and generalization.

The alternative approach, made by Morley (1989) and Silverstone (1994), is to hang on to the relation between media use and social determination but seek this determination in the embedded complex of domestic behaviours such that what is at stake now is no longer the interpretation of messages and their ideological power or effect but the meaning of objects within the power balances of social relations. An interesting question in its own right and based, at least in Silverstone's case, on a specific, object-oriented psychological theory. But now the focus of attention shifts decisively away from the media and to the role of objects of consumption and the meanings attached to them within a general study of social relations of power. Whether the media have any particular or necessary role in this is not at all clear.

In my view three distinct issues are raised by these recent developments in audience research.

(a) The appeal to concepts of the everyday and embeddedness and to ethnography as a preferred methodology raises the problem of generalization and empirical validation.

(b) The question of whether an active audience can necessarily be equated with weak media effects, as is often assumed, and thus how we should assess the power of the media.

(c) The question of the relation between ideas and behaviour and the distinction between behaviour and action, and thus whether it is behaviour or ideas that are the main determinant of social co-ordination and stability. This relates to the discussion of culture in the next chapter because it raises the question of whether it is our shared, habitual routines or our shared meanings that are the main determinant of social co-ordination and stability, and whether the limits of emancipation are primarily behavioural—we can only be reflexive some of the time—or cognitive.

The Ethnography of an Active, Embedded Audience

Let me look first at the way in which the turn to the ethnographic study of the embedded audience raises the problem of generalization and empirical validation and its implications for what audience research can reasonably tell us about the social power of either audience or media. I will then go on to look at the implications for our assessment of the power of the media of conceptualizing the audience–media relation as the activity of consumption and its use in a process of identity construction. In particular I will do this by critiquing the idea that an active audience is necessarily a powerful or resistant audience.

It is undoubtedly the case that the original effects tradition started with a model of media messages affecting individuals, and then conceptualized social effects as the aggregation of these individual impacts. But this was because of the way that the more general social problem was conceptualized. Early effects research was closely linked to mass society, mass audience theory, and to the way the problem had been posed by classical sociology in terms of a transition from mechanical to organic solidarity. By definition the problem was the dissolution of pre-existing social bonds and their replacement as socializing structures by more general processes of social communication between isolated, anonymous, anomic individuals. But the research itself soon showed that this was not a realistic picture. From the work of the Chicago school in urban sociology—which stressed the role of newspapers in building and reinforcing the bonds of local community—onwards, audience research increasingly stressed the ways in which the effects of media were mediated through group affiliation, or rather the ways in which effects were mediated by other pre-existing effects of social structure and location. The issue in dispute thus became not whether we had to see the audience as socially constructed and any effects as socially mediated, but what in any given case were the appropriate social markers. Were they class, gender, ethnicity, age, geographical location, etc.? This is a problem that no audience researcher can escape, since unless the audience is conceived in terms of isolated individuals and any effects are conceived as entirely random, some structuring of the sample to be studied has to take place and such a structuring will, of course, be prescribed by one's hypothesis as to what the most relevant social structural mediations are likely to be. If one is concerned with class power then class will be top of the list, if with gender relations then gender, and so on. One way of seeing recent developments in 'ethnographic' studies of the audience, developments which Morley very even-handedly and judiciously assesses in *Television, Audiences and Cultural Studies* (1992), is as a struggle with this problem. This tradition, stemming from a concern with the role of the media in the operation of hegemony in class societies, starts with Morley's nationwide study, which attempts to map the relationship between variant decodings of a media message and class location. The problem for Morley's critics was the loose fit between interpretations and class location.

But the apparent rich variation in actual audience interpretations and their theorization as an active resistant audience then led ironically, in the name of an 'ethnography' of the embedded audience, not just to the disappearance from research of the intervening social structural variables that the whole effects tradition had developed to explain variations in effects, but also, as Ang's title *Desperately Seeking the Audience* indicates, the disappearance of the audience as anything other than a random collection of individuals so embedded as to dissolve into the huge complexity of the everyday.

This appeal to the everyday and embeddedness dominates recent developments in ethnographic studies of the 'active' audience, and gives the impression, as is intended, of attention to the real experiences of ordinary folk and thus a rejection of both intellectual elitism and of the reifications of sociology.

Radway talks of 'a new object of analysis—the endlessly shifting, ever-evolving kaleidoscope of daily life and the way in which the media are integrated and implicated within it'(1988: 366). Morley writes that 'For audience studies, when it comes to television, the key challenge lies in our ability to construct the audience as both a social and a semiological (cultural) phenomenon, and in our ability to recognise the relationship between viewers and the television set as they are mediated by the determinations of everyday life' (1992: 197), and argues that 'the focus on the embedded audience must certainly now be a priority for media research'. Nightingale writes that 'Self-everyday life is the larger relation where what is studied as audience-text finds its rationale' (1996: 131).

The problem with this invocation of everyday life and of embeddedness as the final destination of the long march through the social determinants of audience interpretations and of the media's effects upon audiences is that a set of analytical distinctions and evaluative stances are being smuggled in without the necessary supporting argument, and in a way which avoids the crucial analytical problems. In my view the mobilization of everyday life involves three different conceptual and evaluative issues.

(a) The use of the distinction between the life world and the systems world, in its turn just another version of the agency/structure problem, in a way which privileges the life world as authentic and free as against the dominating power of rationalizing structures. It is thus part of the Romantic revolt against the implications of modernity and against the necessary role that generalized systems play in social co-ordination, a role that is beneficial as well as detrimental, and is certainly unavoidable.

(b) The mobilization of an opposition between popular and elite culture, with the everyday firmly on the popular and positive side of the balance, accompanied by a related view of the intellectual or researcher as an outsider always in danger of failing fully to appreciate or understand the rich diversity of this culture. There is operating here a quite clear *nostalgie de la boue*, a powerful trope in contemporary media and cultural studies.

(c) This is in turn related to an evaluative schema which opposes pleasure to rational analysis very much in pleasure's favour, again another of the tropes of Romanticism. Pleasure, desire, the unconscious are seen as the Dionysian forces constantly welling up from below to undermine the repressive, disciplining, dominating Apollonian forces of rationality and structure.

All these positions in turn relate to a methodological suspicion of generalization as a misleading abstraction from the diversity of reality, and an accompanying suspicion, if not refusal, of sociology and of the establishment of social and structural facts that are its essence.

These evaluations and refusals are very clear in the works from which this move to everyday life takes its inspiration, those of Lefebvre and De Certeau. Lefebvre explicitly sees everyday life, in Nightingale's words, 'as the source of an audience-generated critique of culture; the origins of a critique of modernism'. As he himself put it, 'there the rationality of economism and technicity produces its opposite as their "structural compliment" and reveals its limitations as restricted rationalism and irrationalism pervade everyday life, confront and reflect one another' (Lefebvre 1984: 83). The underlying positions are made even clearer in De Certeau (1984), who equates the productivity of everyday life with *parole* in contrast to the *langue* of the dominant culture. He writes of the trajectories that 'trace out the ruses of other interests and desires that are neither determined nor captured by the systems in which they develop' (1984: p. xviii), and he explicitly argues that 'statistical investigation grasps the material of these practices, but not their form; it determines the elements used, but not the phrasing produce by bricolage (the artisan-like inventiveness) and the discursiveness that combines these elements which are in general circulation and rather drab . . . the power of its calculation lies in its power to divide, but it is precisely through this analytic fragmentation that it loses sight of what it claims to seek and to represent' (1984: p. xviii). Finally, in claiming the utopian potential of popular culture, he praises the 'opacity of "popular culture" . . . a dark rock which resists all assimilation'.

While the determinations involved in the construction of audiences and in the audience–media relation are indeed complex, and while there is no doubt that in the process of generalization and the search for typical instances of more general processes or structures one undoubtedly loses in complexity what one gains in clarity, to invoke everyday life and embeddedness in this way is to give up on understanding altogether.

The Status and Use of Statistics: A Methodological Digression

Underlying the debate about media effects is a debate about the use and relevance of statistical methods of audience measurement. This is a field where the methodological issues cannot be avoided because they reflect underlying conceptual issues of central importance. The currently ascendant ethnographic turn in audience studies broadly rejects the validity of statistical sampling on the grounds that, from the perspective of the micro contexts of everyday life, all audience members are fundamentally hetero-geneous. That to take an approach that assumes that any individual's interpretative response is representative, and thus open to statistical sam-pling, in order to give a more general and generalizable picture of audience responses is to repress the individual, to fail to recognize her or his differ-ence. This goes along with the view, expressed by Hartley, that the audience is a fiction with no real existence. Now while this view is based on the true perception that audiences do not exist in a state of nature—they have no ontological existence, but are constructed either by institutions or by the research project itself—this is also to use a very special sense of real which in fact draws precisely on the ontological tradition which it appears to deny. That is to say, much of the reality of modern society, precisely be-cause social relations are mediated, is abstract. It can only be captured sta-tistically as patterns of probability. Indeed this is the very definition of a social fact in Durkheim's sense. It is something that *cannot* be explained in terms of individuals and a methodological individualism which sees all social phenomena as merely the sum of individual actions. To claim that audiences are real social entities is not to fall into a structural functional-ism. Indeed the problem with Giddens's critique of structural functional-ism in terms of his theory of structuration is that, while it takes account of the ways in which social structures are iteratively constructed through the actions of intelligent agents, it does not take account of either the differ-ence between behaviour and action, that is to say the ways in which sub- or semi-conscious routines necessarily structure co-ordinated social action, or of the ways in which the sum of a set of intelligent actions produces an overall result which is not what the actors wanted or intended but which has determining or constraining effects upon them. These effects are in part identified and measured in terms of probabilities.

The rejection of statistically based audience measurement methodolo-gies is a part of that wider Romantic, counter-Enlightenment strand of thought which rejects modernity as alienating and is in permanent pursuit of the authentically plural and different. This, in my view, is simply to deny a necessary and defining feature of modern society and to reject the possibility of analysing the ambivalences between the liberating and repressive effects of rationalization and abstraction. In the end ethno-graphic audience research fetishizes direct experience and the everyday. The descriptions get ever thicker—in Geertz's term—but to what end, since they can only result, as in the Borges story, in a map that is physically coterminous with the world it is designed to describe? In the end the whole purpose of social scientific enquiry is to disembed the social phenomenon under investigation. Without such a disembedding no explanation is possible.

The Politics of the Embedded Audience

Thus, while Ang and Hermes (1996) call for 'an unravelling of the intricate intersections of the diverse and the homogenous', it is difficult to see how this could ever be done if one starts with their assumption that a more radical 'anthropologisation' of the study of media consumption needs

to go beyond the boundaries of reception analysis and develop new forms of 'consumption analysis'. In everyday life media consumption cannot be equated with distinct and insulated activities such as 'watching television', 'reading a book', 'listening to a record' and so on. Since people living in (post)-modern societies are surrounded by an ever-present and ever-evolving media environment, they are always-already audiences of an abundance of media provisions, by choice or by force. Thus media consumption should be conceptualised as an ever-proliferating set of heterogeneous and dispersed, intersecting and contradicting cultural practices, involving an indefinite number of multiply positioned subjects. (1996: 340)

But it is not just a question of methodology that is at stake here. In the end it is also a political question. This is well illustrated by the position to which Ang and Hermes are themselves driven in the same article. They ask in the context of studying the relation between media consumption and gender whether

a wariness of generalised absolutes and observance of the irreducible complexity and relentless heterogeneity of social life . . . doesn't make theory and politics impossible? Doesn't post-modern particularism inevitably lead to the resignation that all there is left viable are descriptions of particular events at particular points in time? And doesn't radical endorsement of particularity and difference only serve to intensify an escalating individualism? If we declare 'women' to be an indeterminate category, how can a feminist politics still assert itself?

Their answer is revealing. They argue that 'the dangers of easy categorisation and generalisation, so characteristic of mainstream traditions in the social sciences (including mass communication theory and research) are greater than the benefits of a consistent particularism'. While arguing that post-modern feminism has adopted a profound sense of gender scepticism, they go on to equate categorization with assuming a fixed unity. It does nothing of the sort. But this then enables them to continue to use the terms 'women' and 'sexism' as organizing categories for their thought, while it is no longer clear what meaning or relevance such terms could have unless grounded in some generalized category, however defined. In fact any feminist theory or politics has no alternative but to work with a sociological generalization such that relations of power between groups can be posited, let alone analysed. The issue therefore is not whether it is necessary to generalize from the particular and the heterogeneous, but what generalizing principles are relevant for the analytical or political purposes at hand.

Consumption, Identities, and Lifestyles

But what De Certeau's work, and much of the audience research derived from it, does usefully turn our attention to is the major alternative tradition in audience research which focuses on the audience's use of the media rather than on the impact, however mediated, of the media on the audience. Again it is not useful in my view to see this tradition in terms of a radical or critical shift from a functionalist uses and gratifications, passive audience approach to an active audience, resistance, identities approach. Indeed the continuities in this way of looking at the audience–media relation is well illustrated by comparing Herzog's study of radio soaps in the 1940s (Herzog 1944) with feminist-inspired work within the more recent 'active' audience tradition such as that of Hobson (1982) or Ang (1985) on soaps and serials, or that of Radway (1987) on Romance novels. The methods and conclusions are essentially similar. It is not the reality, escapism, or repressive nature of the content that is crucial, but on the contrary the ways in which women use these media forms to escape from the pressures of their male-, and child-rearing-, and housework-dominated domestic lives. But in my view the continuities are more wide-ranging than that and can best be illustrated by examining the ways in which consumption in relation to identity has been mobilized as a way of thinking about the audience–media relation, and its deep roots in post-Enlightenment thought.

Consumption, Identities, and Commodity Fetishism

The lifestyle approach that glorifies consumer choice and the freedom of the consumer to satisfy tastes and construct identities within the process of consumption in fact shares the same model of identity construction as the commodity fetishism approach it thinks it is rejecting. One can identify a long tradition of thought, which stems originally from Hegel's notion of identity construction through projection and objectification, and then develops into Marx's concept of commodity fetishism, which focuses on the formation of human identities, and thus the motivation of social action, through praxis. The intentional self is created through a process of objectification which involves interaction in production with the external material world and a dialectical reflection of oneself in the response of others within social relations. Thus for Marx commodity fetishism was supportive of the social status quo because it led individuals and groups to find themselves, to create their identities, in a particular form of alienated and reified production and consumption. It thus disguised from them their own deeper and freer potentials. This was then developed by the Frankfurt School, with the addition of the insights of Freudian psychoanalysis, into an analysis of the social effects of the consumption of a commoditized culture. Thus for the Frankfurt School the ideological effect of the media lay not in the rationalized content of their messages, but in the practice of a particular form of alienated consumption. One can criticize this view, but not on the basis that it works with the model of a passive audience. Indeed the difference between it and supposedly new more radical and liberatory current versions of consumption, identities, and lifestyles research is not in the activity or agency granted to the audience, but in the evaluation, from an emancipatory perspective, of the identities and lifestyles actively constructed.

This does not mean that there are not crucial differences of approach and theory at stake within the consumption/identities approach. First, as part of the so-called cultural turn, there is a shift in focus from seeing the commodity as an external object in the world, as part of second nature, through the appropriation of which we come to know ourselves and thus form our identities, to a position which combines the Weberian status competition of distinction with an ethnographic Maussian view, largely mediated via Mary Douglas, of gift exchange, whereby commodities lose all use value except as tokens of social status and their exchange is seen as a process of both status competition and social bonding. A crucial point needs to be made here. The shift to a view of token-based status competition derives from a view of identity as formed by preassigned social roles and one's socialization into them, as in Bourdieu's theory of habitus, and sees token exchange as a means of mediating, in a misrecognized way, the potentially socially dysfunctional conflicts between roles and status positions. While in both cases the audience member is active, the implications of the action and its degree of 'freedom' or 'resistance', and thus the nature of identity construction involved, are very different. As we can see in Bourdieu's work, which draws heavily on this tradition, it sees identity as relatively non-malleable and resistance to the effect of the 'cultural arbitrary' as very difficult to envisage. In my view both the commodity fetishism and the gift exchange positions tend to explain how active intentional individual agents form identities which conform with rather than resist social norms. They both fall, for different reasons, at the behaviour end of the behaviour/action divide and reveal, correctly in my view, the limits to human freedom.

Second, there is a crucial difference in the stance taken towards pleasure. The problem of the relation between reason and pleasure goes back to the sources of the ethical tradition within which this book argues we should work. As we shall see in Chapter 7, it is a key issue in how we evaluate media content. There is no question that the commodity fetishism school is working within a paradigm which sees pleasure as a problem and broadly places it at the animal end of the animal/human divide, around which much thinking within this broad tradition works. From this perspective, as in Kant, the autonomous reasoning moral subject needs to emancipate him- or herself from a slavery to the animal appetites, passions, and desires (it is for this reason that Kant distinguishes the pursuit of freedom from the pursuit of happiness) and thus emancipation involves a process of the construction of an emancipated identity. This is why, within this tradition, education plays such an important role.

Achievement of such emancipation, and of the moral social life based upon it, is always seen as both difficult and fragile. Within a Hegelian projection tradition, our socially constructed identities can be either good or bad, rational or irrational, and again as we shall see in Chapter 7, this is why art came to be seen as a privileged and morally and socially beneficial form of objectification. The alternative tradition saw the animal instincts and desires as broadly good and as subsequently corrupted or repressed by reason and society. The task then became not the control of pleasure by reason, but the liberation of desire from reason. Within this argument, as I am sure must be clear by now, I am firmly on reason's side. This is not to say that the need to discipline the passions has not been used throughout history as an excuse for, and a disguise of, attempts to maintain domination and suppress not passions, but alternative and oppositional ways of moral life. Nor is it to deny the important role that the search for happiness plays in the search for justice. But it is to question whether all pleasures are 'good', much less socially progressive, and whether the active pursuit of pleasure cannot be the basis for social control and manipulation as easily as for liberation.

The key question at issue is the relation between the objects offered for consumption and the identities created by their appropriation. A theory which wishes to stress the autonomy or freedom of consumers has to argue, based often upon an arbitrary theory of representation, that the relationship is random. That production has no determinate influence whatsoever on consumption. But is such a view credible? If we come to know ourselves and at the same time create ourselves in the process of appropriation is there not likely to be a difference—I don't for the moment wish to argue whether one or the other is better—between the human potentials realized in appropriating a political debate, a soap opera, an advertisement for Nike shoes, a novel, or a sports event. To take one example, many scholars have cogently argued that the book as a form enabled the development of individual, private, and domestic appropriation, which itself helped to develop both the Kantian Enlightenment view of humans as intellectually autonomous and the revaluation of the relation between the private and domestic and the public, between fiction and the feminine on the one hand and male and the political on the other. It is this view that forms of consumption are in complex ways embodied in different forms and institutions, and that they in their turn reinforce certain personal and social character traits, that is the rational core of McLuhan's theories, which in their turn derive from studies of the ways in which the development of printing and reading and the shift from orality changed society and the individuals within it. If so much is granted then we also know that the production and distribution of cultural commodities, what is made available for consumption and to whom, is structured—and intentionally structured—in specific, determinate ways. If the connection to individual and group identity formation is granted, then how that power of structuring works and with what effects becomes a matter of legitimate interest. This is what Thompson has called 'the double-bind of mediated dependency'. 'While the availability of media products serves to enrich and accentuate the reflexive organisation of the self, at the same time it renders this reflexive organisation of the self increasingly dependent on systems over which the individual has relatively little control' (Thompson 1995: 214).

The Neo-classical Demand Model, Utilitarianism, and Needs

Within the consumption perspective a key issue is the relationship between producers and consumers, or supply and demand. It is, I think ironic, that the consumption as freedom school, in its hasty desire to reject the producer model and its supposed economic determinism, in fact adopts uncritically central tenets of the neo-classical view of markets. The autonomous consumer or audience member is, in fact, the utilitarian pleasure-maximizer beloved of the neo-classicals. This model of the consumer has been criticized on a number of grounds within economics and within a philosophical critique of utilitarianism. First it is argued that it presents an unrealistic and narrow view of human nature which exaggerates consumer rationality and the pursuit of individual interest at the expense of the altruistic side of human motivation. It is an asocial view of consumption because the desires, wants, or utilities sought through consumption are seen as incommensurable. It does not allow for the comparison of people's utilities or for so called externalities—the effect of one person's utility maximization on that of others. There have been in particular two directions of critique which are of relevance to debates over media consumption. The first, pursued by Sen and others (Nussbaum and Sen 1993), is a move from a theory of consumption based upon consumers' desires to one based on needs. The argument put simply (for an expansion of the argument see Garnham 1999) opposes the notion of the incommensurability of consumer wants and argues that we can in fact agree socially on a range of basic needs, or what Sen calls capabilities, which any social system that aspires, as at some level all post-Enlightenment societies do, to a notion of equality should satisfy. Crucially, these may be needs or capabilities which at first the individual consumer or group of consumers does not recognize, if only because of the human propensity to make the best of a bad job, whether this is ideologically reinforced within the given system of social domination or not. As I have argued elsewhere, this has major implications for how we think about media consumption because it allows us coherently to argue why certain ranges of cultural products should be made available even if, at least at first, no audience demands them. A classic case would be education.

The second line of critique of neo-classical utilitarianism in consumption raises the question whether, in economists' terms, our wants are endogenous or exogenous. Neo-classical market theory assumes that wants are exogenous, that is to say they derive from somewhere outside the system of commodity consumption itself. Where they come from is a mystery. In some theories they would be basic, timeless attributes of human beings. But the crucial point is that for the model of consumer freedom to hold they must be exogenous. However, it is clear that consumer wants are to an important extent determined by the system of production and consumption itself. Thus, as Marx and many others have argued, what at any one time we take to be an acceptable standard of living and how therefore we define poverty is a historical and cultural variable. But more specifically the form of our desires will be shaped by what is actually available for consumption. Indeed the whole identity creation in consumption position depends upon the notion that our desires are formed and we come to know them in the process of consumption itself. In addition, of course, there are all the additional, explicit powers and effects of advertising and marketing which it is hardly credible to argue have no effect at all. In so far as one of the wants we satisfy in consumption is that of social sharing, or what is expressed in its reverse as the concept of relative deprivation, the spread of a cultural practice or of a specific audience or consumption group may be self-reinforcing. There is a point at which, for instance, we need to consume television because most other people in our society do. Indeed it is upon this fact that the whole game of positional goods and status-based consumption is based (for a further discussion of this whole issue in relation to broadcasting policy see Pratten 1998).

7 | Culture, Ideology, and Aesthetics: The Analysis and Evaluation of Media Content

No study of the media can bypass the complex and difficult questions posed by their content, by the symbolic forms they create and circulate. Their effects, whether of agency or structure, are worked, unavoidably, through the symbolic. This is one of the things that makes the mode of persuasion distinct from those of either production or coercion. Here the inducements and sanctions through which power works are and can only be symbolic.

The Problem of the Symbolic

Western culture, probably all cultures, has been troubled by the symbolic—what is the status and function of these strange, miraculous entities that both stand for other material realities and cause action at a distance? The dominant semitic religious tradition of the West—Judaism, Christianity, and Islam—places its central emphasis on the problem of interpreting the word of God through the book, a tradition which includes the dangers of knowledge expressed in the myth of the Fall and the eating of the fruit of the tree of knowledge, and which has built a tradition of hermeneutics and iconography around the 'now you see it now you don't', entangling, enticing, enthralling, but elusive nature of divine revelation presented to human eyes, as it must be, indirectly—direct vision would be blinding—through the veil of language. This ambivalence about the status of symbolic forms is beautifully captured in the ceramic traceries of Islamic religious architecture where the spider's web, which was also the veil that saved the Prophet from his pursuers as he hid in a cave, and the calligraphic representation of the word of God, intermingle to dazzling and dizzying effect. This tradition in its turn has inspired one of the major strands of Western philosophy, feeding, via Thomism, on the one hand into modern scientific method itself and on the other into the general problem of hermeneutics within the human sciences. At the same time the metaphysical tradition stemming from Greek philosophy, having with Parmenides severed thought from being, the conceptual and rational from the sensual, has remained troubled by the relationship between the two. Plato's suspicion of the power of poetry and the potentially corrupting power of art which, in its appeal to the senses and emotions, was the siren song which distracted humans from the pursuit of truth, which lay hidden in the shadows of perception and direct experience, fed through to Kant's fear of the distorting effect of the *Schwärmerei* of fantasies on the necessary discipline of autonomous reason in its passage from intuitions to understanding or judgement, from feelings to the duties of the moral imperative. This problem and this fear then in their turn both motivated and structured Kant's *Critique of Judgement*, from which so much contemporary aesthetic and cultural analysis still flows, and lies behind continuing debates about the relative merits of media genres such as news or entertainment, fears about dumbing down or the decline of educational standards, and moral panics which readily compare the effect of the media to that of a drug. Indeed the whole debate between modernists and post-modernists is inscribed upon and across this distinction and this fear, each side reversing the evaluative terms of the debate, modernists supporting reason and truth against emotion and the aesthetic, the post-modernists vaunting the sensual, the particular, the aesthetic against what they see as the generalizing, abstracting drive of conceptual reason.

In this chapter therefore I want to look at current debates about how we think about the symbolic level of social life and their implications for how we analyse and evaluate the symbolic forms that the media produce and circulate. But theories of the symbolic, or, as they are more generally called, theories of representation, also have central implications for social theory generally precisely because so much contemporary social theory, theories of a broadly discursive, hermeneutic, post-modern type, has not only pursued the so-called linguistic turn with enthusiasm, but in so doing has in general simply implicitly assumed that this turn is both desirable and well founded, without argument. Indeed as can be seen from much of the relevant literature, although it may claim to be anti-foundationalist and reject truth claims as merely the attempt to impose one particular language game upon another, it in fact accepts unquestioningly the truth of the particular linguistic and philosophical model upon which its turn is based, and deploys it as the unquestioned foundation for its theoretical arguments and for any social or political practice that may spring from them. I want in this chapter to question this comfortable assumption, flowing as it does from deeply flawed theories of both culture and language.

The Concept of Culture

The use of the concept culture was designed to highlight two things. First, the intelligence of human agents; the fact that all human action is endowed with and motivated by meaning (although, as I have stressed, this tends to neglect the problem of the habitual and the non-conscious wellsprings of human action). Second, the role of shared belief systems, the mode of persuasion, rather than the mode of production, as the foundation of society. It was mobilized as a challenge on the one hand to one version of the theory of ideology, to what were seen as overly deterministic, materialist accounts of social structure and process—particularly so-called economistic Marxism in its base/superstructure form—and on the other to functionalist or behaviourist interpretations, in terms of effects, of the relation between symbol and action.

As Gellner noted many years ago in a discussion of the influence of Wittgenstein,

The sociological concept of culture (the nearest equivalent in public language to Wittgenstein's private notion of a 'form of Life') is a kind of proto-concept, useful enough as a shorthand indication of a certain cluster of phenomena, but in no way precise enough to constitute, when used on its own, any kind of serious explanation of anything. it can cover anything from the shared assumptions of a small guild to the shared assumptions of all mankind (the looseness and pliability of this key explanatory concept of the whole system is not unconnected with its popularity). (Gellner 1985: 178)

In short the problem with the use of culture as an analytical concept as it has developed within culture and media studies is that it has become entirely vacuous. If it refers to the meaning-endowed nature of all human action and all social structure then it cannot be used analytically to discriminate either between sets of actions or structures, for instance between a television programme and a given state of the labour market, or between symbols and what symbols are used to represent or express. Culture then designates everything and thus nothing. As Stuart Hall has expressed this position, 'culture is involved in all those practices . . . which carry meaning and value for us, which need to be meaningfully interpreted by others, or which depend on meaning for their effective operation. Culture, in this sense, permeates all of society' (Hall 1997: 3). In this anthropological form the concept culture was developed to study other cultures—to study societies that were not our own from the outside. Thus, if only implicitly, the concept did in fact have a notion of analytical discrimination built in from the start, the difference between them and us. While this distinction may have been used, again more often implicitly than explicitly, for evaluative purposes—their 'primitive' culture is being judged from the perspective of 'our' 'advanced' or 'developed' culture—its primary purpose was descriptive and explanatory—what exactly was the system of cultural norms and practices that distinguished this social group as a distinct social group, and why was it this way rather than another? And then perhaps also, does this particular cultural form fit into a wider taxonomy of human cultural organization? Importantly also, the anthropologist's gaze was in general directed at, and developed in order to analyse, social formations that had not experienced the division of social labour in a highly developed and complex form—especially the creation of a specialized social realm for cultural production and circulation in its modern form. In short, to use Durkheim's terminology, it was developed for and appropriate to the analysis of mechanical solidarity where it made some sense to think in terms of culture and society as coterminous, as a single form of life. Thus it was a concept ill fitted to deal with the analysis of culture from within, where the analyst was a participant within the language game and where the problem was not one of the analysis of a culture predefined as a social whole but of the relations between differentiated social groups and cultural forms within a fragmented social formation within which both the existence and desirability of a common culture was in question and indeed where the survival of the social form itself could not be assumed. In making a critical analysis of such societies from within we need to be able to make two crucial distinctions. First, the whole emancipatory thrust of the Enlightenment project and of any social science worth its name depends on being able to make a distinction between a social practice and the meaning it has for the participants, such that the explanation of that practice is not exhausted by the accounts of the participant actors in the practice. It is often the case that we know why we are doing something but not what we are in fact doing. We need therefore to have a conceptual apparatus that enables us to distinguish between social structures and actions on the one hand and the meanings they have on the other. But, second, we also need to be able to distinguish between the meanings embedded in and borne by practices but which are not coded, on the one hand, and meanings which are coded into symbolic forms and created and circulated in that form on the other. Both are covered by the term culture but the difference between them is crucial.

In short we need to distinguish between culture as describing a set of meanings and values circulating within a society and other social processes and relations, with which they may be implicated but from which they can be distinguished. We also need to be able to distinguish between different specific sets of social practices involving the use of symbolic forms in order to ask why and how humans use symbolic forms, for what purposes and with what effects. The concept of culture which has come to dominate much of the social and human sciences does neither. It is also the case that it is often used, in just the way that art has been used, to smuggle in an evaluative judgement, something which this use of culture is supposedly designed to supersede. That is to say, to use the term culture is too often also to make a claim for the ethical, political, or human superiority of this approach as opposed to that of those who study, say, economics or social structure.

Theories of Language

Within the so-called linguistic turn a particular model of language has been used in the same way and with the same effect. Since inter-subjective systems of communication or media, in particular language, are indispensable tools of reflexivity, it is hardly surprising if disputes about the nature and function of such systems of communication lie at the heart of social science and of the debate about modernity that increasingly dominates that field of intellectual enquiry.

I will take one very influential recent example to illustrate the ways in which the use of a very partial and flawed theory of language blocks the possibility of, indeed attempts to render illegitimate, a range of necessary evaluations. But I think the example is representative of a widespread orthodoxy within cultural and media studies. In *Theories of Representation* (1997), Hall starts by arguing that we can have three possible approaches to the analysis of the role of symbolic forms or language—the reflective, the intentional, or the socially constructed. He then argues, on the basis of the Saussurean model of language, that language is both arbitrary in relation to what it represents and at the same time socially constructed and determining on the individual language-user, because you cannot have a private language and because the language we use pre-exists us. It is pre-formed and already shared by a pre-existing community of language-users into which we are born or into which we later move by learning that language. But Hall then goes on to argue that this means that both the reflective and intentional theories of language are untenable. The problem is that this is simply not true. Let us take first the question of arbitrariness. While it is clearly the case, as can easily be demonstrated by comparing two languages, that any word in a language has a purely arbitrary relation to its referent, in terms of the language in social use the relationship is not arbitrary at all. If I point to a woody, leafy object growing in a field and say 'boot' any modestly competent English speaker knows I am wrong and that I am not conveying the meaning intended. Indeed it is precisely for this reason that Wittgenstein argued that meaning lies in social usage. Thus the mimetic power of symbol systems is established and constantly reanchored in social use. A symbol system can be mimetic so long as it continues to work mimetically, and thus the question within a given language community as to whether a given discourse represents the truth, at least according to the criteria of truth in its mimetic, reflective sense established by that community, is a perfectly proper and socially answerable one. Whether this truth can be translated between languages and language communities is a different and more difficult question, but one which in my view is also subject to an affirmative answer. Thus one of the socially constructed functions of language is to reflect true representations of other realities. As Habermas puts it in his critique of Derrida, 'Linguistically mediated processes such as the acquisition of knowledge, the transmission of culture, the formation of personal identity, and socialisation and social integration, involve mastering problems posed by the world: the independence of learning processes that Derrida cannot acknowledge is due to the independent logics of these problems and the linguistic medium tailored to deal with them' (Habermas 1987: 205). Indeed were this not possible it would not just be the translatability between language games that would be at issue but the very possibility of interpersonal communication and thus the developed forms of collaborative and co-ordinated social interaction we call societies. When we talk to someone else, or communicate with them through other symbol systems, we assume, with good warrant in the accumulated experience of human culture, that we are transferring a meaning with relative accuracy such that we can share it. Without that ability we would be trapped within our private worlds. This for me is an image of hell, and certainly no recipe for any sustained social life, but it appears in much post-modern writing, with its worship of the inexpressible sublime and difference, as the utopia to be actively sought beyond 'power'.

However, the major problem with the reflective theory of language arises in situations, which are increasingly common, where the 'reality' is itself discursively constructed—there is thus either no available external reality to point to as a test (in Kant's terms no intuition outside the symbolic system), or the 'reality' referred to is not open to the independent witness of the receiver of the linguistic exchange or message. If I have never seen and can never see a tree I clearly have no means of knowing whether the mimetic effect is true or false. But nonetheless we do have socially acceptable and indeed accepted tests for deciding adequately whether say a news item adequately represents the truth it purports to represent. Moreover, news as a form would cease to exist if this were not the case. Once you reject in principle the possibility of language in particular, and symbol systems more generally, reflecting or accurately portraying a reality external to the symbol system itself, you are rapidly led to the position of a media theorist like Baudrillard, who argues that there is no longer any such thing as reality and thus we cannot say that the Gulf War really took place. We are faced here, of course, with a more general epistemological point that applies to all truth claims, whether in physics or sociology. The socially established rules for the social acceptance of the warrant to truthfulness will be different in each sub-field, or 'game' if one chooses to use that vocabulary, but in social evolutionary terms the game will only continue to be played, in cases where such a warrant is important, so long as it continues to work, just as scientific theories can be said to be true so long as planes continue to fly and radio transmitters to send messages. Thus languages can and do work mimetically so long as it is socially necessary for them so to do. Thus reflection and social construction theories of language are not mutually incompatible, as Hall and others seem to think, since adequate mimesis is itself created by and grounded in social practice.

The same can be said of intentionality. Here we need to distinguish two issues. There are two grounds for the attack on intentionality. On the one hand the failure of intentionality is seen as stemming from the source of the discourse, on the other it is sought in the nature of discourse itself and its undetermined relation to both what it represents and how it is interpreted.

If discourses are socially constructed does that mean that they speak their subjects and that thus there is no room for authorial intentionality? Is our phenomenological experience of intentionality merely an illusion, since what we can think and say is in a strong sense predetermined by the discursive order, or what Foucault called a regime of truth, in which we find ourselves? Thus is it society that speaks through us, not a founding Cartesian *cogito* which speaks using language as a tool? Is the failure of intentionality located at the source of the utterance? This is of absolutely central importance because Kant, and thus the whole theoretical and political tradition that stems from him, based the very idea of autonomous reason, defined as purposive rationality, or the margin, however small, for the exercise of free will, and thus of emancipation, upon the grounding phenomenological experience of intentionality within self-consciousness itself (see Bowie 1990).

Thus our view of the nature and possible reach of intentionality will rest in part on our theory of the nature of the individual subject—a problem encapsulated in the term identity. Thus a different attack on intentionality arises from an attack on the coherent subject as a source of discourse, rather than as continually formed and reformed in and between discourses. I would want to argue that any theory of human agency which wishes to avoid total determinism must retain a space for intentionality, that there is a subject, sufficiently stable through time and internally unified, to serve as the foundation for a relatively conscious relation with both the world and discourse, and thus able to form discourse with the intention of (a) conveying one meaning rather than another, and (b) having a specific effect as a result of that discourse. And as with mimesis, the existence and success of intentionality are demonstrated in practice. This does not mean that all discourse is intentional or that all intentions are realized. It does mean that when language, or other discursive forms, is used intentionally that intention is realized sufficiently frequently to socially confirm the possibility of intentional communication. Indeed if that were not the case it would once again be difficult to explain how intelligent agents sustain socially collaborative actions at all. It would certainly be difficult to explain why those who control or work in the media do what they do rather than something else. It would be impossible to criticize their actions, there being no responsibility without intentionality.

On the other hand the failure, the impossibility, of intentionality can be located in the necessarily ambiguous, incomplete, constantly slipping relationship between language and meaning such that what we can variously think of as reception, decoding, or interpretation is radically arbitrary. Whatever meaning we intend to convey is inevitably so garbled in transmission that it bears little or no relation to the meaning actually conveyed.

Again no mediating system is perfectly transparent. That is clear. It is also clear that any discourse we employ is a constant social process in construction. We are indeed born into pre-existing cultural traditions, conceptual schema, and so on. As in other realms we construct our discourse, but not in conditions of our own making. However, those conventions are resources out of which we construct the infinite variability of *paroles*. This has two implications. First, the structure does not determine the individual specificity of each utterance, and the adequacy of the relation between intended meaning transmitted and meaning actually received is constantly tested and adjusted within the process of linguistic communication itself such that two humans can agree that they share, if not absolutely, at least adequately, a meaning, although this agreement is always provisional since the meaning is always open to revision in the light of further utterances. Second, each use of a language has the potential to change the conventions themselves. Indeed that is what many theorists would argue is one of the functions and effects of the 'artistic' use of language.

Far be it from me to exaggerate the role of individual intentionality in the creation and circulation of meaning in society. But we should note in passing that it is difficult to reconcile an emancipatory theory of difference with such a socially determinist position and that post-modern cultural theory attempts to combine two incompatibles—a reflection theory of identity such that identity and thus intentionality is never formed or fixed within the endless mirror process of signifiers, and a theory of vitalism drawn from Schopenhauer via Nietzsche, whereby it is Dionysian nature, and the will to power that it excretes, that drives and explains human identity as projection, a drive that can never be captured or corralled within language or indeed conceptual thought.

This debate is important because it is upon the ground of these theories of culture and language that contemporary theory of a post-modern type mounts its challenge. Questions of evaluative judgement in relation to either the truth, justice, or beauty of symbolic forms are all rendered non-questions with a wave of the post-modernist wand. In particular the linguistic and cultural turn taken by structuralist and post-structuralist social theory has posed a relativist challenge to evaluation which now lies at the heart of debates about the social function and the power effects of the symbolic.

Evaluation and Function

The attempt to distinguish between good, bad and indifferent work in specific practices is, when made in full seriousness and without the presumption of privileged classes and habits, an indispensable element of the central process of conscious human production (Raymond Williams, quoted in Hoggart 1995: 83)

In the dominant intellectual, political, and cultural climate views such as those of Williams are deeply unfashionable, as is the conviction he expressed in *The Long Revolution* and held throughout his life that inherited artistic traditions, what are sometimes referred to, usually now derogatorily, as the canon or heritage, were repositories of human wisdom which we ignored at our peril. The works could not be simply dismissed on the grounds that they were the ideological product of a dominant class or gender or race, nor could their appreciation be dismissed as necessarily elitist, patriarchal, or ethnocentric. Indeed Williams's effort throughout his career was to widen rather than to narrow the range of work to be evaluated and the social access to that work and that evaluative process.

This chapter is, therefore, centrally about the problem of aesthetic evaluation. It focuses on the question of whether we can make evaluative judgements of media content which are more than the expression of our personal taste. In the current relativist and individualist intellectual climate there is widespread discomfort with such evaluative judgement whether as to truth and falsity, right and wrong, or beauty and ugliness. The question we face, following the cultural and post-modern turn in the social and human sciences, is whether these judgements can be anything other than the determined and historically constructed expression of a social position or of a distinct way of life.

In practice the exercise of evaluative judgement is unavoidable. We make such judgements every day within the various roles we fulfil. Cultural consumers make judgements between symbolic forms as the basis of their present and future choices. Producers make judgements as they are faced with the choices involved in deciding what to make and how to make it. Policy-makers, politicians, and citizens make judgements in their assessment of the performance of media institutions. Academics make judgements when deciding what books to recommend to students. Students make judgements when deciding what, where, and with whom to study. The question, therefore, is not whether we should or do make such evaluative judgements, but the criteria against which such judgements are made and validated. When we say of a television programme, a piece of music, a book, or a painting that it is good or bad, or better or worse than another example, what do we mean, and to what extent can such criteria and such judgements have force for anyone but ourselves? Above all at present this question is raised in terms of the relative value of so-called high as opposed to popular culture, in terms of the supposed elitism involved in intellectuals passing any critical judgement on the cultural tastes or activities of anyone else and in terms of the ethnocentrism of cross-cultural evaluations. It finds expression in differing approaches to media, cultural, and educational policy. For instance, this issue of cultural value judgements has been central to debates in the United States about political correctness and the content of the curriculum. It is also the ground for the debate over the legitimacy and future development of media and cultural studies within British higher education, where politicians, journalists, and their allies in academia, many of whom should and probably do know better, argue that the novels of Jane Austen are a proper object of university study while soap operas are not.

All evaluation rests upon a prior definition of function. How well we judge something is being done depends upon what we think is being done. To judge a novel against the same standards of truth or falsity as a news story or to apply the same standards of ethical judgement to an action and to a statement about an action is to commit what philosophers would call a category error. It is thus a mistake to look for a single function, whether we call it art or communication, or a single standard of evaluation. Different forms of communication may have been endowed with different human intentions or have different functions, whether intentional or not. For instance they may be designed to tell others about a state of the world, to convey a truth. They may be designed instrumentally—to achieve a given action at a distance—an order or instruction. They may be designed to create and/or reinforce a group identity, i.e. their function may be primarily phatic. They may be designed and used for self-expression—to convey inner truth but at the same time to help people understand by projection who they are. They may be designed for pleasure. In each case the ways in which they work and judgements about how well or badly they work will be different. For instance, just because messages/symbolic forms may be distributed on the same media system—by broadcast television for instance—does not mean that they have the same function and should be judged by the same standards. From this perspective genre plays an important role in the evaluative process; news is not the same as drama, education is not the same as entertainment. Evaluative arguments are often in fact questions of genre confusion. Should docu-soaps be judged, and are they in fact judged by their audience, by the truth standards of documentaries or the dramatic and narrative standards of dramatic fiction? Do newspapers fulfil a primarily political or entertainment function? Arguments over tabloidization or 'dumbing down' revolve around this definitional issue.

In relation to all these possible types of evaluative judgement two further questions are raised. First, to what extent are these judgements socially constructed; i.e. can we explain either the similarity or variance between such judgements in terms of other social factors such as class, and if so does that in fact mean that evaluative judgements are merely the expression of, or *post hoc* rationalization of, a given pattern of cultural consumption and the pleasures or other benefits to be derived from them? This is the sociological version of *de gustibus non disputandum est*. Second, are evaluative judgements, and any attempt to justify them as anything more than personal taste, really expressions of social interest and exercises of what Bourdieu calls symbolic violence, i.e. the mobilization of evaluative power within a wider hegemonic struggle between social interest groups? Here a crucial issue, as we saw in Chapter 5, has been whether the kind of exercise in which I am engaged in this chapter, indeed in this book, can be more generally socially and philosophically legitimated or is merely the attempt of an intellectual to exploit and at the same time reinforce the advantages to be gained from his membership of a social group possessing high levels of cultural capital and the power to impose their evaluations on others.

The Sociology of Art

The roots of the contemporary sociological, social constructivist approach to art and its critique of evaluation can be traced back to Hegel's critique of what he saw as Kant's excessively individualist and asocial conception of the judging subject. This led Hegel to stress sociability at the expense of the unsocial, and to focus on the problem of what he called *Sittlichkeit*, that set of social norms or customs that made, he argued, the social possible. The problem within Hegelian praxis theory, from the point of view of the problem that Hegel took over from Kant of creating a viable human community out of rational reflexive subjects, was that the forms of creative projection and objectification that praxis philosophy posited could not be guaranteed to produce social unity. It is for this reason that some have seen Hegel's later thought as increasingly socially conservative. In response to this problem he stressed the ways in which general structures of thought and their objectification in symbolic and institutional forms expressed and therefore at the same time created greater social rationality, or rather the concordance of the social with the rational. Within this line of thought Hegel saw art as the new religion, or as it became more generally known within this philosophical tradition, 'the new mythology'. There is not space here to go into the complex debate within the philosophical discourse of modernity about the need or possibility of creating a new mythology or a new religion as the necessary medium of social bonding out of the shards of a destroyed doxa and the principled refusal of dogmatic theology; its relation to an analysis of the art and mythology of classical Greece and the resulting mobilization, most famously in the work of Nietzsche, of the contrast between Dionysus and Apollo. This has been well done by Bowie and Hawthorn among others, and is the subject for a thesis in its own right. Suffice it to say here that the arguments that postmodernists think so novel go back to the very beginning of modern Enlightenment thought, and the problems it raises are genuinely difficult both philosophically and sociologically and cannot be resolved by the fiat of excoriating the 'subjectification of Being' or logocentrism, as so many contemporary cultural theorists seem to think. What can be said is that it reveals a complex relation to the question of tradition and its value and that, although in the end Hegel proclaimed the death of art in the face of the superior power of philosophy, his aesthetics was the foundation and remains the fount of all sociologies of art. In its historical development his

149

theory of art as an expression of society and its development was combined first with Herder's theorization of culture, and in particular the symbolic form of language, as the expression of a distinct people or *Volk* and its way of life, and then with Durkheim's development of Kant's notion of a priori categories of thought, as the necessary basis for thinking as such, into a concept of the a priori categories as the symbolic expression of pre-existing social bonds transmitted not explicitly but via ritual reinforcement. Here the conscience collective that ensures social co-ordination and the reproducibility of a viable social whole is not the product of purposive interaction, nor is it a reflective construct of either pure or practical reason. It is the projection of the social structure itself. From such a perspective all value judgements are internal to the categories of thought of a given culture or society and cannot therefore be criticized either from within or from without. Truth and falsehood or any question of the variable relation between symbolic forms and the structures of social power within the society are by definition ruled out of court. They cannot be thought within this paradigm. This is the problem and the paradigm now underlying much that passes for cultural theory and is one warrant for the flight from evaluation. The tensions and difficulties, indeed in the end the insurmountable problems, that arise from trying to combine this position with an ideology critique derived from Marxism's development of Hegelian praxis theory, as in their various ways many postmodern theorists now try to do, by combining an apparent ideology critique of signifying practice or discourse in the service of power, while at the same time arguing from within a Durkheimian, Herderian theory of culture and conscience collective as socially determined and determining, is clear in the work of Bourdieu, perhaps the most heroic, intelligent, and theoretically aware attempt to combine the two traditions. It is these tensions and difficulties that are continually in play in the contemporary analysis and evaluation of the symbolic forms which the media produce and circulate.

Modernity and the Specialization of the Aesthetic Sphere

The questions that the analysis of symbolic forms still poses for us were handed down to us from the Enlightenment in two ways. First the process of modernization, as Weber and Cassirer argued, institutionally split off the world of art from other social practices as part of the general process of social specialization. Second, in parallel with this social development, Enlightenment philosophy, especially in the work of Kant, created aesthetics as a specific mode of cognition and evaluation. The social specialization was mirrored by epistemological specialization. Thus was created both the set of problems in sociology and aesthetics with which we have still to deal and at the same time the set of conceptual tools for thinking about those problems, including the very concepts of art and of aesthetics, with which, however uneasily as I will show, we now work. It is this double movement that, for the case of Britain, Williams examines in *Culture and Society* and *The Long Revolution*: 'The attempt to distinguish "art" from other, often closely related, practices is a quite extraordinarily important historical and social process. the attempt to distinguish "aesthetic" from other kinds of attention and response is, as a historical and social process, perhaps even more important' (Williams 1981: 126).

The process of specialization then in its turn created a specialist social group and associated institutions—artists, critics, galleries, museums, etc.—whose job and interest it was, as sociologists such as Becker (1982) and Bourdieu (1984, 1993, 1996) have analysed, to create the self-sustaining worlds of practices and values, and an associated public that Becker calls 'art worlds' and Bourdieu 'artistic fields'. This in its turn has led to the whole tradition of the sociology of art which attempts to explain the creation and evaluation of art in social and historical terms. It is this historicist and social constructivist tradition of sociology that has dominated recent thinking about the symbolic, and which continually calls into question the process of evaluation. The knowledge that this work has produced is real and valuable and its challenge to evaluation has to be faced. What, then, are its main propositions? Here I will take the work of Bourdieu as the type case, although by no means all sociologists of art would support all parts of his theory.

All sociology is a process of demystification, the unveiling of the 'truth' behind the taken for granted of everyday social existence. The historical sociology of art thus demystifies and in so doing tends to relativize evaluation on four grounds. First it shows how distinctions between realms of symbolic production, consumption, and their associated value regimes have been historically and socially created such that the evaluative distinctions that are widely used in our society and which underpin, in a taken-for-granted way, much evaluative debate, between art and science, between high art and popular art, between art and craft, between literature and other forms of writing, and so on, can be shown to vary historically and cross-culturally. It thus challenges the idea, central to a range of cultural evaluation, of the autonomy of the aesthetic, that there is a special realm of art which is the repository of either universal or superior human values against which various cultural and social practices can be judged. It is important to stress that this challenge can work both ways. It challenges the idea not just of the specificity and autonomy of art, but also of the specificity and autonomy of science and thus lays the ground for the post-modern challenge that all our relations with the world are in some sense aesthetic and our cognitions in some sense fictions.

Secondly it shows how within each specialized field the producers and consumers of art (or indeed science) are involved in the creation precisely of what Bourdieu calls fields, that is to say socially bounded sets of power relations which constitute interpretative communities and associated value regimes. The crucial point here is that these fields are historically and socially contingent and variable. Central here is the demonstration of the ways in which the division between High Art and Popular Culture, as both a division of publics and those producing for them and a division of value regimes, was created and of the role played in this division and these relative evaluations of the relation to the economic. It thus claims to show that criteria for evaluation are socially produced and socially variable and on that basis tends to argue that they are therefore arbitrary. That all one can say about an evaluation is that it is an evaluation appropriate to that value regime and that products, audiences, and valuations are produced by a mutually reinforcing process within the field. As I will try to show, this is not, in my view, a necessary consequence.

Third, it demonstrates the indubitable historical fact of shifting tastes even within such fields. It may also try and explain those shifts, whether in terms of the internal dynamics of the field through a constant struggle for distinction and thus a necessary and perpetual process of differentiation, or in terms of external social determinants.

Fourth, in some versions, of which Bourdieu's is the most notable example, it then goes on to argue that society itself can be seen as a field and a value regime within which the practice of evaluation works always and exclusively ideologically. The criteria for the relative evaluation of cultural products and the consumption practices of different classes, in particular in Bourdieu's case the aesthetic criteria stemming from Kant of high art as a repository of superior values, especially those of disinterestedness in respect of other social and economic interests and of separation from gross, immediate and short-term gratification and the pleasures of the flesh, work at the same time to reinforce the social inferiority of the dominated classes by condemning their cultural tastes and practices as the product of their lack of intelligence, sensibility, even moral worth, while at the same time defending the privileges of intellectuals as the monopolizers of these legitimate evaluations.

Now there is no question in my view that this general approach gives us real knowledge and that any defence of evaluative criteria as anything other than the expression of a contingent and arbitrary personal taste or the ideological expression of a social position and interest has to meet its challenge.

This can be done on the following grounds. The social constructivist approach tends to collapse art and its evaluation too easily into ideology in three ways. First, by allying itself with the structural linguistic approach, it neglects the mimetic function of symbolic forms and thus their evaluation on that basis. One function that art works may have is to tell us 'truths' about the world, even if those truths are carried in 'fictional' form. Thus we might want to defend an evaluation that criticized a work on the basis of the accuracy of its portrayal of some aspect or other of life. And this is true not just of overtly factual genres such as news or documentaries but of a narrative fiction which it may be perfectly appropriate to evaluate on the basis of the realism or lack of realism of its portrayal of either character, social milieu, patterns of motivation, plot outcomes, and so on. The crucial point is that we make such judgements all the time and the criteria are neither socially arbitrary nor purely internal to the interpretative community, unless that community is defined as all human beings. The claims are tested against evidence from outside the specific field of art. Indeed the continuing problem that the non-mimetic aspects of art have raised would not exist unless we could make and operationalize these distinctions.

Secondly, by focusing on shifting tastes and regimes of value it avoids the question of what makes types of symbolic form or cultural practice special and why humans invest time and effort in either their production or consumption. In describing the historical process of the specialization of spheres and shifts of taste, it does not explain why across this historical process humans have continued to produce a range of forms and genres, paintings, sculpture, drama, architectural styles, and so on, which have no obvious and immediate social purpose, but which persist across the historical and cultural record. As Hennion puts it in a discussion of Haskell's work on the shifting evaluation of classical sculpture, 'the stabilisation of objects is as difficult to explain as the variation in the categories of their appreciation' (1995: 254). Thus it may be that as to both practices and criteria of evaluation there is more constancy in the social and historical record than social constructivism allows for. There may be genres, objects, practices, and modes of evaluation that in Hume's words 'have survived all the caprices of mode and fashion, all the mistakes of ignorance and envy'.

Third, by seeing taste and its evaluation as both arbitrary and as the socially constructed outcome of symbolic struggle it fails to explain what motivates this process and thus neglects the crucial question of aesthetic pleasure. As we have seen, the culturalist approach sees all social life from the perspective of a struggle over meaning. In Bourdieu's case and those of his epigones, even those like Frow, who criticize him for his continuing attachment to class as the major organizing concept around which these struggles are waged, this is combined with a Weberian status competition position and a Durkheimian position whereby the struggle is not over specific meanings but over the systems of basic categories of thought which determine the distinctions which, in their turn, are mobilized to legitimate social stratification. In Bourdieu's case social location is determining in the sense that it is through the habitus that these categories are internalized in relation to dispositions and competencies which govern the ways in which these categories are operationalized. Now what such an approach does, and has to do by definition, is leave out of account any concrete specificity to social practices themselves, since they are only used as necessarily arbitrary differential social markers within the overall system of socially produced categories. Within such an analytical schema any practice is as good as any other for the ideological purpose of carrying the work of social classification and acting as a field for status competition. Thus it can explain how both practices, in the case under consideration art and evaluative schema, in this case Kantian aesthetics, are used, but not why they come into existence in the actual form they did in the first place, nor why these particular practices and schema of evaluation should be used rather than any others. Or rather in Bourdieu it is precisely because art has a completely arbitrary relation to 'reality' that it is so powerful in its ideological use. What none of this allows for is the apparent fact that people gain specific pleasures, or however you want to describe the use value of aesthetic consumption, of some sort or another from the aesthetic or from symbolic forms that are different from those they gain from other forms of social practice. The difficulty in fact of maintaining Bourdieu's sociological perspective on the arbitrariness of cultural distinctions is demonstrated in his own work, where an implicit, but quite strong and clear, positive evaluation of popular taste and a corresponding negative evaluation of bourgeois taste are continually invoked.

These possible objections to Bourdieu's position allow us to turn back to Kant in order to re-examine the arguments not just for the autonomy of art and of aesthetic judgement but for the positive social value of such autonomy.

Aesthetic Value

'The sociology of art has in some ways exceeded its own brief, in so far as it fails to account for the "aesthetic". Indeed the central theme of this book is the irreducibility of "aesthetic value" to social, political or ideological co-ordinates' (Wolff 1993: 11). As Wolff argues in her succinct and insightful analysis of the field, the sociology of art fails to explain 'why particular ideological texts should afford aesthetic gratification'. 'The critique of art as ideology seems to have resulted in the disappearance of art as anything but ideology and there are many reasons why this will not do' (1993: 23).

One way of resisting this reduction of the aesthetic to the social and of aesthetic judgements to the ideological is to return to the Kantian arguments for the autonomy of the aesthetic and for the positive political and moral evaluation of art as both a mode of cognition and a practice that stems from them. Kant's concern with the aesthetic stems from his concern with the imagination. (In the following section I am indebted to Bowie.) The problem was that human reason and moral consciousness was based upon the faculty of imagination. It was imagination which both created a preliminary ordering out of the chaos of the immediate impressions of the senses with which reason could then work and which created, as part of the intentionality upon which human moral being was based, worlds which did not yet exist. Thus imagination was the essential human faculty, but, as well as the possibility of moral intentionality and the projection of alternative future courses of action it also created the danger of misleading fantasy. The category of autonomous, 'disinterested' art was created to deal with this problem. Art was the exercise of the 'free' imagination. This had two opposed implications. On the one hand it was a mode of cognition that bridged the sensual and rational sides of humans. It was thus an activity within which one could gain access to, and thus express or produce knowledge of, those sides of self-consciousness that were both the basis for, and at the same time not accessible to, reason. On the other hand it was also an activity that enabled humans to escape from the constraints of the world of necessity and the interests derived from it and to embody alternative moral worlds within which the categorical imperative could be given free rein and happiness and virtue could be combined. As Schiller wrote, 'Only the communication of the beautiful unites society because it relates to what is common to them all' (quoted in Bowie 1990: 13).

From this position there then developed two different theories of the value of the autonomy of art. The first, via German Romanticism, argued for the value of art on the grounds of its resistance to rationality and thus as a refuge against the disenchanting effects of the Dialectic of Enlightenment. Stressing the relation between aesthetic pleasure and the sensual, art was seen as an expression of the particular rather than the universal of scientific thought and as an expression of the endless uncontrollable creative plurality of life forms. That strand of thought then developed into the vitalism of Nietzsche's will to power, whereby all human activity should be judged by aesthetic standards.

On the other hand, when combined with Hegel's praxis, projection theory of the formation of human subjectivity, and the search for a new mythology, art was seen as a realm of moral education and as a realm within which the possibilities of social emancipation could be experienced and thus held open, if only as a utopian possibility. Hegel argued that human subjects came to know themselves and the natural and social world through purposive interaction with those worlds—the process that came, within Marx's development of Hegel's thought, to be known as labour. Within this theory of praxis symbolic forms are seen as an objectification and projection of this interaction between subjects and the worlds of nature and of other humans, an interaction within which individuals and societies came to know themselves by creating themselves and a necessarily shared social reality. This is a view that informs, for instance, the aesthetic analysis of Lukács. For our purposes such a theory was then linked to theories of social interest and struggle to develop within the Marxist tradition a theory of ideology based upon the alienation of labour, such that humans could no longer recognize themselves and therefore their interests in the symbolic objectifications they produced. This then developed into a theory of art, most notably with the Frankfurt School and especially Adorno, which combined the praxis approach with the resistance to disenchantment and instrumental rationality of Romanticism. The Frankfurt School argued that the value of true art lay in its unalienated conditions of production, and therefore in its possibilities as a true and non-reified and utopian objectification of human possibility. It developed a critique of the culture industry and its products as ideological because producing alienated art and shaping, through these objectifications, alienated humans unaware of their own best possibilities. The point I would wish to stress here is that it is beside the point to criticize this approach, as is now orthodox in cultural and media theory, as elitist. It is a critique based upon a theory of commodity fetishism and simply has nothing to do, one way or the other, with elitism and the class basis of art. As Bowie has admirably analysed, it is a position which bases its arguments for the need for autonomous art on a historically grounded philosophical debate not about class, but about the nature of self-consciousness, a self-consciousness which must of necessity be the ground for autonomous rational action. Based upon Kant's analysis of the sublime as an expression of the Unsayable, or the truth of the sensual particularity of our experience of ourselves and nature which cannot be captured in the generalizing and abstracting moves of conceptual thought and its categories, and upon later

German idealist and Romantic developments out of it, it argues for the necessity of autonomous aesthetic production as refusing and resisting any ultimate collapse of the individual into the social, or the particular into the general, or the sensual into the rational, and thus dialectically keeps open the possibility, if only as a utopian hope, of a viable, non-dominative community of free, autonomous, rational persons. In spite of Bourdieu's attempts to reduce this whole tradition of aesthetic thought to the status of ideology, the case it makes for the role of art and of aesthetic pleasure as not reducible to the ideological, and of their specificity and autonomy as not the veil for power, but carriers of the combined emancipatory possibilities of both happiness (identity formation) and virtue (a morally acceptable social world), needs to be taken seriously.

It is this general position, which underpins an ethical approach to the validation of symbolic forms, to which I now turn.

Art as Moral Education

Such an approach has close affinities with another deeply unfashionable approach to the evaluation of symbolic forms as sites of moral education. Kant had written of art 'as the visible expression of moral ideas' and Hegel that man (*sic*) 'enjoys in the shape of things an external realisation of himself'. Such an approach derives initially from the Greeks, but was expressed most forcefully in the modern era by Schiller, who argued that works of art provided a site for human play. His notion of play was deeply serious. What he meant was that the very separation of art from life, but at the same time its ability to produce lifelike fictions, enabled humans to use art as a means of working out life experiments. 'Art arouses a middle disposition, in which our nature is constrained neither physically nor morally and yet is active both ways' (quoted in Habermas 1987: 48). 'In the middle of the awful realm of powers and of the sacred realm of laws, the aesthetic creative impulse is building unawares a third joyous realm of play and of appearance, in which it releases man from all the shackles of circumstance and frees him from everything that may be called constraint, whether physical or moral' (quoted in Habermas 1987: 137–8).

Such a view of art links of course to an interactionist, pragmatist view of the formation of human and social identity, of life as a project whereby we only come to know the nature both of ourselves and of external reality when it is externalized, objectified, and reflected back to us in action. For Schiller, and those who think like him, the symbolic constructions that we have come to call art are a special privileged form of the general human process of externalization and objectification precisely because, as Kant argued, they have no purpose. Because moral action is not directly at stake we can afford to take experimental risks that would be unacceptable in 'real life'. We find a similar view expressed in Ang's analysis of the audience for *Dallas*, where she argues: 'producing and consuming fantasies allows for a play with reality, which can be felt as "liberating" because it is fictional, not real. In the play of fantasy we can adopt positions and "try out" those positions, without having to worry about their reality value' (Ang 1985: 130). We can find a similar argument for a concept of quality in television in Mepham (1990), where he argues that it is the duty of television to supply narratives which can help us live our lives, a matter ultimately of ethical rather than aesthetic concern. This view of the value of literature and the need to make discriminatory literary judgements also underpins Leavis's whole critical effort. The most sophisticated recent formulation of this position is that of Nussbaum in *Love's Knowledge* (1990). Here from a neo-Aristotelian position which wishes to put forward the superiority of Aristotelian practical reasoning over Kantian categorical moral impera- tives within ethics, she argues, using a selection of novels as exemplars, that novels provide us with privileged examples of practical moral reasoning the experience of which improves, or at least gives us the resources to im- prove, our moral reasoning. Again this seems to me a position that we need to take seriously and not just dismiss out of hand from a sociological or de- constructionist position.

Philosophical Anthropology of Art

We need also to remain open to another approach to the problem of aesthetic value and its universality, that of a philosophical anthropology of art. A discursive approach to common cultural standards does not, in short, rule out the possibility that certain aesthetic functions and the standards we therefore apply to judging them relate to common universal human attributes and problems. Current trends which stress the arbitrary nature of the discursive, and a cultural relativism based upon it, are left with either an excessive individualism of taste as the only standard of judgement or with a dogmatic social constructivism which, in its retreat from materialism, makes human nature and human life excessively mal- leable and rules out a priori any explanation of cultural practices or aes- thetic judgements in terms of human nature or the relatively unchanging characteristics of the human condition. Ironically that school of post- modern thought which stresses the autonomy of consumption and the centrality of pleasure in the experience of cultural forms uses a model of the consuming, pleasure-seeking individual which bears remarkable similarities to the utility-maximizer familiar to Utilitarian and neo-classical economic thought. In such a view all pleasures are equal and they are exogenous to the process of consumption itself. But in considering whether aesthetic functions and their related standards are or are not potentially or actually universal we need to take seriously that strand of aesthetic argument which relates aesthetic pleasures and judges aesthetic forms in terms of an appeal to basic human nature and a response to certain cross-cultural human needs. As Williams has put it in his characteristically gnomic style, 'I say it is wholly necessary to reject the notion of aesthetics as the special province of a certain kind of response, but we cannot rule out the possibility of discovering certain permanent configurations of a theoretical kind which answer to it' (Williams 1979: 325).

What does he mean by this? As he makes clear in *Politics and Letters*, he was very influenced by the materialist Marxism of Timpanaro who, in a wide-ranging critique of structuralist Marxism and the Saussurean language theory upon which it was based, argued that

the task is to construct a 'theory of needs' which is not reduced to a compromise between Marx and Freud, but which confronts on a wider basis the problem of the relation between nature and society. The accusation of 'biologism' or 'vulgar materialism' is, at this point, obvious and foreseen . . . If what is meant is the denial of the conditioning which nature continues to exercise on man; relegation of the biological character of man to a kind of prehistoric prologue to humanity; refusal to acknowledge the relevance which certain biological data have in relation to the demand for *happiness* (a demand which remains fundamental to the struggle for communism); then these pages are deliberately 'vulgar materialist'.

He went on to cite as constant dimensions of human experience 'the sexual instinct, the debility produced by age (with its psychological repercussions), the fear of one's own death and sorrow at the death of others' (Timpanaro 1975: 10, quoted in Wolff 1993: 96). As Wolff puts it, 'he does not claim that these are eternal, or that they have any metaphysical or meta-historical status, but that they are long-lasting, and have much greater stability than historical or social institutions' (1993: 97). It is to these constants founded in biology that Williams points in the phrase 'permanent configurations'. As he wrote in *Politic and Letters*, 'there is a very deep material bond between language and body, which communication theories that concentrate on the passing of messages and information typically miss: many poems, many kinds of writing, indeed a lot of everyday speech, communicate what is in effect a life rhythm' (Williams 1979: 340).

Peter Fuller, another critic influenced by both Timpanaro and Williams, when criticizing what he saw as John Berger's excessively ideological interpretation of painting, related the 'specificities of painting' to the 'reality constant underlying the human condition', and argued that

> the aesthetic constitutes a historically specific structuring of relatively constant, or long-lasting elements of affective experience . . . the material basis of the 'spirituality' of works of art is not so easily dissolved. I think that it may lie in their capacity to be expressive of 'relative constants' of psycho-biological experience, which, however they may be structured culturally, have roots below the ideological level. (Fuller 1980: 29–30, quoted in Wolff 1993: 99)

Such an approach draws on Kant's conception of the beautiful as a perception of the harmonious relationship between human imaginative judgement and the rhythms and structures of nature, and of the sublime as an access to a level of human reality beyond the grasp of the rational mind. Such an approach can be applied to the forms of art—to rhythm, proportion, colour, and so on—and can be found in the aesthetic philosophy, for instance, of Suzanne Langer, who argues that our pleasure in music relates to the way it expresses our relation to the rhythms of our own bodies. Or it can be applied to a judgement of art as a vehicle for the universal sharing of human emotional truths and to an evaluation based on the sincerity and depth with which those emotional realities are handled and the extent to which—the cathartic theory of art—it helps us to handle the inescapable constraints of human life by objectifying them.

As Marcuse argued in his later work, 'by virtue of its transhistorical, universal truths, art appeals to a consciousness which is not only that of a particular class, but that of human beings as "species beings", developing all their life-enhancing faculties' (1978: 29).

The accuracy and validity of such judgements have to be tested in the public sphere of criticism, but it does open up the possibility for both cross-cultural and cross-temporal aesthetic pleasures and judgements which are more than the expression of an individual taste, whether socially and culturally constructed or not. The pleasures may be formal, such that one can experience not just the formal pleasures of a Christian cathedral, an Islamic mosque, or a Japanese Zen Buddhist temple garden, but also, even as an atheist, the different ways in which the formal means create a certain contemplative attitude as part of a universally available human cultural experience, or they may be emotional and cognitive and relate to the sharing of common human dilemmas and experiences. Both possibilities point to a canon which has survived, not just the atrophy of time, which may be accidental in its effects, but the test of the experience of the life world over a period of time and under differing social conditions. From this perspective culture, and the surviving artefacts and texts that are its product, can justifiably be thought of as a human learning resource as, in Arnold's famous phrase, 'the best that has been thought and said', a re-source whatever its original social source—whether temple, court, bour-geoisie, or popular carnival—that is potentially open to all human kind. The social challenge then is as part of the construction of a common cul-ture to ensure that potential access becomes actual—that cultural capital in that sense is equally distributed. Here clearly education is a large part of the answer, but other media also bear a heavy responsibility. In short, we should not allow a misplaced cultural relativism with its rejection of value and an ideological suspicion of the ways in which elites mobilize high cul-ture to their own social advantage to block out a priori the possibilities of a true cultural democracy and the opportunities for learning and the sat-isfaction of aesthetic needs that wider access to the world's artistic heritage offers.

Evaluation, the Interpretative Community, and the Public Sphere

Judgements of value and truth are relative to a social position of enunciation and to a set of conditions of enunciation . . . 'Better' and 'worse' will be meaningful terms to the extent that a framework of valuation is agreed, and that the authority of speakers is accepted, at least provisionally within it. (Frow 1995: 153)

Whether this is true, or rather the wider implications of it being true, depends on how we define 'social' and 'conditions' and on where we draw the boundaries of the valuing community or value regime within which the framework is to be agreed and the authority accepted. The tendency is to draw them narrowly, and indeed in Frow's case to adopt a very class-determinist stance on the question of social position, and the perspecti-valism that is derived from it. Thus for Frow by definition the people or the popular is an opaque Other to the intellectual. This creates for Frow what is a totally false and politically damaging dilemma:

The central aporia that I see for cultural studies in confronting these questions of value, the impossibility either of espousing, in any simple way, the norms of high culture in so far as this represents that exercise of distinction which works to ex-clude those not possessed of cultural capital; or, on the other hand, of espousing, in any simple way, the norms of 'popular' culture to the extent that this involves, for the possessor of cultural capacity, a fantasy of otherness and a politically dubious will to speak on behalf of the Other. (Frow 1995: 158–9).

The great advantage of opposing a Kantian view to this perspectivalism is that it enables us to at least posit the human as the proper social position of enunciation—evaluations offered for confirmation within a *sensus communis* and thus based on the needs, aspirations, and potentialities of a common humanity—rather than denying it a priori; and to see the condition of enunciation as one of a public sphere within which valuations are confirmed, modified, or overturned within a general ethics of discourse, the authority of the valuation being that of the human community. None of this is to deny the barriers that access to cultural capital or the exercise of various forms of power can place on arriving at these shared valuations. But it is to offer an analysis that makes them remediable, if only as a hope of a common culture. It is also to deny that the norms of high and popular culture can be so easily contrasted. Indeed it is to deny that is the relevant distinction for these purposes.

It is central to my argument that, contrary to most contemporary cultural theory, we need to take seriously the possibility of standards that are more than merely the temporarily valid expression of either personal taste or a position of ideological power, but that such standards can only be revealed and validated within the wider discourse ethic that underlies this book's approach. That is to say, the movement of criticism and evaluation is never a 'this is so', but, as Leavis always claimed for literary criticism, a ' this is so isn't it?' such that standards of taste can be communally arrived at, as Kant argued they must be, within a *sensus communis*. This then poses the problem of standards within modern media in a different way.

Now the problem is created by the institutional structure of mass communication and the historically widened split both between creators and consumers and between the consumers themselves, such that the discourse space for creating standards, or for discovering what indeed those standards are, exists only in the weakest possible form. This returns us of course to the question of the relation of intellectuals to the emancipatory project, and in particular places media criticism at the heart of the problem of standards.

Thus the problem of the evaluation of symbolic forms is itself a part of the more general problem of creating viable communities for autonomous agents under the conditions of modernity. Modernity has had three possible effects on the interpretative community and thus on the possibility of common standards. First, it has broken the cultural doxa of tradition and by so doing called the universality or sharing of standards in to question; second, it has created within the social division of labour increasingly distinct social classes or status groups each with differential cultural resources and constituting themselves as distinct interpretative communities or class cultures—thus social stratification and judgements of taste became partially fused; third, it has widened the distance within most interpretative communities between producers and consumers (this has above all been the effect of the growth of the culture industries) thus both creating uncertainty as to function and evaluative standards and making the need for explicit evaluations as a guide to both production and consumption more necessary and at the same time more difficult.

It is this historical development that has produced the crisis of value and at least the plausibility of a historicist and social constructivist relativism. The question is whether this rules out all possibility of a common culture as a project for a viable community based upon the construction of a *sensus communis*.

We can agree with the historicist, social constructivist tradition that evaluative standards are created and applied within socially constructed interpretative communities. They depend upon a set of socially shared and legitimated practices and discourses within which that set of distinctions and related evaluations makes sense. It is this that the whole post-Herder tradition terms a culture or way of life. But this is not the end of the argument, only its beginning. For we then need to ask what are the boundaries of these interpretative communities and whether there can be communication between them such as to arrive at a common set of distinctions and evaluations. The problems with the broadly post-modern, perspectival, value-relative position is that it finds it difficult to demonstrate that the monadic communities or identities upon which its cultural relativism must be based have an actual empirical existence. Discursive regimes of value which, by their very nature, are open to argument, are confused with concrete communities of actors which by their very nature either exist or do not exist.

As Frith has usefully, perceptively, and cogently argued in respect to the high- and low-culture argument, what we find in fact is not distinct interpretative communities but a range of what he calls discourses of value which do not map onto socially distinct and concrete groups, practices, or types of symbolic forms. This leads him to three conclusions. First, that while we may sociologically be able to identify and explain a relationship between distinct social groups and distinct patterns of cultural consumption, distinguishing therefore an audience for opera from an audience for rock music, at the same time, contra Bourdieu, both sets of audiences are applying the same set of hierarchical value judgements to their chosen form. Second, that many of the relations between social distinction and aesthetic valuation that Bourdieu identifies as operating across society, and above all around the high art/popular art divide, actually operate within so-called taste publics, within the varying cultural practices and associated audience formations of popular culture itself. Third, that this distinction between discourses of value, cultural practices, and consuming publics enables one to continue to use standards of cultural evaluation across the board such that, for instance, in his case he, as I, would wish to defend cultural practices that extend human potential and hold out a utopian hope as against those that do not (Frith 1996). From this perspective the great failing of an approach like Frow's which, from its perspectival position, re-erects the distinction between high and low culture in terms of an insurmountable barrier between the enunciatory position and thus evaluative discourse of intellectuals and that of 'ordinary' people is, ironically given its discourse-based, broadly post-modern position, that it works with a very strongly determinist theory of social position. In effect the class position of intellectuals determines absolutely their evaluative position, and this evaluative position can have nothing in common with that of those from other social positions nor is it open to transitive modification in the light of a shared public sphere of argument over values. What Frith's argument does, I think, is move us from a position where aesthetic evaluations are necessarily ideological and where interpretative communities, however socially defined, are Leibnizian cultural monads, not merely resisting, but impervious to, external cultural influence and change, as a result of exchange with other interpretative communities and debate across value regimes, and towards a position where the problem of aesthetic value is no longer one of the power relations between incommensurable value regimes—whether read as resistance or domination—but of evaluation as a social learning experience and of the development of common values within a public sphere of critical debate. Towards the development of a common culture and a respect for those cultural differences, but only those cultural differences, that have been tested in comparison and debate with alternative interpretations and evaluations. Within such a process the media themselves are of crucial importance as the public sphere within which alone such a *sensus communis* can be created.

8 | The Media and Politics

It is clear that many of the questions asked about the media, both in general public debate carried by the media themselves, within Parliament and the wider political sphere and within the community of communication scholars, concern the political role of the media and the relationship between politics and the media. These range from a concern with immediate effects—did the *Sun* lose the 1992 election for Labour with its celebrated 'Turn the Lights Out' headline?—to the more systemic—have the rise of spin doctors and the sound bite led to a dumbing down of politics at the expense of issues and long-term coherent political policy, or, as Meyrowitz for instance argues in his influential book *No Sense of Place* (1985), have the electronic media led to an undermining of all authority figures including political leaders and policy experts? They also include the issue of the legitimate role of state regulation of the media. Should there be censorship, and if so in what forms? Should privacy be protected? To what extent should information be kept secret in the public interest? In these debates both the media, politicians, and interested citizens commonly mobilize arguments with a venerable heritage. Politicians mobilize arguments of the public interest and their elected, representative status to defend their interests against what they see, or at least represent as, the increasingly invasive and irresponsible media—a view famously summed up by Balfour's accusation that the press exercises the prerogative of the harlot down the ages, 'freedom without responsibility'. On the other side the media mobilize arguments for free speech and a free press to defend the pursuit of commercial objectives and what is often a wanton disregard for any public interest, and the exploitation of defenceless individuals for the public's vicarious delectation. Since the premises of these arguments remain in general unexamined—a supposed inheritance of 'our' enlightened democracy, and one which, in the United States, is given constitutional protection under the First Amendment and is thus defended against attack from anyone but lawyers working within a narrow legal tradition—this debate is in general a debate of the deaf.

In this chapter I will argue that the relationship between communication and democracy is indeed central, but that in the current debates it is not our ideas about the media that are at stake so much as our vision of democratic politics and of the position and role of politics in social life more generally. Indeed it is the very definition of the political that is at issue. The kinds of demands we make of the media as political institutions, and of journalists and others as political actors, and the kinds of critical questions we pose as to their current structure or performance, will depend upon our vision of politics. Thus any emancipatory theory of the media from a political perspective must not only be informed by but must be a part of political theory.

Politics and the Enlightenment

The systems and processes of social communication have always been integral to both the theory and practice of politics, the sphere in which the mode of coercion and the mode of persuasion coalesce. As we saw in Chapter 2, questions about the relationship of the mode of persuasion to the modes of coercion and production lie at the heart of attempts to understand the varying and evolving forms of human societies since the beginning of historical time and across the range of the anthropological record. But these questions have taken on a specific importance under conditions of modernity where, with increasing differentiation of social spheres and roles and generalized reflexivity concerning norms and roles, the task of social co-ordination is necessarily increasingly borne by the mode of persuasion and takes on a discursive form.

A vision of democratic politics as the ultimate exercise of practical reason has been integral to the Enlightenment's emancipatory project from its origins. Alongside freedom from natural necessity and freedom from religious dogma was sought freedom from the coercive rule of others. In particular absolutism was the political enemy. On the other hand politics was the realm where the inherent tension in Enlightenment thought between individual personal autonomy on the one hand and rational and transparent forms of necessary social co-ordination on the other had to be thought through and fought out. As we shall see, that battle still continues and is at the heart of debates about the media and politics.

This debate takes place both within Enlightenment thought itself and between Enlightenment and counter-Enlightenment thought. Within Enlightenment thought there is both an idealist, hyper-rationalist, and a critical realist strand. It is the former which has been criticized, with much justice, by post-modernists and communitarians. But what has been neglected is the source of Enlightenment thought in doubt, critique, and thus in the limits of reason. In a tradition going back to the Stoics, this strand in Enlightenment thought—as in Kant—confronts the limits of politics and does not ask too much of it. In contrast much post-modernist critique stemming from Haman, Herder, and Nietzsche, by extending the realm of aesthetics to cover all of social life and its judgement, including politics, gives to politics too extensive a realm. With its roots in a supposed community, or *Volk*, politics covers everything, but it is now a total, non-transparent politics, impervious to argument.

Politics and Media Studies

From its very origins in the analysis of *Publizistik* by Weber, media studies has been concerned with the role of the media in modern politics. The problem presented by the rise of the modern, capitalist democratic state in the nineteenth century was how to ensure or create popular consent to the development of necessarily increasingly complex, and thus not immediately transparent, processes of social co-ordination under the control of specialist experts.

We can then identify two approaches to this problem. It is these antagonistic approaches that have dominated the study of the media and politics. One was essentially pessimistic. It argued, for instance classically in the case of Walter Lippman, that the gulf between the people and the expert could never be bridged and that modern democratic politics under the influence of the media would become increasingly irrational, charismatic, and possibly plebiscitory. This tradition then developed in one direction within mass society theory by merging with a Marxist critique of dominant ideology. Within this tradition the institutions of so-called bourgeois democracy are seen as a sham—the state is either the executive committee of the ruling class or of an elite of experts—and the question is why the people continue to accept this rule as legitimate. The answer is because of the ideology largely propagated by the media.

It is not my purpose here to examine the more general role of ideology critique in media studies. But it is important to note two major problems with this tradition of thought. First it is based upon an assumption that ideology and political conflict only arise from conflicts of material interest and that therefore, once those conflicts are resolved, politics will become in effect redundant. This is, in its turn, based upon the productivist core of Marxist theory which assumes that social conflict is caused by a material scarcity which the immense productive capacity of the industrial system has abolished, or will shortly abolish. This position is rightly in my view subject to Isaiah Berlin's critique based on the irreducible incompatibility of values (Berlin 1979, 1990; see also Gray 1995b). The second problem, which links it to the more widespread cynical anarchist strand in post-modernist thought stemming from Nietzsche, is that this Marxist position is based on the centrality of the concept of alienation, and thus an inherent suspicion of forms of intermediation (including those of representative politics) and of the necessary fragmentation and specialization of modern life. This position is famously caught by Marx's own brief vision of the communist future, where we will 'hunt in the morning, fish in the after-noon, rear cattle in the evening, criticise after dinner' (Marx 1963). Such a vision has no room for any institution of politics except direct democracy, and simply has no tools with which to think through either the scale prob-lems or information-flow problems of this position. It can only make everything political by denying politics and the necessary limits, choices, and compromises this involves. Its danger, as of course is well attested, is to allow the socially necessary levels of large-scale co-ordination to become systems of unaccountable administration.

The second liberal-pluralist approach was optimistic. In opposition to both Marxism and mass society theory it saw capitalist development as broadly positive for democracy within a general whiggish view of histori-cal progress. Drawing on the Lockian strand in Enlightenment political theory it took for granted the liberal, rights-based model of politics, par-ticularly as institutionalized and operationalized in the United States, as the *ne plus ultra* of democratic development. The media/politics problem was seen as one of the relations between media that were supposedly free because they were market-based and the institutions of representative party democracy. From this perspective politics was conceived as a strug-gle for influence, and the control over state power granted by election vic-tory, between a plurality of social interests. The media were and are then seen as the channels by which interest groups communicated within and between each other and as two-way channels of communication between politicians and those they represented, between government and people. Here the research questions were how voters were influenced, how politi-cal agendas were set, how well the media fulfilled their function of provid-ing relevant political information, and so on.

The Turn Against Marxism and Liberalism

But in recent years, both within political theory and in thinking about the media and their political role, we have witnessed a critique of both the Marxist and liberal traditions and a return to the central questions of En-lightenment political thought. This return has focused on concepts of the public sphere, civil society, citizenship, and identity. It has in particular pitted those, such as Habermas, who see the emancipatory project of the Enlightenment as unfinished business and wish, in a movement of immanent critique, to hold liberalism to its emancipatory ideals, against a range of communitarians and post-moderns who, in the name of various versions of identity politics, see liberal, rights-based political theories as inherently repressive and claim to have rumbled their emancipatory and universalizing tendencies (Gray 1995a; Rorty 1989).

The Public Sphere

It is easy, I think, to understand the attraction of the public sphere approach. It provided, against the background of the turn away from Marxism associated with the collapse of 'actual existing socialism', an alternative to theories of dominant ideology or hegemony as an explanation for the coincidence, within what used to be called 'bourgeois democracies', of growing social inequality and political apathy on the one hand with the relative stability and increasingly consensual, non-ideological nature of representative party politics on the other. Its emphasis on discursive practices and on communicative action as central to democratic practice and legitimation fitted well with the wider 'linguistic turn' in the human and social sciences and the associated growth of what Nancy Fraser has called the politics of recognition (Fraser 1992). At the same time its use of the spatial metaphor of the sphere, and its stress on the necessary institutional foundations for the realization of those citizen rights to free expression and debate central to democratic theory, addressed both the problems arising from the perceived empirical reality in the mature democracies of an increasingly media-saturated plebiscitory politics dominated by public relations, image manipulation, and political marketing (and the associated growth of both political cynicism and apathy) and the problem of constructing the institutions and practices of democracy at the level of both state and civil society in newly democratized countries with little or no historical traditions of democracy to call upon.

Drawing upon a Kantian heritage that links freedom to a personal autonomy grounded in the exercise of public reason, Habermas and his followers have stressed the role of the public sphere as a site within which the formation of public opinion, and the political will stemming from and legitimized by such opinion, is subject to the disciplines of a discourse, or communicative ethics, by which all views are subjected to the critical reasoning of others. At the same time a democratically legitimate public sphere requires that access to it is open to both all citizens and all views equally, provided only that all participants are governed by the search for general agreement. This general model is then applied as a normative test against which the performance of contemporary media, in terms of political effects and democratic potential, can be judged in terms of either the rationality of their discourse or in terms of the range of views or speakers accorded access.

This view of the public sphere has then been criticized on three main grounds. First, that its procedural rules are too rationalist—that the persuasive use of rhetoric can never, and indeed should never, be excluded from political communication—and that to impose such discursive norms in practice excludes from the public sphere as illegitimate not just a range of culturally specific discursive forms but also those who do not possess the cultural capital required to mobilize those discursive forms. Here we find the criticism that the model of procedural rationality being deployed is in fact a model of a certain intellectual practice and thus excludes, in a movement of symbolic violence, those who are not members of the social group who are the carriers of that practice, whether conceived as intellectuals or as the white male bourgeoisie, and that it leads to a privileging of certain genres of media, especially to an assumption that news and overt political coverage are 'serious' and thus to an evaluation of their absence as a sign of 'dumbing down' or 'refeudalization', at the expense of entertainment and its role in the formation of publics and as a site for the development of an understanding of issues of public importance or, à la Bakhtin, the carnivalesque subversion of imposed norms and hierarchies of significance. Secondly, the public sphere model of procedural rationality is criticized for drawing the distinction between public and private in such a way as to exclude both key groups of citizens, for example women, or key matters of potential public political concern, for example the regulation of domestic, intra-familial, or sexual relations. Thirdly, it is criticized on the grounds that it has valued general agreement around a set of universal values or norms, however rationally discursively arrived at, which, its critics argue, derive in turn from a liberal model of proceduralism, abstract individual rights, and ethical neutrality which prioritizes the just over the good and thus denies difference and thus the inevitability of perpetual normative conflict within modern societies. This in its turn, so critics argue, leads to an over-centralized model of *the* public sphere incompatible with the politics of identity in multicultural societies, whereas what is needed is a decentralized model of multiple public spheres expressive of each distinct collective identity, culture, or form of life.

In this chapter I wish to examine these issues through the optic of the distinction between public and private. It is clear that the use of the concept of the public sphere mobilizes this distinction, and critics of

Habermas's position and that of his followers have rightly pointed to the ways in which this distinction operates normatively as well as descriptively; to how the conceptualization of the boundary between public and private has shifted historically and to the ways in which the boundary has been mobilized to exclude both topics for debate and action and social actors from legitimate participation in the public realm. The key argument here is that we can only clarify what is at stake in these arguments—what it is that the protagonists are actually talking about—if we go behind this apparently simple distinction and begin to unpick the range of meanings, both descriptive and normative, that these terms mobilize, and the differing intellectual traditions, or strands of thought and associated problems, from which those different meanings are drawn.

In particular in current debates about the media the concepts of public, and private as its opposite, are mobilized in three ways. First around the concept of the public sphere within a general institutional debate about the practice of democratic politics in general. Second in a debate about the content and practice of the mass media which focuses on issues of privacy. Third in debates about media regulation which, in the face of technological convergence and the growth of the Internet, turn on the distinction between the rights and obligations attaching to public and private communication respectively. In each case two issues are at stake. Where to draw the boundary between the public and private, both generally and within specific spheres of social action, which in its turn depends upon the ways in which we choose to distinguish the public from the private. And what relative normative valuation to attach to each sphere—that is to say do we regard, for instance, the private as a sphere to be protected against the encroachment and domination of the public, or, on the contrary, do we regard the public as a sphere of superior shared social values to be fostered at the expense of selfish, corrupting private interests? Because both the boundaries and the relative evaluations are in fact mobilized both for intellectual analysis and political debate in shifting, confused, and often mutually contradictory ways it is necessary, I think, to unpack the roots of these distinctions and evaluations in order to clarify their entailments.

The debate on the validity and usefulness of the concept of the public sphere uses the distinction between public and private in two ways related to two distinct defining attributes of the public sphere—one epistemological and the other institutional. The public sphere is defined, for instance classically in the writings of Habermas, as being public in two senses; because the opinions, 'truths', or agreements arrived at within it have to be validated by publicly presented and challengeable arguments, and because the sphere is equally open to the access of all citizens. The reason that this distinction is important is because advocates of differing positions within the debate around the public sphere may place their emphasis on one or the other, and the two sets of values may be in conflict. Thus those who stress the discourse or communicative ethics side will stress the importance of public standards of argument—of a certain procedurally based form of rational rhetoric, but by so doing will, either implicitly or explicitly, exclude those who are not prepared to obey or are incapable of obeying those rhetorical rules. It is on this basis, for instance, that one form of feminist critique of the public sphere approach has been mounted on the grounds that the form of discourse defended as appropriate for public dispute and opinion formation is inherently masculine. Similarly debates over the evaluation of the political implications of talk shows, or over the so-called 'dumbing down' or tabloidization of news and political reporting in both newspapers and broadcasting, have in part turned on a difference between those who stress the populist and emotive nature of the discourse as dangerously anti-rational and thus anti-democratic on the one hand and, on the other, those who stress the democratically positive nature of the increased access of 'ordinary' people to arenas of public debate previously dominated by political and intellectual elites. It is easy to see how defenders of a discourse ethics approach can at a minimum be blind to the ways in which socially created cultural incapacities—such as those extensively analysed by Bourdieu—create barriers to full and effective access to the public sphere and maximally can lead to the elitist defence of rule by experts. On the other hand a stress on access can easily lead to the defence of demagogic populism and the view that the lowering of material or cultural barriers to access is *ipso facto* democratic—the kind of argument that is only too easily mobilized by the Murdochs of this world in defence of the *Sun* or Sky TV against the toffs, the chattering classes, the educated middle-class professionals running broadsheet newspapers or the BBC.

The debate over privacy in particular and media ethics more generally is now pervasive. It is in essence a debate about what subjects, in both senses of the word—persons and subjects of discussion—should be the legitimate object of media coverage and thus of public exposure or display. This issue has recently been raised by the moral panic surrounding the role of the paparazzi in the death of Princess Diana, and by so-called Zippergate in the United States, which has raised the issues of what areas of behaviour it is or is not appropriate to subject to the glare of 'publicity' and of the relationship between the President's 'private' sexual behaviour and the performance of his 'public' political duties. Similar issues are currently raised in the UK over the 'outing', that is to say the publication of the legal sexual preferences and behaviours of, gay politicians which they, for whatever reason, would prefer to keep 'private'. We can see played out here a more central drama of our times, namely the increasing stress on the personal and individual and on inter-personal relations as the supreme source of value on the one hand and the obsession with celebrity on the other—on both of which the media feed and the latter of which they are crucial in creating and sustaining. This was one of the paradoxes of the media discourse in the wake of Princess Diana's death. On the one hand there was the condemnation of the hounding paparazzi and the ecstatic praise for the personal, 'touchy-feely', 'feminine' values that Diana supposedly represented and expressed, in opposition to what were represented as the repressive, formal values of traditional public life and duty. On the other there was condemnation of the Royal Family for its failure to mourn in public for popular delectation, coupled with a more general claim to the socially therapeutic role of the public expression of private feelings.

Thus in the debate over privacy and media reporting we find on the one hand those defending privacy against media intrusion—including celebrities and 'public' figures such as politicians objecting to intrusions in their 'private' as opposed to their 'public' lives—on the other hand the media defending their behaviour as in the 'public' interest because it makes publicly available information necessary for the making of informed political judgements as to the suitability for public office of the individuals concerned. What is at issue here are two different distinctions between public and private. On the one hand there is the issue of whether in the case of a given individual private and public behaviour can or should be distinguished. On the other whether there is a range of subject-matter (or behaviour) which is appropriate or inappropriate for discussion and/or display in public. And in both cases whether morality is a public or private matter.

The third example of the mobilization of the public/private distinction to which I want to draw attention is the regulatory debate set in motion by so-called convergence and the development of the Internet mode of communication. To date two models of communication have underpinned regulation. On the one hand the traditional mass media of the press and broadcasting have been seen as media of public communication and thus as institutions straddling the private economic sphere and the public political sphere in a way that legitimized public policy intervention to ensure that these media fulfilled their public functions, functions ultimately underpinned by a liberal freedom of expression theory. To what extent this involved an intervention by the state in the private economic activities of corporations, and if so what forms of intervention, has been and remains a matter of continuous political debate. On the other hand telecommunication networks developed as carriers of private communication between individual private persons. While regulation of the network was considered legitimate, any regulation of the messages passing over the network was and is regarded as an illegitimate infringement of individual freedom, autonomy and privacy, as indeed an infringement of the right to free speech. Within the Internet environment these two traditions of thought now come into conflict because it is possible, for instance, to regard a website as either, because of the individual addressability and transactional nature of each communicative relation with the site, a site for a series of private individual transactions on the model of the market or, because of its general accessibility, as a site for public communication within the public sphere with associated rights and responsibilities for those who control and use it. Which view we take will make a difference to the normative evaluations of the activity and any resulting regulatory policy we might wish to advocate or impose.

This brings me to the complex ways in which the public/private distinction can be defined and then normatively mobilized. Let me start by very schematically laying out a set of binary distinctions which are, I think, in play across this field, each of which has a long history and deep roots, at least within Western post-Enlightenment thought. I want to argue that the difficulties and confusions of the debates in this area arise from the ways in which the use of the distinction public/private inescapably carries with it a range of cross-cutting and sometimes mutually contradictory evaluative distinctions derived from these underlying associated dichotomies. In each case the first term can be mapped, depending on the circumstances, onto the private and the second onto the public.

individual	social
family	society
economy	polity
civil society	state
life world	systems world
agent/action	structure
everyday life	structure/system/power
nature	culture
feelings	reason
freedom	power
arts	sciences
personal	political
negative freedom	positive freedom

The radically ambivalent nature of the public/private distinction and thus the need to specify very carefully in any specific case which value vector is being mobilized can be illustrated if we look at the ways in which the relative evaluation of public and private action can be reversed when they carry with them opposing distinctions between freedom and necessity. The classic liberal view of politics sees the private realm of negative freedom as positive and the public realm as a perhaps regretfully necessary negative constraint on that freedom and thus to be reduced to the minimum. The public is there to serve the superior interests of the private. The classic civic republican tradition, as most clearly represented in recent political philosophy by Hannah Arendt, sees the private domestic economy of the family as the realm of necessity and the public realm of the political as that of freedom within which alone humans can forge autonomous identities by making free choices.

I want to argue that uses of the terms public and private and the differential valuations applied to each by different commentators and in different situations register our deep unease over, and the conceptual difficulties that arise from, this set of distinctions. The result of the complex conceptual, cultural, and political history within which those distinctions were developed and used is that the same term can shift radically in its evaluative entailments both between users and situations.

Let me take an example from Habermas's work. Habermas operates, as is well known, with a distinction between life world—the realm of communicative rationality—and systems world—the realm of instrumental rationality. From this conceptual base the problem of the media and democracy is set up as one of bringing the systems world under the control of the life world by means of the use of communicative rationality in the public sphere. Conversely the problem of the decline of the public sphere—or rather the failure to realize the ideal potentials contained within the bourgeois public sphere for the democratization of modern life—is posed as a problem of the colonization of the life world by the systems world in a process that Habermas calls refeudalization. Habermas sees feudalism as a politics of public display whereby rule is based upon personal allegiance to the lord, who is in his person a displayed representative of the body politic and of the god of which this body politic is in its turn a representation. Thus feudal politics is both entirely private because personal and at the same time entirely public. Its public nature is well illustrated by the customs of the court at Versailles, where what we would now regard as the most private aspects of the sovereign's personal life, his daily toilet, took place in public and as public ceremony. The point here is twofold. First that, as Habermas himself argues following Hegel, the creation of what we now call public involved, and depended upon, the simultaneous creation of the private, an intimate sphere of personal, family life which was not only to be excluded from the public gaze and from the rules of public procedure and valuation, but was in the Habermas version, a necessary foundation for a new type of public person or citizen. 'The public's understanding of the public use of reason was guided specifically by such private experiences as grew out of the audience-oriented subjectivity of the conjugal family. Historically the latter was the source of privateness in the modern sense of a saturated and free interiority.' It is of course this version of the public/private divide that has been forcefully criticized by feminists and that is at stake in the slogan 'the personal is political'. Thus the move from feudalism to bourgeois modernity on this model involves a complex realignment of public and private or rather the creation of the distinction along a number of different dimensions. On the one hand the liberation from feudal rule involves a shift from private personal rule to rule by public, impersonal systems, in particular law. On the other hand, looked at through the civil society optic, it involves the development of private realms—not just of affective life, but also the market—free from the control of the ruler, who has now become a more abstract form of public authority—the state.

Given that, within the Habermasian model, the market is set up as a threat to the public sphere, the way in which the market/public sphere maps onto the public/private divide is of central importance. Central to the systems world that is supposedly colonizing the life world and thus destroying the space of the public sphere is the medium of money, a medium of social co-ordination and communication through which instrumental rationality operates. The public sphere is distinguished from the private sphere of the market on the grounds that, following Hegel, individuals pursue their private, competitive interests in the market, whereas in the public sphere their actions are oriented to reaching uncoerced agreement on the common good (or public interest). We similarly make a distinction between the private and public sectors within an economy—the one privately owned the other owned by the state on behalf of the general public or body of citizens. Two problems arise here. First that Adam Smith's classic defence of the market, from which our core ideas about the market in relation to politics still derive, was that it was public, as opposed to the private corporate monopolies of the mercantilist absolutist feudal state. It was public in two senses. It was open to everyone and anyone (in economists' jargon there were no barriers to entry) and, because of the price mechanism, its workings were transparent. Just as Milton argued against censorship on the grounds that only free competition of ideas could ensure the survival of truth, and as Kant argued, as we shall see, that Enlightenment depended upon the public rather than the private use of reason, so Smith argued that public competition between producers ensured optimization of material welfare and thus the pursuit of private interest is transformed into the public interest. So far we have been looking at the relation between the market and the public sphere in terms of a private interest/public interest distinction. But second, a crucial, and largely neglected, aspect of Smith's defence of the market as a public sphere also mobilizes the private/public distinction in terms of the beneficial effect on social behaviour of its public display. But before turning to this issue we need to examine the roots of the central importance given to a discourse ethic within theories of the public sphere and of the democratic political theory based upon it.

The Roots of Public Sphere Theory

We do admittedly say that, whereas a higher authority may deprive us of freedom of *speech* or of *writing*, it cannot deprive us of freedom of *thought*. But how much and how accurately would we *think* if we did not think so to speak, in community with others to whom we *communicate* our thoughts and who communicate their thoughts to us! We may therefore conclude that the same external constraints which deprive people of the freedom to *communicate* their thoughts in public also remove their freedom of *thought*, the one treasure which remains to us amidst all the burdens of civil life, and which alone offers us a means of overcoming all the evils of this condition. (Kant 1949)

The concept of the public sphere, and the related conceptual and normative distinctions between public and private, have been mobilized as normative concepts with which to pass judgement on the performance of the media from the perspective of the creation and maintenance of democracy. In making a judgement of its efficacy from this perspective and of the criticisms made of it we need to be clear about the problem which it addresses.

The problem of the relationship between communication and politics can be traced back to the Enlightenment and the basic paradox that modernity posed, the paradox of what Kant called the 'unsocial sociability' of human beings. We might think of this as the inherent tension between liberty and fraternity. If we take as granted the key characteristics of modernity as the development of ever more complex forms of social specialization associated with a separation between human identity formation and life chances on the one hand and ascribed roles on the other and with the death of tradition as a guide to social behaviour, then we are unavoidably faced by the task of constructing forms of social co-ordination, social bonds, whether seen as polities, communities, or societies, which are compatible with free individual subjects, in the sense of rational reflexive and autonomous beings whose identities and moralities must unavoidably be post-conventional. We do not need to concern ourselves, interesting as that is, with the historical roots of this shift out of traditional societies, nor indeed with its desirability or morality. It is simply the fate with which we are now faced and with which we have to deal.

In essence modern democracy is about how we handle the relationship between individual freedom and moral agency on the one hand and the necessary and unavoidable social norms and structures within which alone such freedom can be exercised on the other. As Rousseau put it in *The Social Contract*, 'the problem is to find a form of association . . . in which each, while uniting himself with all, may still obey himself alone, and remain as free as before. This is the fundamental problem of which the social contract provides the solution.'

Kant's answer was epistemological and placed what has become known as a discourse ethic centre-stage. Thus the key foundation of a democratic polity was the ability and duty to exercise public reason. Free citizens could not depend upon the mere ungrounded opinion of others. They had to think for themselves and subject their opinions to the discipline of public criticism. This argument then linked up with a tradition of political thought stemming from the community of saints and the need to discover the truth of God through the free public exchange of views derived from private faith and conscience to found the liberal social contract theory of democratic legitimacy, within which free expression, and thus tolerance, are the supreme political virtues, and to assert the supremacy of the right over the good. The crucial point is that upon this epistemological foundation is built a theory of the relation between communication and politics which builds a limited sphere for public action upon the prior existence of private, autonomous individual subjects whose individual rights it is the purpose of the public realm to equally protect, but whose autonomy, and therefore potential for freedom, is itself built on public discourse.

The alternative response to the paradox of modernity can also be derived from Rousseau. It stems from the stress that he laid on the centrality for the formation of human identity and the maintenance of social bonds of the human desire for recognition or the love or esteem of others. As Charles Taylor has argued, our modern politics of identity, whether individual or collective, and the problems and disputes surrounding it, stems from the attempt, following Rousseau, to make honour egalitarian. Drawing upon a tradition of civic republicanism the political realm was seen as the realm where the common values of the collective were expressed and where agonistically individual citizens competed for honour and respect—or in modern terminology recognition. This is why for Rousseau in the utopian republic all citizens would be permanently and perpetually on mutual show. If feudalism had been a theatre in which the ruler performed for a spectating public then in an egalitarian republic all citizens were at the same time actors and spectators for each other in a permanent social theatre (Taylor 1994).

This view was then developed by Hegel in his critique of Kant in two key directions. First by developing a theory of human subjectivity as essentially socially constructed in a process of reciprocal interaction and mutual recognition. Second by stressing the problem of what he called *Sittlichkeit*, namely the shared values upon which membership of any social collective not held together by mere force must be based and as that which motivated free individuals to belong to a given collectivity—to feel at home in it—such that they owed loyalty to it and then, in the ultimate test of citizenship, were prepared to subordinate their private interests to the public interest by being prepared to die for their country. From the perspective of public sphere theory this tradition prioritizes fraternity or solidarity. It is out of this tradition that the communitarian critique is mounted against what it sees as the abstract, rationalist, rights-based characteristics of discourse ethics and the public sphere. For these critics the problem of public discourse is one of constructing discourses which recognize cultural and individual diversity and which are capable of motivating and providing a sense of belonging, or *Heimat*, to human agents rather than of fostering critical self-development.

The political problem to which the public sphere tradition of analysis addresses itself is then two-sided, and many of the problems with current uses of the phrase 'public sphere', and criticisms of it, derive from a confusion about which of the two sides of the dilemma is being addressed.

The public sphere involves both questions of discourse and its relationship to the formation of human identities and to the motivation of action on the one hand, and questions of the institutional structures, forms of social relationship, and of the social effectivity of spheres of discourse and action we can call public on the other. In particular, differences between positions turn on the relative weight given within more general views of society, identity formation, and politics to discourse or action. Is then the purpose of the public sphere, and of politics more generally, to reach agreement and substitute persuasion for force as the dominant mode of social co-ordination? Or on the contrary is the public realm, in Arendt's words, 'where freedom can appear' because 'men act in concert'?

Let us start from the side of discourse. Central to Habermas's public sphere theory is a concept of communicative or discourse ethics, and a specific test of rationality applied to communicative interchange appropriate to the public sphere and legitimate as the foundation for public opinion and will formation. And a central criticism of this tradition from communitarians and post-modernists has been that it is based upon the no longer tenable rational subject of the Enlightenment, and also therefore upon the liberal rights model of politics with its supposed denial of differentiated life worlds and the inevitable irreducibility of the relativity of the values that stem from those life worlds.

It is clear that this strand in Habermas's thinking derives from Kant's concept of the relationship between the formation of autonomous individual subjects and the use of what Kant called public reason. As Onora O'Neil has shown in her important book *Constructions of Reason* (1989), Kant's very definition of reason is political. As O'Neil puts it, Kant

sees the problem of cognitive and political order arising in one and the same context. In either case we have plurality of agents or voices (perhaps potential agents or voices) and no transcendent or preestablished authority. Authority has in either case to be constructed. The problem is to discover whether there are any constraints on the mode of order (cognitive or political) that can be constituted. Such constraints (if they can be discovered) constitute respectively the principles of reason and of justice. Reason and justice are two aspects to the solution of the problems that arise when an uncoordinated plurality of agents is to share a possible world. (O'Neil 1989: 16)

It is crucial to stress that Kant's position was explicitly anti-foundationalist. Thus for Kant reason is not the rationalism of Descartes, a rationalism which derives solipsistically from within the thinking subject, and against the imperialism and delusion of which post-modernism has railed as though that disposed of Enlightenment rationalism. For Kant the authority of reason can only be established discursively and recursively within open debate among free citizens. It is thus practical reason that rules and practical reason is itself disciplined by the categorical imperative, because reason is by definition that which could be accepted as authoritative by all free individuals within any possible community, or what Kant calls a *sensus communis*. Kantian, as opposed to Cartesian, reason is not foundational because it is a task and process, not a given. Moreover, it is a task that will never be completed. Since reason must be constantly open to criticism in open debate reason is humble and hesitant, not assured and dominating. The enlightened citizen in Kant is much closer to Lear naked upon the heath, in Kant's case upon what he called 'the plains of experience' than he is to Genghis Khan, trampling all difference beneath the hooves of the horse of the rational subject as in the post-modern tale of modernity.

'Human reason has this peculiarity, that in one species of its knowledge it is burdened by questions which, as prescribed by the very nature of reason itself, it is not able to ignore, but which, as transcending all its powers, it is also not able to answer' (Kant 1781, quoted in O'Neil 1989: 12). Thus for Kant, and I would argue still for us, the pursuit of reason, and thus of a virtuous community, which is reason's only viable home, is a historically given fate which we cannot escape but which is doomed to an always partial failure. The tragic nature of the Enlightenment vision, and of the emancipatory project and thus any politics based upon it, is due to this sense of the limits of reason and thus also the limits of politics.

It has in my view been unfortunate that Habermas has combined a Kantian approach to public reason with a search for a foundationalism in the basic structure of communicative action which is both unnecessary and probably unsustainable. The reason for this move by Habermas is clear. It was an attempt to find a substitute for a need- and interest-based, and thus ultimately instrumental, foundationalism that underpinned Marxist-inspired versions of ideology and ideology critique. We will need to return to this question of interests and the problem of the source of the motivations for political action shortly. But to return to the problem of discourse ethics. It is important to register that for Kant the autonomy of the individual subject and thus her or his freedom, upon which any theory of democracy must rest, and from which much of the liberal tradition of political thought derives, rested upon the ability to think for oneself, which in a situation of all-enveloping doubt involved freeing oneself both from dogmas—the pre-packaged thoughts of others or of society at large, what has become known as ideology—and from the subjectivity of individual desires and the individual point of view. On this view the rationality which was the founding condition for autonomy and thus for freedom depended upon the exercise of public as opposed to private reason. It is important to stress that the distinction does not turn upon the number of people to whom a discourse is addressed or who have access to the discourse, but upon the discursive conditions. For Kant public reason must be offered in such a way that it is potentially acceptable by any other human being, and this in its turn involves the effort of putting oneself in the position of the other. This involves the exercise of reflective judgement or a *sensus communis*, what Hannah Arendt has termed enlarged thinking. This Kant defines as

the idea of a public sense, i.e. a critical faculty which in its reflective act takes account (a priori) of the mode of representation of everyone else, in order, as it were, to weigh its judgement with the collective reason of mankind, and thereby avoid the illusion arising from subjective and personal conditions which could readily be taken for objective . . . This is accomplished by weighing the judgement, not so much with actual, as rather with the merely possible judgements of others, and by putting ourselves in the position of everyone else. (Kant 1964: 151, quoted in Benhabib 1992: 133)

Arendt glosses this passage as follows:

The power of judgement rests on a potential agreement with others, and the thinking process which is active in judging something is not, like the thought process of pure reasoning, a dialogue between me and myself, but finds itself always and primarily, even if I am quite alone in making up my mind, in an anticipated communication with others with whom I know I must finally come to some agreement . . . From this potential agreement judgement derives its specific validity. This means on the one hand that such judgement must liberate itself from the 'subjective private conditions', that is from the idiosyncrasies which naturally determine the outlook of each individual in his privacy and which are legitimate as long as they are only privately held opinions but are not fit to enter the market place, and lack all validity in the public realm. And this enlarged thinking, which as judgement knows how to transcend its individual limitations, cannot function in strict isolation or solitude; it needs the presence of the other 'in whose place' it must think, whose perspective it must take into consideration, and without whom it never has the opportunity to operate at all. (Arendt 1961: 220–1, quoted in Benhabib 1992: 133)

Thus for Kant public reason is closely tied to the categorical imperative and the particular form of universalizability that, in Kant's view, must be the founding condition for any social grouping that does not infringe the autonomy of its members. For Kant this could ultimately be extended to all human beings (indeed the possibility of other reasoning species being included was not excluded). Thus, and this is crucial in the current climate of thought which places such emphasis on identity, for Kant and for that strand of the public sphere tradition which stems from his thought, identity, except in the sense of the most basic and minimal perception of self-consciousness, without which Kant argued we would not be moral beings at all, but merely instinct-driven animals, does not pre-exist social interaction, and the autonomous moral agent who is the necessary subject of democratic politics can only be formed within the exercise of public reason as Kant defined it. The essence of such public reason is that it is always offered for possible critique by others. Public reason is distinguished from private reason—here Kant gives the example of a sermon—on the grounds that acceptance of the sermon depends upon the prior unquestioned and unquestionable acceptance of a range of given religious dogmas. For public reason no issues are off limits. This is why within this tradition intellectual tolerance and free communication are the supreme values.

Reason must in all its undertakings subject itself to criticism; should it limit freedom of criticism by any prohibitions, it must harm itself, drawing upon itself a damaging suspicion. Nothing is so important through its usefulness, nothing so sacred, that it may be exempted from this searching examination, which knows no respect for persons. Reason depends on this freedom for its very existence. For reason has no dictatorial authority; its verdict is always simply the agreement of free citizens, of whom each one must be permitted to express, without let or hindrance, his objection or even his veto. (Kant 1781, quoted in O'Neil 1989: 15)

Thus the publicness of discourse as a condition for a society of agents who are free and autonomous, not in the sense that they are not subject to social and material constraints, but that they think for themselves, is based on the nature of the discourse and its potential accessibility rather than upon the number of people who actually have access to it. Given a Heideggerian twist this is the basis upon which Scannell argues for the democratizing force of broadcasting as a medium which is forced to offer its discourse to a public that is anyone everywhere. For Scannell, in contrast to many theorists of democracy and the media, it is precisely because the media for their survival are forced to appeal to random, anonymous audiences and thus to make general rather than specific appeals that they are both public and democratic.

This is why it is simply beside the point to argue, as critics of this strand in public sphere thinking do, that either most people cannot meet this test of rationality in their discourse or that it denies the importance of pleasure and the particularity of 'difference'. It is certainly the case that this position can be read in a very narrow way and the rationality proposed as the standard of legitimate public sphere communication, or of undistorted communication, can be seen in over-rationalist ways, for instance in terms of linear forms of written communication as opposed to the more iconic forms of visual communication, and as excluding the rhetorical forms of persuasion or the narrative and the spectacular as opposed to the norms of syllogistic logical argument. In my view this is not a necessary presupposition of the exercise of Kantian public reason. It does not predetermine the discursive form, although there has undoubtedly been a bias in the actual literature towards a limited range of communicative forms and genres— news and current affairs as opposed to fiction for instance.

It can also be linked to a tradition stemming from the Stoics, which Kant undoubtedly also shared, which links the public/private distinction to those between mind and body and between reason and passion, and which is suspicious of the autonomy-threatening power of what are seen as the animal passions or desires and thus of emotive appeals. I personally have some sympathy with this strand of thought, but it is not a necessary entailment of the discourse ethics position. The only condition is that, whatever the propositions and however they are expressed, they must be open to discursive challenge according to the standards of argument and evidence accepted by the particular discursive community or culture concerned. Whether such standards are universal or can be universalized is then a secondary question.

Here I think Mayhew's recent effort to combine the irreducible rhetorical element in all communications with a public sphere approach through the concept of tokens of solidarity and a redefinition of the public sphere as forums for the redemption of such tokens, is both illustrative and exemplary. In *The New Public* (1997) Mayhew argues that 'arguments about the efficacy of the public turn on the question of whether public discussion is sufficiently independent of other strong forces—most notably power and wealth—to constitute an integrative force in its own right. Accordingly debates about the integration of democratic society inevitably lead to questions about persuasion, its nature, its role in society and its relation to the basic distinction between reason and coercion.' He then goes on to argue that 'From a sociological standpoint the public sphere does not depend on the unrealistic notion that rhetoric can be banished in favour of fully rational discourse on all issues at all times, but on the institutionalization of forums for the redemption of rhetorical tokens.' What does he mean by rhetorical tokens? He argues that 'there is a modern form of solidarity that partially replaces the strong ties of kin, clan, local community, and traditionally defined deference hierarchies. Modern differentiated solidarity consists in processes of communication.' He goes on to argue, however, that 'there are limitations in the use of reason in rhetorical communication. Effective persuasion relies on appeals to social norms, on ties of solidarity, and on the cultural strength of eloquence', but that rhetoric relies on trust: 'audiences are asked to accept abbreviated arguments, *tokens* of more ample arguments that could supposedly be supplied were time and opportunity available'. Crucial to Mayhew's argument is the attempt to reintroduce appeals to group solidarity as not only a legitimate but an unavoidable aspect of public sphere communication. As he again puts it, 'The novel question of early modern debate about rhetoric and group life centred on the question of whether community can or should be purposively willed or must be conceived as naturally inhering in primordial groups.' He then goes on to criticize Habermas's approach on the grounds that 'Habermas's discourse theory founds social integration on solidarity, but not on the particular communal ties that we normally associate with institutionalised solidarity. Rather, Habermas's discursive solidarity would be universal, created by a union of everyone's common interest in justice, autonomy and emancipation. It would be constructed by a community engaged in rational, unconstrained discussion, *without rhetoric*', thus 'subsuming freedom of speech under an individualistic rather than a communal version of liberalism'.

Mayhew's concept of tokens of solidarity brings us back to the other side of the original dilemma of modernity, namely the construction of sociability by autonomous rational moral agents or the construction of a world to which an autonomous agent could feel it belonged rather than to which it was subjected.

Here we are brought back to the Hegelian concern for *Sittlichkeit* and to critiques of Habermas's public sphere approach from a communitarian and neo-Aristotelian perspective. Here the debate over the public sphere has to be seen as part of the wider debate between advocates and defenders of the theory and practice of rights-based liberalism and the various proponents of communitarianism and identity politics (Benhabib 1992; Gray 1995a; Guttman 1994). What is the problem here?

The communitarian critique is a response to the political dilemma of modernity that stems, as we have seen, from Hegel's critique of Kant and from an alternative response to the dilemma raised by Rousseau. Rousseau posed the dilemma in terms of the relationship between freedom and social conditioning. Having argued that humans were by nature good and altruistic, but had been corrupted by society, he was then faced by the problem of how to create a free society out of agents who had been conditioned to be undemocratic and enslaved. This dilemma is, of course, an old one stemming from Greek thought, which saw the moral life as essentially social and thus socially conditioned. How then could one create a just commonwealth out of an unjust one? The Platonic solution, as is well known, was the philosopher king. But where then to find these philosopher kings remained a problem. But the crucial point is that this leads to the opposite solution to that of social contract theory and the liberalism based upon it. Now political values are social before they are individual. Politics is embedded in, and ideally expresses, a set of pre- existing social values, or a way of life, and the role and legitimacy of the state, or the public realm, is then to foster and uphold those communal values and defend that way of life. The citizens find their identity in and give their loyalty to, not a set of abstract rights, but a way of life, an ethos, that embodies a set of moral values. From this perspective liberalism, and the particular forms of democracy that it supports, is but one way of life among many possible alternatives (Gray 1995a). From this perspective the role of the media is then to foster and defend this shared way of life, sometimes described, in the nationalist model of communitarianism, as national identity or culture.

The communitarian position on the public/private divide, and the approaches to both politics and the media that stem from it, is in a sense contradictory. The core of identity politics—or what Nancy Fraser has called the politics of recognition—is the call for the recognition in the public realm of values hitherto deemed private, both in the sense of being excluded from the public gaze and from public debate but also in the sense of stemming from private group interests and identities rather than from a generally shared interest and identity, and thus for the acquisition of rights that recognition of these values as public entails, while at the same time drawing for its evaluative arguments upon a range of sources which must exclude the very concept of the public, and its liberal valuation of rights and the recognition and equal treatment of the diversity of private interests, that they are demanding.

What Benhabib (1992: 68–88) has called the integrationist strand within communitarianism seeks *Sittlichkeit* in an attempted return to the moral certainties and social unities of traditional pre-modern societies. Here everything is in a sense public; the values that motivate people and give them their social anchorage are derived from and shape a whole shared way of life. In a theocracy there is no room for the individual or the private. Indeed this strand in communitarianism criticizes the liberal tradition precisely for creating, and philosophically justifying as the highest good, social arrangements that separate political or public spheres of action and value on the one hand from private spheres of action and value on the other to the impoverishment, in their view, of both (MacIntyre 1981, 1988).

On the other hand the participationist strand wishes to build its way out of the alienation and formalism of liberalism by both accepting the conditions of modernity which are liberalism's starting-point—namely post-traditional societies and reflexive individuals—while at the same time arguing for a refounding of political communities on the universalization of the discourse ethic and its practices, whereby in a sense the systems world can sink back into the life world. The more post-modern end of communitarianism, which links to so-called new social movements and the politics of identity or recognition, makes this attempt by, in effect, advocating the fragmentation of societies into small-scale or specialized communities of interest or identity, each with their own public sphere. They tend to see more universalistic and unified definitions of the public sphere as repressive of difference and thus anti-democratic. What is at issue here is both whether within a polity we should be looking at one or multiple public spheres and how we think about the relation between public and private. It is clear, I think, that an integrationist communitarianism and the politics of recognition that stems from it demands a unified public sphere and places continuous pressure on the existence of a meaningful private sphere. Its aim is a one-to-one fit between a unitary set of values, a single public sphere (if this term any longer has meaning here), and single polity. If diverse communities exist within a single territory or polity the aim is fragmentation, not co-existence and the toleration of diversity. It is clearly incompatible with the exercise of public reason in the Kantian sense and with media practices and institutional forms in harmony with such an ideal. The case of participatory communitarianism and the identity politics that stems from it is more complex. Here the problem arises from the ambivalence of the liberal value of tolerance vis-à-vis the public/private divide. On the one hand toleration can be taken to mean the acceptance by public authorities of a range of practices and beliefs by defining them as private and outside the realm of public regulation: for instance religious observance. Such toleration of course rests, as the communitarian critics quite rightly point out, on a prior judgement that the practice or belief in question is not in any sense a threat to the public weal or interest. This form of toleration can be rejected by certain advocates of the politics of recognition because it is argued it implicitly downgrades, and thus in some sense fails to fully recognize, the importance or centrality of the practice or belief in question. On the other hand we can also understand toleration as giving public recognition to and bringing into the public realm people, practices, or beliefs to which by so doing we signal we give equal value to those already so recognized and with which we are prepared to live and argue within a shared culture and polity. Thus we need to distinguish those demands for recognition and for multiple public spheres that seek in effect to extend the private so that their group identities remain unthreatened by the risk of corrosion that participation in the critical discourse of the public sphere, and the need for compromise that the agreement on common courses of action inevitably carries, from those that are demands for a widening of the definition of what is public to let them into what remains a common arena for critical public debate and decision-making with the acceptance of the duties and risks that such entry carries with it. In the former case what is being demanded in the name of difference is the dissolution of any shared culture, polity, and set of rights and associated obligations, and here the question is how much of such private fragmentation can any society or polity sustain while remaining viable, and whether in fact we will only regard such demands as democratically legitimate where the group identity claimed is itself subject to the disciplines of the discourse ethic. In the latter case the liberal polity is being asked, rightly, to live up to its ideals and be prepared to accept that those values that it considers central to its way of life must always be held provisionally and be subject to the review of critical discourse. Here we need to distinguish between a truly private realm, the irreducible site of individual autonomy (a realm which from a true social constructivist view does not of course exist) from the multiple public spheres within which we necessarily live and have our being, defined by Benhabib as any occasion or situation where people share views on matters of common interest, multiple public spheres that all contribute to the formation of our identities and which may be more or less democratic in the sense of meeting the requirements of the discourse ethic. The media are integral to these multiple public spheres and should be judged in each case on the basis of the identities and practices they foster. But these multiple public spheres then need to be distinguished from the political public sphere where discussion is necessarily aimed at the common agreement necessary for concerted action within a unified polity. Of course one of the matters legitimately discussible must always be the extent of the reach of such debate and action, in the sense of the proper boundary at any time of the public and the private, and the continuing legitimacy of the particular polity.

Privacy

If the Kantian approach to the distinction between public and private, and the view of politics that stems from it, can be seen as the search for individual autonomy via public discourse, the Hegelian tradition from which the communitarian critique of public sphere thinking is mounted can be seen as a search for an identity that only the recognition and esteem of others can create. If the autonomous identity upon which democracy must be founded is created within the Kantian model by mutual criticism, the bonds of sociality in the Hegelian model are based upon our recognition of ourselves in the gaze of others. As Rousseau then argued, an egalitarian social order must be founded on the equality of public exposure that his metaphor of all citizens being at once performers and spectators in the theatre of life expresses.

This approach leads to a notion that runs continuously through the debates over privacy and the media—namely the role played in the construction of a viable modern social order of the behaviour-controlling effects of public exposure. To return to Adam Smith, his primary founding argument in favour of the market as a public institution and sphere of public behaviour was a moral one. He argued that we could never know how our fellow humans really thought and felt, but that what mattered was how they behaved towards one another. He then argued, on lines similar to Rousseau, that a driving human motivation was the desire to be liked and respected by others and thus that the best way to ensure that people behaved well towards one another was to expose their behaviour to public view. It was this that the market achieved. But one finds a general extension of this view in the wider assessment of urban life and the development of the division of labour as widening the range of both actual, and perhaps more important potential, human interactions outside a person's immediate personal and private sphere, in particular outside kin relations, as a force for civilization, as the root of the word indicates, in the view that urbanity, again with the same root, is a desirable human character trait. One finds perhaps the ultimate development of this view in Elias's *The Civilising Process*, where he argues, drawing ultimately on Durkheim, that it was the increasing density of social contact between strangers, the increased and necessary publicness of modern life, that led to the internalization of a set of socially collaborative norms and greater levels of self-control that made a harmonious and relatively non-violent modern social order possible. Ironically here we find an internalization of social control, its personalization, individuation, and in a sense privatization caused by the increased publicness of social interactions. It is precisely these self-disciplining effects of public display that Foucault and his followers attack, using the metaphor of the Benthamite Panopticon as epitomizing modernity, in the name of a difference whose source and place of refuge they then seek in the privacy of a body which lies outside both discourse and politics.

References

Abercrombie, N. and Longhurst, B. 1998. *Audiences*. London.

Adorno, T. 1977. 'Letters to Walter Benjamin', in *Aesthetics and Politics*, 110–33. London.

—— and Horkheimer, M. 1997. *Dialectic of Enlightenment*. London.

Alpers, S. 1988. *Rembrandt's Enterprise: The Studio and the Market*. London.

—— 1989. *The Art of Describing: Dutch Art in the 17th Century*. London.

Anderson, B. 1993. *Imagined Communities: Reflections on the Origins and Spread of Nationalism*. London.

Ang, I. 1985. *Watching Dallas: Soap Opera and the Melodramatic Imagination*. London.

—— 1990. *Desperately Seeking the Audience*. London.

—— and Hermes, J. 1996. 'Gender and/in Media Consumption', in J. Curran and M. Gurevitch (eds.), *Mass Media and Society*. London.

Arendt, H. 1961. 'Crisis in Culture', in *Between Past and Future: Six Exercises in Political Thought*. New York.

Arthur, B. 1994. *Increasing Returns and Path Dependency in the Economy*. Ann Arbor, Mich.

Bailey, P. 1978. *Leisure and Class in Victorian England: Rational Recreation and the Contest for Control 1830–1885*. London.

Baker, K. M. 1992. 'Defining the Public Sphere in 18th-Century France', in C. Calhoun (ed.), *Habermas and the Public Sphere*. Boston, Mass.

Baran, P. and Sweezy, P. 1968. *Monopoly Capital: An Essay on the American Economic and Social Order*. London.

Bauman, Z. 1987. *Legislators and Interpreters: On Modernity, Post-Modernity and Intellectuals*. Cambridge.

Baxandall, M. 1972. *Painting and Experience in 15th Century Italy*. Oxford.

—— 1985. *Patterns of Intention: On the Historical Explanation of Pictures*. Yale.

Becker, H. S. 1982. *Art Worlds*. Berkeley, Calif.

Bell, D. 1973. *The Coming of Post-Industrial Society: A Venture in Social Forecasting*. New York.

Benhabib, S. 1992. *Situating the Self: Gender, Community and Post-Modernism in Contemporary Ethics*. Cambridge.

Beninger, J. 1986. *The Control Revolution*. Cambridge, Mass.

Benjamin, W. 1970. 'The Work of Art in the Age of Mechanical Reproduction', in *Illuminations*. London.

Berlin, I. 1979. 'The Originality of Machiavelli', in *Against the Current: Essays in the History of Ideas*. Oxford.

—— 1990. *The Crooked Timber of Humanity: Chapters in the History of Ideas*. London.

Bourdieu, P. 1984. *Distinction: A Social Critique of the Judgement of Taste*. Cambridge, Mass.

—— 1993. *The Field of Cultural Production: Essays on Art and Literature*. Cambridge.

—— 1996. *The Rules of Art: Genesis and Structure of the Literary Field*. Cambridge.

Bowie, A. 1990. *Aesthetics and Subjectivity: From Kant to Nietzsche*. Manchester.

Braverman, H. 1974. *Labour and Monopoly Capitalism*. New York.

Brewer, J. 1997. *The Pleasures of the Imagination: English Culture in the 18th Century*. London.

—— and Porter, R. (eds.). 1993. *Consumption and the World of Goods*. London.

Burckhardt, J. 1929. *The Civilization of the Renaissance in Italy*, trans S. G. Middleman. London.

—— 1943. *Reflections on History*, trans. MDH. London.

Cairncross, F. 1997. *The Death of Distance: How the Communication Revolution Will Change our Lives*. London.

Calhoun, C. 1992. 'Introduction: Habermas and the Public Sphere', in id. (ed.), *Habermas and the Public Sphere*. Cambridge, Mass.

—— 1995. *Critical Social Theory*. Oxford.

Callinicos, A. 1995. *Theories and Narratives: Reflections on the Philosophy of History*. London.

Carey, James. 1987. 'The Press and the Public Discourse'. *The Center Magazine*, 4–16.

Carey, John. 1993. *The Intellectuals and the Masses: Pride and Prejudice Among the Literary Intelligentsia 1880–1939*. New York.

Castells, M. 1996. *The Rise of the Network Society*. Oxford.

Chanan, M. 1976. *Labour Power in the British Film Industry*. London.

Chandler, A. D. jr. 1977. *The Visible Hand: The Managerial Revolution in American Business*. Cambridge, Mass.

—— 1990. *Scale and Scope: The Dynamics of Industrial Capitalism*. Cambridge, Mass.

Chartier, R. (ed.). 1985. *Pratique de la lecture*. Paris.

—— 1987. *Les Usages de l'imprimerie (XV–XIX ème siecles)*. Paris.

Clark, T. J. 1973. *Image of the People: Gustave Courbet and the 1848 Revolution*. London.

Coase, R. 1937. 'The Nature of the Firm'. *Economica*, 4: 386–405.

Cohen, G. A. 1978. *Karl Marx's Theory of History*. Oxford.

Colley, L. 1992. *Britons: Forging the Nation 1707–1837*. London.

Collins, R. and Murroni, C. 1996. *New Media, New Policies*. Oxford.

—— Garnham, N., and Locksley, G. 1988. *The Economics of Television in the UK*. London.

Congdon, T., Graham, A., Green, D., and Robinson, B. 1995. *The Cross Media Revolution: Ownership and Control*. London.

References

Corner, J. 1991. 'Meaning, Genre and Context', in J. Curran and M. Gurevitch (eds.), *Mass Media and Society*. London.

Coyle, D. 1997. *The Weightless World: Strategies for Managing the Digital Economy*. Oxford.

Cumberbatch, G. 1989. 'Overview of the Effects of the Mass Media', in G. Cumberbatch and D. Howitt (eds.), *A Measurement of Uncertainty: The Effects of the Mass Media*. London.

Curran, J. 1977. 'Capitalism and Control of the Press, 1800–1975', in J. Curran, M. Gurevitch, and J. Woollacott (eds.), *Mass Communication and Society*. London.

——1990. 'The New Revisionism in Mass Communications Research: A Reappraisal'. *European Journal of Communication* 5: 2–3.

Darnton, R. 1979. *The Business of Enlightenment: Publishing History of the 'Encyclopédie', 1775–1800*. Cambridge, Mass.

——1982. *The Literary Underground of the Old Regime*. Cambridge, Mass.

David, P. 1975. *Technical Choice, Innovation and Economic Growth*. Cambridge.

——1985. 'Clio and the Economics of QWERTY'. *American Economic Review*, 75: 332–7.

De Certeau, M. 1984. *The Practice of Everyday Life*. Berkeley, Calif.

De Sola Pool, I. 1984. *Technologies of Freedom*. Cambridge, Mass.

Di Maggio, P. 1982. 'Cultural Entrepreneurship in 19th-century Boston: The Creation of an Organizational Base for High Culture in America'. *Media, Culture and Society*, iv/1. London.

Dosi, G., Freeman, C., Nelson, R., Silverberg, G., and Soete, L. 1988. *Technical Change and Economic Theory*. London.

Duby, G. 1978. *Les Trois Ordres ou l'imaginaire de feodalisme*. Paris.

Dutton, W. (ed.). 1996. *Information and Communication Technologies: Visions and Realities*. Oxford.

Eisenstein, E. 1979. *The Printing Press as an Agent of Change*. 2 vols. Cambridge.

Elias, N. 1994. *The Civilizing Process*. Oxford.

Elliott, P. 1986. 'Intellectuals, the "Information Society" and the Disappearance of the Public Sphere', in Collins *et al.* (eds.), *Media Culture and Society: A Critical Reader*. London.

——1974. 'Uses and Gratifications Research: A Critique and a Sociological Alternative', in J. G. Blumler and E. Katz (eds.), *The Uses of Mass Communication*. London.

European Commission. 1994. *Europe and the Global Information Society: Recommendations to the European Council, Brussels*. May.

——1997a. *Constructing a European Information Society For All: Final Report of the High-Level Experts Group*. Luxembourg.

——1997b. *Green Paper on Convergence*. Brussels.

Ewen, S. 1979. *Captains of Consciousness: Advertising and the Social Roots of Consumer Culture*. New York.

——and Ewen, E. 1982. *Channels of Desire: Mass Images and the Shaping of American Consciousness*. New York.

Febvre, L. and Martin, H. J. 1990. *The Coming of the Book: The Impact of Printing 1450–1800.* London.

Fine, B. and Leopold, E. 1993. *The World of Consumption.* London.

Fiske, J. 1989. *Reading the Popular.* London.

Flichy, P. 1995. *Dynamics of Modern Communication: The Shaping and Impact of New Communication Technologies.* London.

Fraser, N. 1989. *Unruly Practices.* Minneapolis, Minn.

—— 1992. 'Rethinking the Public Sphere: A Contribution to the Critique of Actually Existing Democracy' in C. Calhoun (ed.), *Habermas and the Public Sphere.* Cambridge, Mass.

—— 1997. *Justice Interruptus.* London.

Freeman, C. 1996. 'The Two-edged Nature of Technological Change: Employment and Unemployment', in W. Dutton (ed.), *Information and Communication Technologies: Visions and Realities.* Oxford.

Frith, S. 1996. *Performing Rites: On the Value of Popular Music.* Oxford.

Frow, J. 1995. *Cultural Studies and Cultural Value.* Oxford.

Fukuyama, F. 1992. *The End of History and the Last Man.* London.

Fuller, P. 1990. *Seeing Berger: A Reevaluation.* London.

Garnham, N. 1998. 'Information Society Theory as Ideology: A Critique'. *Loisirs et Société,* 21/1. Quebec.

—— 1999. 'Amartya Sen's "Capabilities" Approach to the Evaluation of Welfare: Its Application to Communications', in A. Calabrese and J.-C. Burgelman (eds.), *Communication, Citizenship and Social Policy.* Lanham.

Gellner, E. 1983. *Nations and Nationalism.* London.

—— 1984. 'Tractatus Sociologico-Philosophicus', in S. L. Brown (ed.), *Objectivity and Cultural Divergence.* Royal Institute of Philosophy, Lecture Series 17.

—— 1985. *Relativism and the Social Sciences.* Cambridge.

—— 1988. *Plough, Book and Sword.* London.

Ginzburg, C. 1985. *The Enigma of Piero: Piero della Francesca.* London.

Gitlin, T. 1994. *Inside Prime Time.* 2nd edn. London.

Glasgow Media Group. 1976. *Bad News.* London.

—— 1980. *More Bad News.* London.

—— 1995. *Reader,* vol. ii: *Industry, Economy, War and Politics.* London.

Gombrich, E. 1994. *Ideals and Idols: Essays on Values in History and in Art.* Oxford 1979, repr. London.

Gouldner, A. W. 1976. *The Dialectic of Ideology and Technology: The Origins, Grammar and Future of Ideology.* London.

Graham, A. and Davies, G. 1997. *Broadcasting, Society and Policy in the Multimedia Age.* London.

Gramsci, A. 1971. *Selections from the Prison Notebooks.* London.

Gray, J. 1995a. *Enlightenment's Wake: Politics and Culture at the Close of the Modern Age.* London.

—— 1995b. *Berlin.* London.

Grossberg, L., Wartella, E., and Whitney, C. 1998. *Media Making: Mass Media in a Popular Culture.* California.

References

Guttman, A. (ed.). 1994. *Multiculturalism*. Princeton, NJ.

Habermas, J. 1987. *The Philosophical Discourse of Modernity*. Cambridge.

—— 1989. *The Structural Transformation of the Public Sphere*. Cambridge, Mass.

Hall, S. 1982. 'The Rediscovery of Ideology: Return of the Repressed in Media Studies', in M. Gurevitch, T. Bennett, J. Curran, and J. Woollacot (eds.), *Culture, Media and Society*. London.

—— 1997. 'Introduction', in S. Hall (ed.), *Representation: Cultural Representation and Signifying Practice*. London.

Halsey, A. H. 1992. *The Decline of Donnish Dominion*. Oxford.

Harding, S. 1991. *Whose Science? Whose Knowledge?* Ithaca, NY.

Hartley, J. 1987. 'Television Audiences, Paedocracy and Pleasure'. *Textual Practice*, 1(2): 121–38.

Harvey, D. 1989. *The Condition of Post-Modernity*. Oxford.

Haskell, F. 1980. *Patrons and Painters*. rev. edn. Yale.

—— 1981. *Taste and the Antique: The Lure of Classical Sculpture 1500–1900*. Yale.

—— 1993. *History and its Images*. Yale.

Hawthorn, G. 1987. *Enlightenment and Despair*. 2nd edn. Cambridge.

Hennion, A. 1995. 'The History of Art. Lessons in Mediation'. *Reseaux*, 3/2. London.

Herzog, H. 1944. 'What Do We Really Know about Day-time Serial Listeners?' in P. Lazarsfeld and F. N. Stanton (eds.), *Radio Research 1942–43*. New York.

Hewison, R. 1987. *The Heritage Industry: Britain in a Climate of Decline*. London.

Hobsbawm, E. and Ranger, T. (eds.). 1983. *The Invention of Tradition*. London.

Hobson, D. 1982. *Crossroads: The Drama of a Soap Opera*. London.

Hodgson, G. 1993. *Economics and Evolution: Bringing Life Back into Economics*. Cambridge.

Hoggart, R. 1995a. 'Why Treat Us Like Dimwits?'. *Independent on Sunday*, 19 Feb.

—— 1995b. *The Way We Live Now*. London.

Home Office. 1986. *Report of the Committee on Financing the BBC* (Cmnd 9824). London.

Horowitz, R. 1989. *The Irony of Regulatory Reform*. New York.

Huizinga, J. 1965. *The Waning of the Middle Ages*. Harmondsworth.

Innis, H. 1964. *The Bias of Communication*. Toronto.

—— 1972. *Empire and Communication*. Toronto.

Johnson, P. 1988. *The Intellectuals*. London.

Jones, P. 1995. 'Williams and "quality": a response to John Corner'. *Media, Culture and Society*, 17: 317–22.

Jonscher, C. 1983. 'Information Resources and Economic Productivity'. *Information Economics and Policy*, 1(1): 13–35.

Kant, I. 1992– . *Kritik der reinen Vernunft* (1st edn. 1781), vols. iii and iv, in *Gesammelte Schriften*, 29 vols. Berlin.

—— 1949. 'What is Orientation in Thinking ?', in *Kant's Critique of Practical Reason and Other Writings on Moral Philosophy*, trans. L. W. Beck. Chicago.

—— 1964. *The Critique of Judgement*, J. C. Meredith. trans. Oxford.

—— 1970. *Kant's Political Writings*, ed. Hans Reiss. Cambridge.

—— 1991. 'What is Enlightenment?', in J. Schmidt (ed.), *What is Enlightenment? 18th-Century Answers and 20th-Century Questions*. Berkeley, Calif.

Kennedy, M. 1991. 'The Intelligentsia in Civil Society in Post-Communist Regimes'. *Theory and Society*, 21/1.

Lasch, S. and Urry, J. 1994. *Economies of Signs and Space*. London.

Latour, B. 1987. *Science in Action: How to Follow Scientists and Engineers through Society*. Cambridge, Mass.

Le Roy Ladurie, E. 1980. *Carnival: A People's Uprising at Romans 1579–1580*. London.

Lefebvre, H. 1984. *Everyday Life in the Modern World*. New Jersey.

McChesney, R. 1993. *Telecommunications, Mass Media and Democracy: The Battle for the Control of US Broadcasting*. Oxford.

MacIntyre, A. 1981. *After Virtue*. London.

—— 1988. *Whose Justice? Whose Rationality?* Indiana.

McKendrick, N., Brewer, J., and Plumb, J. H. 1982. *The Birth of a Consumer Society: The Commercialization of 18th-Century England*. London.

McLuhan, M. 1964. *Understanding Media: The Extensions of Man*. New York.

McQuail, D., Blumler, J. G., and Brown, J. R. 1972. 'The Television Audience: A Revised Perspective', in D. McQuail (ed.), *Sociology of Mass Communication*. Harmondsworth.

Mann, M. 1986. *The Sources of Social Power*. Vol. i. Cambridge.

—— 1993. *The Sources of Social Power*. Vol. ii. Cambridge.

Marcuse, H. 1978. *The Aesthetic Dimension: Towards a Critique of Marxist Aesthetics*. Boston, Mass.

Marx, K. 1963. *The German Ideology*. London.

Mayhew, L. 1997. *The New Public*. Cambridge.

Mepham, J. 1990. 'The Ethics of Quality in Television', in G. Mulgan (ed.), *The Question of Quality*. London.

Meyrowitz, J. 1985. *No Sense of Place*. New York.

Miege, B. 1989. *The Capitalization of Cultural Production*. New York.

Morley, D. 1980. *The Nationwide Audience: Structure and Decoding*. London.

—— 1989. *Family Television: Cultural Power and Domestic Leisure*. London.

—— 1992. *Television, Audiences and Cultural Studies*, London.

Mosco, V. 1996. *The Political Economy of Communication*. London.

Mukerji, C. V. 1983. *From Graven Images*. New York.

Mulgan, G. 1991. *Communication and Control*. Oxford.

Nava, M., Barker, A., Macrury, I., and Richards, B. 1997. *Buy This Book: Studies in Advertising and Consumption*. London.

Negroponte, N. 1995. *Being Digital*. London.

Neumann, R. W. 1991. *The Future of the Mass Audience*. Cambridge.

Nightingale, V. 1996. *Studying Audiences: The Shock of the Real*. London.

Noam, E. 1987. 'The Public Telecommunications Network: A Concept in Transition'. *Journal of Communication*, 37/1: 28–48.

Noble, D. 1979. *America by Design: Science, Technology and the Rise of Corporate Capitalism*. Oxford.

Nussbaum, M. 1990. *Love's Knowledge*. Oxford.

References

Nussbaum, M. and Sen, A. (eds.). 1993. *The Quality of Life*. Oxford.

O'Brien, C. C. 1993. *The Great Melody*. London.

Oftel. 1995. *Beyond the Telephone, the Television and the PC: Consultative Document*. London.

O'Neil, O. 1989. *Constructions of Reason: Explorations of Kant's Practical Philosophy*. Cambridge.

Ong, W. 1982. *Orality and Literacy: Technologizing of the Word*. London.

Panofsky, E. 1951. *Gothic Architecture and Scholasticism*. Philadelphia, Pa.

——1966. *Meaning and the Visual Arts*. Princeton, NJ.

——1991. *Perspective as Symbolic Form*. London.

Perkin, H. 1987. *The Rise of Professional Society: England Since 1880*. London.

Philo, G. 1990. *Seeing and Believing*. London.

Pratten, S. 1998. 'Needs and Wants: The Case of Broadcasting Policy', *Media, Culture and Society*, 20/3 (July).

Quah, D. 1994. *The Invisible Hand and the Weightless Economy*. Centre for Economic Performance, Working Paper. London.

Radway, J. 1995. *Reading the Romance: Women, Patriarchy and Popular Literature*. 1st pub. London, 1987.

——1988. 'Reception Studies'. *Cultural Studies*, 2: 3.

Rorty, R. 1989. *Contingency, Irony and Solidarity*. Cambridge.

——1991. 'Intellectuals in Politics: Too Far In? Too Far Out?'. *Dissent* (Fall): 483–90.

Rosen, J. 1994. 'Making Things More Public: On the Political Responsibility of the Media Intellectual'. *Critical Studies in Mass Communication*, 11/4: 363–88.

Runciman, W. G. 1983. *A Treatise on Social Theory*. Vol. i. Cambridge.

——1989. *A Treatise on Social Theory*. Vol. ii. Cambridge.

——1997. *A Treatise on Social Theory*. Vol. iii. Cambridge.

Said, E. W. 1994. *Representations of the Intellectual*. New York.

——1995. *Orientalism*, rev. edn. London.

Samuel, R. 1994. *Theatres of Memory*, vol. i: *Past and Present in Contemporary Culture*. London.

Scannel, P. 1996. *Radio, Television and Modern Life*. Oxford.

——and Cardiff, D. 1991. *A Social History of British Broadcasting: Serving the Nation*. Oxford.

Schiller, H. 1992. *Mass Communication and American Empire*. 2nd edn. Boulder, Colo.

Schramm, W., Lyle, J., and Parker, E. B. 1961. *Television in the Lives of Our Children*. Stanford, Calif.

Schudson, M. 1978. *Discovering News: A Social History of the American Newspaper*. New York.

——1998. *The Good Citizen: A History of US Civic Life*. New York.

Sennet, R. 1993. *The Fall of Public Man*. London.

Silverstone, R. 1994. *Television and Everyday Life*. London.

Simon, J. P. 1995. 'Mediation and the Social History of Art'. *Reseaux*, 3/2. London.

Smith, A. 1980. *Goodbye Gutenberg*. Oxford.

Smythe, D. 1981. *Dependency Road: Communication, Capitalism, Consciousness and Canada*. Norwood, NJ.

Sokal, A. and Bricmount, J. 1998. *Intellectual Impostures*. London.

Sparks, C. 1998. 'Are Newspaper Prices Inelastic? Lessons of the UK Price War', in Picard (ed.), *Evolving Media Markets: Effects of Economic and Social Change*. Finland.

Storper, M. and Salias, R. 1997. *Worlds of Production*. Cambridge, Mass.

Streeter, T. 1996. *Selling the Air*. Chicago.

Sweezy, P. 1968. *The Theory of Capitalist Development: Principles of Marxian Political Economy*. New York.

Szeleny, I. and Martin, B. 1991. 'The Three Waves of New Class Theories and a Postscript', in C. Lemert (ed.), *Intellectuals and Politics*. Newbery Park, Calif.

Taylor, C. 1994. 'The Politics of Recognition', in A. Gutman (ed.), *Multiculturalism*. Princeton, NJ.

Thompson, J. 1995. *The Media and Modernity: A Social Theory of the Media*. Cambridge.

Thompson, E. P. 1963. *The Making of the English Working Class*. Harmondsworth.

—— 1967. 'Time, Work Discipline and Industrial Capitalism'. *Past and Present*, 38.

Thurow, J. 1997. *Breaking Up America*. Chicago.

Toffler, A. 1980. *The Third Wave*. London.

Walzer, M. 1988. *The Company of Critics: Social Criticism and Political Commitment in the 20th Century*. New York.

Wasko, J. 1982. *Movies and Money*. Norwood, NJ.

Weber, E. 1979. *Peasants into Frenchmen: The Modernisation of Rural France, 1870–1914*. London.

Webster, F. and Robbins, K. 1986. *Information Technology: A Luddite Analysis*. Norwood, NJ.

Wiener, M. J. 1981. *English Culture and the Decline of the Industrial Spirit 1850–1980*. Cambridge.

Williams, R. 1958. *Culture and Society*. London.

—— 1973. *The Country and the City*. London.

—— 1974. *TV, Technology and Cultural Form*. London.

—— 1979. *Politics and Letters: Interviews with 'New Left Review'*. London.

—— 1981. *Culture*. Glasgow.

—— 1983. 'Intellectuals behind the Screens'. *Times Higher Education Supplement*, 21 Jan.

Williamson, O. 1975. *Markets and Hierarchies: Analysis and Anti-Trust Implications*. New York.

—— 1985. *The Economic Institutions of Capitalism: Firms, Markets, Relational Contracting*. New York.

Winston, B. 1998. *Media Technology and Society, a History: From the Telegraph to the Internet*. London.

Wolff, J. 1981. *The Social Production of Art*. London.

—— 1993. *Aesthetics and the Sociology of Art*, 2nd edn. London.

Wolgar, S. 1996. 'Technologies as Cultural Artefacts', in W. Dutton (ed.), *Information and Communication Technologies: Visions and Realities*. Oxford.

References

Wright Mills, C. 1963. *Power, Politics and People: The Collected Essays of C. Wright Mills*, ed. I. Horowitz. New York.

Yeo, E. and Yeo, S. (eds.). 1981. *Popular Culture and Class Conflict 1890–1914: Explorations in the History of Labour and Leisure.* Brighton, Sussex.

Index

Index

Index